The Power of the Written Word

Studia Classica

Anthony Podlecki
John C. Overbeck
General Editors

Vol. 1

PETER LANG
New York • Bern • Frankfurt am Main • Paris

Alfred Burns

The Power of the Written Word

The Role of Literacy in the History of Western Civilization

PETER LANG
New York • Bern • Frankfurt am Main • Paris

Library of Congress Cataloging-in-Publication Data

Burns, Alfred
    The power of the written word : the role of
literacy in Western civilization / Alfred Burns.
        p. cm.—(Studia classica ; vol. 1)
        Bibliography: p.
        1. Writing—History.   2. Literacy—History.
3. Civilization, Occidental.   4. Technology and
civilization.   I. Title.   II. Series: Studia classica
(New York, N.Y.) : vol. 1.
    Z40.B85   1989   652'.1—dc19   88-23061
    ISBN 0-8204-0896-4   CIP
    ISSN 0899-9929

CIP-Titelaufnahme der Deutschen Bibliothek

Burns, Alfred:
The power of the written word: the role of literacy in the
history of Western civilization / Alfred Burns. –
New York; Bern; Frankfurt am Main; Paris: Lang, 1989
    (Studia classica; Vol. 1)
    ISBN 0-8204-0896-4
NE: GT

Printed by Weihert-Druck GmbH, Darmstadt, West Germany

In memoriam Stellae

uxoris dilectae

Table of Contents

Preface

The theme of this book is the original impact and the continuing influence of literacy, especially Greek literacy and ideas, on the intellectual development of Western civilization from its beginnings to the present. My study explores the specific ways in which literacy and literature shaped concepts and modes of thought during the most creative periods in Western history. The concluding chapter is concerned with the present state and the future of literacy.

The World Literacy Drives of UNESCO and the concern with the decline in literacy in the U.S. and the U.K. have generated a great debate and a number of books on the subject of literacy.

On one side are studies which ascribe to literacy a major role in the cultural and material developments of the West. Since 1965 the United Nations have considered the propagation and expansion of literacy an essential prerequisite for economic development in the Third World and for the solutions of problems confronting the world as a whole.

On the opposite side are a number of sociologists and anthropologists who consider literacy an effect of cultural advance rather than a cause of it. Furthermore these writers see no advantage of literacy for those who have no immediate economic need for it.

This book is not intended as a comprehensive history of Western civilization. As my purpose is to show the specific interrelationships between advances in literacy and cultural developments, I have concentrated on those milestone periods in which the connection appears most clearly and which had the most lasting influence on the western world: The beginnings of civilization in the Near East and the Aegean; the Greek-Roman urban civilizations to which I have devoted the most space because of their continuing formative effects; the Renaissance; and (in the epilogue) to our own era.

When I summarize historical events to put cognitive developments into their chronological and cultural context I do not consider it necessary to provide extensive annotation as long as I review generally accepted material which can be found in most pertinent textbooks. Only when I present dissenting and potentially controversial views, do I cite the sources on which my reasoning is based. Since almost the whole book deals with the thought processes of the historic past I choose not to use the vocabulary of sexual equality. Although I am a fervent believer in equal rights of the genders I would consider modern cliches like "he or she" not only awkward but also a crass anachronism when dealing with the patriarchic past. Thus "man" or "mankind" will be used in its original Germanic linguistic meaning to denote the species, including both sexes.

I want to express my thanks to all those who helped to make my project a reality: John B. McDiarmid of the University of Washington, for many stimulating discussions, my friends Hoyt Barnebey and Heinz Betzler for their unflagging encouragement, the editors Anthony J. Podlecki and John C. Overbeck for their many helpful suggestions, and to Dorothy Aspinwall and Dorry Wollstein for their help with proofreading.

1

Introduction

This study examines the part played by the technology of writing in the early phases of Western civilization. Material and intellectual progress did not proceed in a continuous linear upward direction. Throughout history general cultural conditions remained static for long periods in most regions of the world, and great cognitive advances occurred only in a few places during relatively brief spans of time. Concentrating on some of these milestone periods and areas, this study will lead to the conclusion that usually they were associated with significant advances in the art of writing.

It is hardly ever possible in the examination of history to prove unambiguous cause-effect relationships, because in complex cultural systems changes are the result of a multiplicity of interacting social, economic and traditional forces. Still, it is often possible to discern one factor that is stronger than others and acts as a catalyst. The stimulating effects of writing and literacy on cognitive processes have been taken for granted throughout history. Recently, however, some voices have been raised denying any conceptual advantages derived from writing; they consider literacy a result of cognitive advance rather than a cause of it.

A decision of the dispute may come soon from an unexpected source: a review of current findings in neurological research seems to indicate that the acquisition and exercise of literacy in childhood are powerful stimulants in individual mental development. This should come as a surprise to no one. After all, literacy is an extension of the language capability, the most uniquely human characteristic. Notwithstanding the current experiments with primates in primitive forms of verbal communication, geneticists agree that the development and spontaneous use of language is the cardinal trait

that separates the species of *homo sapiens* from its hominid ancestors. This trait was developed during a period of less than two million years (perhaps only two hundred thousand years according to
the latest fossil finds) and was accompanied by an increase of about
fifty percent in the size of the cerebral cortex. Even if a question
remains whether the use of language produced the genetic pressure for larger brain capacity or whether language is the result of a
higher level of cognitive processes facilitated by the larger brain,
the salient fact is that the two steps were taken concurrently and
seem inextricably connected. The physiological connection between brain development and language is further confirmed by the
lateralization of the human brain and the partial localization of the
speech function in the left hemisphere. Lateralization underlines
the unity of the evolutionary processes which simultaneously produced the size and complexity of the human brain and the language
capability.

Thus language was at the heart of the evolutionary step which
created the species of *homo sapiens*. And apparently human evolution stopped with its creation. In the 30,000 years since paleolithic
man left his sophisticated paintings and ingenious tools in the caves
of France and Spain, no further evolution is discernible. As the
eminent geneticist G. G. Simpson[1] observes:

> Cro-Magnon man, who appeared in Europe some 35,000 years ago (give or
> take a few thousand), would look as normal in a space capsule as any astro-
> naut and, given equivalent training, would doubtlessly manage just as well.

All further developments were not evolutionary but cultural, with
each individual using his genetic gifts of learning ability and language to contribute to his community's oral heritage of experience
and ability to cope with the environment.

With the help of articulated language and the communal efforts
that language made possible man mastered the rigors of the glacial
periods of Eurasia and North America and the drought cycles of
Africa, preying on animals many times his own size and overcoming
their strength by the ingenuity of his weapons and his cooperative

hunting methods. Next he met a different challenge: starvation caused by the disappearance of the large animals after the recession of the large glaciers. Endowed with intelligence and the ability to communicate through language, mankind accomplished the revolutionary transition from food gathering to food raising: the domestication of animals and the planting of food-grains. A new cultural pattern of agricultural villages and permanent settlements emerged. This was the first great cultural breakthrough and seems to have occurred at different times in different places, but generally in most regions of Asia, North Africa, and Europe during the sixth millennium BC. It was also the last significant achievement by purely oral societies.

Considering the part played by language in the human genetic evolution, and subsequently in cultural developments, the hypothesis seems plausible that literacy, an extension and refinement of the language capability, may have been similarly instrumental in furthering ontogenetic conceptual abilities. This seems confirmed by studies of the seminal periods in western history. Just as the auditory symbols of oral language had raised humanity to a settled, more secure and organized way of life, so the visual symbols of written language would be increasingly involved with further material and intellectual progress.

Many of the advantages of literacy are obvious and have been generally recognized for a long time. Knowledge and experience no longer died with their possessor, but could be passed on to future generations. To some degree oral tradition, too, had that capability, but its keepers were subject to death, memory lapses and misunderstandings. There was always the possibility of arbitrary "forgetfulness" or changes due to personal whims or outside pressures. Written material alone had the ability of faithful transmission over not only time but also long distances. With writing the store of knowledge became permanent and cumulative with an unlimited potential for growth through subsequent contributions.

Furthermore, ever since antiquity there has existed an empirical belief that in addition to the practical benefits of literacy the learning process involved in the acquisition of literacy, especially multilingual literacy, is an important mental discipline, a valuable "training of the mind." More and more, the findings of modern neurological and psychological research tend to confirm the validity of this traditional assumption. That literacy is an integral part of civilization has long been taken for granted. I. J. Gelb[2] observes:

> I have reached the conclusion that writing is of such importance that civilization cannot exist without it and conversely, that writing cannot exist without a civilization.

This raises the question as to what is meant by the term civilization. Clyde Kluckhohn[3] defines civilization thus:

> societies characterized by at least two of the following features: (1) towns upwards of, say, 5000 inhabitants; (2) *a written language*; (3) monumental ceremonial centers. (The italics are mine)

Stuart Piggot[4] explains civilization as follows:

> Definition is perhaps not easy, but we should surely not be far from the mark if we thought of civilized societies as those which worked out a solution to the problem of living in a relatively permanent community, at a level of technological and social development above that of the hunting band, the family farmstead, the rustic self-sufficient village or the pastoral tribe, and with a capacity for storing information in the form of *written documents* or their equivalent. Civilization, like all human culture at whatever level, is something artificial and man-made, the result of making tools (physical and conceptual) of increasing complexity in response to the enlarging concepts of community life developing in men's minds. (The italics are mine)

Colin Renfrew[5] in his definition observes that in the pastoral and agricultural village, man mainly interacts with the ecosystem, with the natural environment, but...

> Civilization is the self-made environment of man which he has fashioned to insulate himself from the primeval environment of nature alone. All the artifacts which he uses serve as intermediaries between himself and this natural environment and, in creating civilization, he spins, so to speak, a web of culture so complex and so dense that most of his activities now relate to this artificial environment rather than directly to the fundamental natural one.

Literacy is certainly a part of this web. Two of the definitions we have quoted include literacy as one of the characteristics that define a civilization.

It was, of course, only a fairly large community with sufficient resources that could provide the division of labor and social organization needed to free certain groups from having to raise their own food, and thus to enable them to devote their time to higher intellectual pursuits. The city had the capability to collect surplus commodities from the producers and to redistribute them among those in other occupations or to barter them in foreign trade for material not available locally, and thus to raise the general level of material well-being. All this required a system of administration that could hardly exist without written records, especially in the absence of any equivalent medium of monetary exchange. Indeed 90 percent of early written documents are records of economic transactions and inventories of a type which some scholars, disappointed in their search for great literature, have dubbed "laundry tickets." Still, we owe our knowledge of ancient economic life to such records, and if future historians were to examine our myriad pieces of paper, they would probably find that our ratio of "laundry tickets" to literature is 99 to 1 as credit cards and computers are again replacing money with records.

In the West, civilization from its beginning has been associated with large urban communities-- with cities. Both of the words, city and civilization, derive from the Latin word *civitas*, which denotes an urban community as well as membership in it, the condition of being a *civis*, a citizen. Citizenship implies privileges conferred by the city as well as obligations towards it. From *civis* the adjective *civilis* is formed, which meant behaving like a citizen-- that is, according to civic duty, which includes treating fellow citizens with consideration and politeness, as in English "civil behavior." Civilization, then, means the education to proper civic and civil conduct as well as the resulting cultural conditions and practices in addition to the criteria mentioned above. From this it is clear that the Romans, just as the Greeks before them, and we not so long ago, had a strong conviction that urbanization had raised life to a new ethical level. As we shall see later, to the Greeks their city-- the *polis*-- was the dispenser, the fountainhead of all humanizing influences, and there are indications that the inhabitants of the earliest cities, the Sumerians, had already developed that feeling.

Urban civilization and writing appeared on the scene of history at the same time. Essentially five important phases in the history of literacy can be discerned: (1) the first formulation of the concept of communicating through pictographic signs, (2) the development of word-syllabic phonetic writing, (3) the invention of the alphabet, (4) the technological breakthrough to the printed book based on the invention of the printing press and the introduction of paper, and (5) most recently, the computer.

Primitive pictographic writing apparently arose naturally among many peoples in various places at various times. It was simply the conveying of a message by means of a series of pictures. Pictures, however, had the inherent limitation that they could represent only concrete noun-objects. The difficulty was partly overcome by the use of thought association and expansion of the meaning of the image. For instance, a picture of the sun could also represent the concept of light or of day; a series of footprints or the image of two striding legs could convey the meaning of walking. Thus the image became the symbol of an idea, an *ideogram*. The signs gradually became more simplified, often denoting the object only by a characteristic feature. Thus an ox could be represented by a pair of horns. In early Sumerian writing, a triangle resting on its base would denote a mountain, a triangle standing on its apex with a vertical line in its center (a schematized vulva) would represent the noun woman or the adjective female; a combination of the two signs would indicate a slave-girl since most of those were imported from the mountainous areas of Anatolia.

According to a more recent hypothesis, Sumerian ideographic writing evolved from numerical notation in response to the needs of foreign trade. Symbols for numbers generally seem to have preceded other writing. Paleolithic engravings on a bone from a cave in France have been interpreted as an early primitive lunar calendar. Later, with the advent of agriculture, calendars were a most urgent requirement. In Sumerian foreign trade, sealed pottery vessels were labeled to indicate their content by commodity and quantity. According to Schmandt-Besserat's theory, the symbols on the identifying labels which denoted numbers, units of measurement, and commodities were the beginning of the ideographic script.[6] The evidence for this theory has not found universal acceptance, but parallels in other cultures seem to lend it plausibility. For example, the Meso-American scripts, except the Mayan, seem not to have gone much beyond numbers, calendars, and proper names.

Eventually in the continuing process of schematization the signs lost all resemblance to recognizable objects The shapes which the signs finally assumed were largely determined by the writing materials, instruments and drawing methods. Sumerian cuneiform writing was dissolved into its characteristic wedge shapes because the signs were incised in clay by oblique stabbing motions of a stylus while the Aegean linear signs owed their curved narrow lines to continuous movements of a stylus over a soft surface, and Chinese characters to the use of brush and ink on paper. Cursive Egyptian writing was shaped by the use of a reed pen on papyrus.

The next important step in ideographic writing was "phonetic transfer," which eventually led to the development of syllabic writing: the written sign became the symbol not only for the object or idea, but also for its name in the spoken language. Thus the visual signal became an auditory signal, a word. The ideogram became also a logogram. Each sign stood now for a combination of sounds, and could represent homophones or similar sounding words. If we were to use an artificial example from English, the sign for horse could also denote hoarse; or the sign for the animal bear could also represent the verb to bear or the adjective bare. Obviously exact homonyms are not always available. In that case similarity of sounds would suffice; the sign for pig might also serve for big or pick or peek or peak. A system of this kind is manageable for a language using mainly monosyllabic words such as ancient Sumeric or Chinese. When Semitic peoples adopted the Sumeric cuneiform script for their own polysyllabic languages, they used the Sumeric word-signs to represent similar sounding syllables in their own

Semitic language. The Japanese in like fashion adapted Chinese logograms to denote Japanese syllables.

As there are almost innumerable ideas to be communicated between human beings, an ideo-logographic system requires the memorization of thousands of signs. Chinese writing has a repertory of 50,000 signs, and to be reasonably literate requires the knowledge of at least 3,000. Consequently throughout China's history literacy has been the privilege of a small elite, and the invention of printing never had the revolutionary impact that its introduction in Europe would have two centuries later. The complexity and large number of the Chinese characters still constitute an enormous obstacle to modernization. Recent attempts at reform have been defeated by tradition and national pride.

The syllabic scripts evolved gradually out of ideographic writing, but many ideograms remained in use in otherwise syllabic scripts. Eventually all the Near Eastern civilizations developed or adopted syllabic writing. When syllabic systems were fully developed, they constituted a tremendous simplification over ideographic scripts requiring several thousands of signs. Most mature syllabaries consisted of 65 to 110 signs representing a corresponding number of syllables. Syllables usually consisted of a vowel or a vowel combined with a consonant, as for instance *a*, *ba*, *ga*, *da*, etc., or *i*, *bi*, *gi*, *di*, and so forth, according to the number of vowels in the language. Such systems were well suited to languages consisting mainly of open syllables such as the Semitic languages or Japanese, which has the only syllabary still in use. But when a syllabary of this kind was borrowed for use in an Indo-European language with many consonants in groups of two or three without intervening vowels (as in Greek) it offered considerable difficulties. Since each sign represents a syllable in which a vowel is attached to a consonant, a cluster of consonants cannot be rendered in writing without the retention of unnecessary vowels between them or by omitting some consonants altogether. The Mycenaean scribes resorted to both expedients. They omitted consonant word-endings in some cases, in others, words had a superfluous vowel attached to them. Thus in addition to linguistic difficulties the Mycenaean Linear B tablets confront modern scholars with many ambiguities, as some words or sign-groups can be read in two or three different ways. The orthography must have been difficult even for the scribes working in their native Greek dialect. This may explain why they retained many ideograms for frequently used words.

But the scribes had also other reasons. Mastery of the mixture of syllabic and ideographic signs required many years of training and made the art of writing a highly specialized skill. In the centralized empires of Mesopotamia and Egypt the scribal bureaucracies maintained control of taxation and the allocation of resources, of the compensation of workers and the exchange of goods internally as well as in foreign trade. The representations of economic activities on Egyptian monuments invariably show a scribe in a prominent location keeping track of the operation. Because of their importance in the economic and political administration, the scribes held a respected and privileged position. Therefore they had no interest in simplifying their arcane art, thus making it more accessible to potential competitors. In spite of their complexity, the mixed ideographic and syllabic scripts were an efficient means of record keeping and communication and remained dominant for over 2000 years. Cuneiform writing was used by Sumerians, Akkadians, Babylonians, Hittites and Assyrians. Egyptian writing survived into Roman times with very little change since its beginnings around 3000 BC.

It took the advent of the simplest, the most accurate, and still today the most efficient writing system, the alphabet, to supersede syllabic writing in the Near East. The Semitic alphabet appeared about 1,000 BC in the region that now comprises Israel, Jordan, Syria and Lebanon. Its exact point of origin and process of derivation are still a matter of dispute. The most plausible theories, advanced by I. J. Gelb and F. Householder, suggest that the alphabet came into being by dropping the vowels from an existing Semitic syllabary.

The West Semitic alphabet consisted of 22 letters expressing consonants only, and was written from right to left. The absence of vowels made the script adaptable to all Semitic languages in which sequences of consonants essentially determine the meaning of words, while different vowels may appear in different positions between the consonants. The Canaanite, Hebrew and Aramaic alphabets derived from it at about the same time, initially with little difference between them in the shape of the letters. The names of the letters and their sequence remained the same. David Diringer considers the Semitic script a true alphabet, but not yet carried to its full perfection. He defines the principle of an alphabet as follows:[7]

> Perfection in an alphabet implies the accurate rendering of phonemes, that is, each sound must be represented by a single constant symbol, not more than one sound to the same symbol.

Since vowels are not represented by any symbol in the Semitic alphabet, groups of consonants can be, and frequently are, pronounced differently depending on the vowels the reader might supply. I. J. Gelb[8] is of the opinion that the West Semitic system was not a true alphabet, but rather a syllabary with undifferentiated vowels. Householder[9] notes that a typical consonant-plus-vowel syllabary consists of 65 to 110 signs (e.g. 65 in classical Greek Cypriot, 90 in Linear B). He considers the Semitic script "a vowelless alphabet or an unvocalized syllabary" and calls it a "mad simplification" based on the relative scarcity of vowels in the Semitic languages. The arithmetic admirably fits Householder's observation. In a syllabary comprising 110 open syllables, each consisting of one consonant paired with one of five vowels, the number of signs would be reduced to one fifth, equaling 22, if the differentiation by vowels were to be abandoned. In other words, if one reduced the signs for syllables *ba*, *be*, *bi*, *bo* etc., *ga*, *ge*, *gi*, *go*, etc. to simply b, g, etc., all the signs left would be one for each consonant. Actually the number of letters, as we may call them now, in the West Semitic alphabet was 22 with no vowels. (I have oversimplified somewhat since some of the phonemes are half vowels, which the Greeks later on used as vowels).

Thus the Semitic alphabet economized in the number of signs at the expense of accuracy and left many ambiguities and uncertainties to the reader who was faced with the difficulty of determining the pronunciation of many words in any unfamiliar text. Very often he was confronted with a choice between several words or different readings that could be obtained by supplying different vowels. Consequently reading was still a difficult and time-consuming task requiring a great amount of practice and thus the province of professional scribes. In the Hebrew community, where religious, social and political life revolved around strict interpretation of scriptures and laws, a whole establishment of learned scribes held a position of power based on their ability to expound and interpret the sacred texts.

Despite its shortcomings, the 22 letter West Semitic alphabet was so superior to the previous writing systems in simplicity and adaptability that directly or indirectly it became the ancestor of all subsequent alphabetic scripts. All Asiatic alphabets, such as Persian, Sanskrit, modern Hindi, and Arabic developed from Aramaic, all European alphabets from the Greek writing system which was derived from the Canaanite (Phoenician) alphabet. Eventually most ethnic groups who adopted the alphabet learned to deal with the vowel problem through diacritic signs or other means. All authorities agree that the alphabet was and remains the greatest advance in the history of writing, even if the ideal of the unvarying one-letter-to-one-sound relationship has never been fully realized in any language. In addition, changes in the language subsequent to the formulation of the alphabet often have blurred the one-to-one relationship even further. The worst offender in this respect is modern English, which never has reformed its spelling to keep pace with changes in pronunciation, so that today the same letters or combination of letters often may denote from three to five different sounds, or the same sound may be represented by several different letters or letter combinations. This is one source of the problems in English speaking schools, because an inordinate amount of time has to be spent on spelling in comparison with most Romance or Germanic language countries. Geoffrey Sampson, however, believes that the spelling difficulties for the writer are compensated by greater ease for the reader.[10] In any event the time when reform was possible has passed. Today, when English speaking countries are scattered all over the world, any agreement on spelling changes would be impossible and the language would be fragmented.

The Greeks were the first to develop a fully vocalized alphabet. When they adapted the Phoenician alphabet to their own language sometime in the 8th century BC, they converted some of the Phoenician letters which represented sounds that had no exact equivalent in Greek into the five vowels they needed. Eventually they changed the direction of writing from the Semitic right- to-left, to the left-to-right direction. The Greek and the closely related Roman alphabet probably came closer to the ideal of a one sound to one letter relationship than any other since. For the first time it was possible to render human speech in writing without ambiguities by use of fewer than 30 signs. The Greek alphabet was the most efficient writing system devised to this day. No improvements have ever made been made to the alphabet since.

The next great advance in literacy was not in the art of writing itself, but in the technology of dissemination. Printing and the use of paper in relatively cheap books made universal literacy possible, at least theoretically, and almost a reality.

Today we find ourselves in the midst of the electronic revolution, a change with a potentially greater impact on literacy than all preceding developments. It is much too soon to evaluate the effects of high speed computing and instant world-wide communications with all their cultural ramifications. The last chapter of this book examines some of the questions posed by the electronic age.

Literacy had first evolved in Sumeria and neighboring Elam from where, at least by idea-transmission, it spread outward to Syria and Egypt in the west, Anatolia and possibly Crete to the north, and Iran and the Indus valley to the east. The first written documents in Sumeria date from the second half of the fourth millennium BC, in Egypt from the early third, in Mohenjodaro and Harappa on the Indus and in Crete from the early second millennium BC. As far as we know, Chinese writing originated independently. The earliest Chinese inscriptions date probably from the 14th century BC, and are thus contemporary with the Cretan Linear B tablets. In the New World the earliest known date of Mayan inscriptions is AD 320. In the second millennium BC, not surprisingly, literacy seems to have been most advanced in breadth and depth where it had been established earliest, i.e. in Mesopotamia and Egypt. By breadth and depth are meant the numbers of literate persons and the variety of uses of writing.

The following chapters will examine the ways in which different phases of literacy influenced Western cultural history during its milestone periods of creative innovation. One of the most salient impressions will be the undiminished survival and influence of classical Greek literacy and literature throughout the lifespan of Western civilization.

Notes

.

1. G.G. Simpson, *Biology of Man* (New York 1964), 110- 119

2. I.J. Gelb, *A Study of Writing* (Chicago 1963), 222

3. C.H. Kraeling & R.M. Adams, edd, *City Invincible* (Chicago 1960), 400

4. Stuart Piggot in preface to M.E.L. Mallowan, *Early Mesopotamia and Iran* (London 1965), 7

5. Colin Renfrew, *The Emergence of Civilization* (London (1972), 11

6. "From Tokens to Tablets", *Visible Language* 15 (1981), 321-44; "An Ancient Token System: The Precursor to Numerals and Writing", *Archaeology* 39 (1986), 32-39

7. David Diringer, *The Alphabet*, (3d ed., London 1968)

8. Gelb, *A Study of Writing*, 147-152

9. F. W. Householder, "More on Mycenaean", *Classical Journal* 54 (1959), 379-383

10. Geoffrey Sampson, *Writing Systems*, (Stanford 1985), 213

2

Mesopotamia: The First Civilization

The first known urban civilization developed together with literacy in Sumer, the southern part of Mesopotamia (today's Iraq) in the 4th millennium BC. There, in the alluvial plain of the lower Euphrates and Tigris, early agricultural settlers had found a rich soil, renewed by spring floods every year and easily worked with primitive tools. Once they had learned to control the floodwaters to an extent and to irrigate the soil during the dry season, relatively small areas could support fairly large populations. Archaeological investigators have found many levels of occupation in the area and in adjacent parts of Iran. From the 5th millennium BC on, several successive Neolithic cultures have been identified by their characteristic pottery types and named after the sites of their discovery:

Eridu, named after a later Sumerian city, is dated to ca. 5000 BC.

Hajji Mohammad, named after a modern place name, occupies five successive building levels at Eridu and flourished about 4750 BC.

Ubaid is an important culture because it preceded the Sumerian period known as *Uruk* (the Erech of the Bible). It is not known whether the Sumerians established themselves in the area during the Ubaid or the Uruk period. During the Ubaid period, around 4350 BC, the first large urban settlements appeared. The cemetery at Eridu contained more than 1,000 graves. Metals make their first appearance in the form of cast copper axe heads and gold jewelry. Also during the Ubaid period we find the beginning of monumental architecture, using mud-bricks. At Eridu a temple was built on a raised platform with a stairway leading up to the door, clearly a forerunner of the pyramid-shaped ziggurats which later became so typical of Mesopotamia, e.g. the "Tower of Babel." Excavations show several foundation levels indicating that the first building goes back to about 4 000 BC.

By about 3500 BC during the Uruk period, the Sumerian civilization seems to have been in the full process of development. The first known pictorial writing was found on a stone tablet from Kish, soon to be followed by the earliest collection of inscribed clay tablets from Uruk itself. The middle of the fourth millennium also marks the development of an elaborate architecture, sculpture, and other new technologies in many Mesopotamian towns. The first intelligible documents from Uruk, Ur, and Jemdet Nasr are in the Sumeric language and mark the protoliterate period, ca. 3200-3100 BC. Although with the proliferation of written records after 3000 BC we gain considerable insight into the cultural life of the Sumerians, many problems remain. One which might never be solved is the ethnic identity of the Sumerians. Although their agglutinative language has become quite well known through the decipherment of some bilingual texts in the Sumeric and Semitic Akkadian languages, no relationship between Sumerian and any known language family has been found. Connected with this problem is the question of the geographic origin and the time of the arrival of the Sumerians in Mesopotamia. The consensus of scholars seems to be that the Sumerians were not the first inhabitants, because the names of rivers and places are not Sumerian; neither are they Semitic and thus they seem to indicate that the original inhabitants belonged to a third, unknown, linguistic group. There are, however, many Semitic proper names and loanwords in even the earliest deciphered Sumeric texts (in the following, "Sumerian" will refer to the population while "Sumeric" designates the language and the script). The question of ethnic affiliation loses whatever importance might be attached to it because Sumer seems to have been settled by a mixture of peoples of different geographic and linguistic origins. Some time during the Ubaid or the Uruk period the Sumeric language and culture with their characteristic features became dominant in southern Mesopotamia, the land of Sumer, the Shemer of the Bible. At the beginning of the literate period there seem to have been no social or rank distinctions between people of

Sumerian and Semitic origin, since as many officeholders with Semitic as with Sumerian names are found in the records. Several Semitic names appear among the early rulers of Kish; Sargon, an Akkadian, was cupbearer to the Sumerian king of Kish before usurping the royal power. In the northern cities of the Sumerian cultural orbit like Mari and Lagash the dominant spoken language was Semitic Akkadian. But regardless of their native tongue, the inhabitants of all the Mesopotamian cities made the Sumerian civilization their own. Even a thousand years later, the Babylonians considered Sumeric their classical language and continued to study and write it long after it had disappeared as a spoken language.

When written texts lifted the curtain on historic time, the Mesopotamian cultural complex embraced about a score of city-states strung out along the Euphrates and the Tigris from the Persian Gulf northwards as far as Mari on the Euphrates and Assur on the Tigris, with extensions to the east as far as Susa, the future capital of the Persian empire, and in the west (as recent excavations have shown) as far as Ebla. Some of the important cities were Eridu, Uruk, Ur, Larsa, Lagash, Umma, Shurupak, Isin, Nippur and Kish. All these cities, whether the Sumerian or the Semitic element predominated, shared similar religious, economic, and social characteristics. The unifying cultural cement of this civilization was Sumeric cuneiform writing and its rich literature. Both the assets and the deficiencies of the environment had played an important part in the Sumerian civilization. The yearly spring floods of the rivers provided a fertile alluvial soil offering an abundant food supply. For the first time it was possible not only to support large concentrations of population, but even to produce surpluses beyond the subsistence level that could be used to maintain specialized craftsmen, priests and administrators and reserves for future emergencies or trade. The absence of rain required extensive irrigation during the dry season and flood control during the inundation periods. The large scale construction of ditches, dikes and reservoirs could be achieved only through an elaborate social organization with planning and management of the necessary communal effort. The surplus of agrarian products and the lack of basic raw materials such as stone, wood and metals stimulated an active trade with the neighboring highland people to the east. All these developments required, and would have been impossible without, a system of writing and record keeping.

Sumerian writing by the beginning of the 3rd millennium had evolved into the cuneiform script. It was essentially syllabic, but contained also hundreds of ideograms. The cuneiform writing system was successively adapted to Akkadian, Elamite, Babylonian, Hittite, and Assyrian, and remained the dominant mode of writing in western Asia for two thousand years until it was replaced by alphabetic writing.

In a complex urban society without coined money or other convenient means of exchange, the administration of the economy depended on written records. Land had to be measured and allotted, the appropriate amounts of seed grain had to be allocated, taxes and lease-rents assessed according to yield. Property records, inventory records, records of the distribution of rations, of trade and other transactions had to be maintained. Obviously the administration of such a system required a large specialized professional clerical establishment.

From the physical remains and the literary sources it is possible to form a picture of the Mesopotamian civilization which moves into sharper focus as literacy progresses during the 3rd millennium. The cities were built from brick, centered on the temple and the palace of the ruler, and surrounded by protective walls. Some indications exist that in the early Sumerian stage the city-states may have enjoyed a degree of self-government, with a council of elders and a popular assembly, which under the pressure of continual inter-city warfare gave way to an increasing centralization of power. The underlying concept was totally theocratic. Each city was the possession of a god. The gods had created mankind to feed and serve them. The ruler was the gods' earthly representative, responsible for keeping the citizens at their assigned tasks working for the gods. Civilization itself was a gift of the gods, who had taught mankind agriculture and all the other crafts in order to enable them to give the gods their due.

The division of labor had been accomplished at an early stage. There is not only the evidence of artifacts for highly skilled craftsmanship in many trades, but also records listing farmers, cattle breeders, boatmen, metalworkers, carpenters, leather-workers, weavers and others. There are teachers, judges, nobles, and merchants and, of course, priests and priestesses. The Sumerians invented the wheel, in both uses-- as potter's and as wagon wheel; they were the first to use draft animals. Oxen and asses pulled wagons and boats, and plows-- another Sumerian invention. Trade played an important part in the Sumerian economy. Surplus wool, grain and manufactured items such as cylinder seals were exchanged for stone, wood, metal and slaves. Cylinder seals were a hallmark of Sumerian decorative craft and apparently a popular trade item, as they have been found from India to Egypt and from Crete to the Persian Gulf. Conversely the types of stone for their manufacture were imported from the same far-flung areas. There is much other evidence of the profound influence of the Sumerian civilization on the evolution of the other early cultures in the Nile and Indus valleys with which the Sumerians maintained communications by land and sea. Beyond all of these accomplishments in material progress, in the words of Henri Frankfort:[1]

> The most important single innovation is the introduction of writing. In the opinion of many scholars the whole history of writing in the West derives from this discovery since they hold (as does the present writer) that the invention of hieroglyphic writing in Egypt was stimulated by a knowledge of Sumerian writing as it existed in the last part of the 'protoliterate' period. Egypt was at that time in contact with Sumer.

In spite of contests for leadership and temporary hegemonies the Sumerian cities, on the whole, seem to have retained their independence until 2371 BC when Sargon the Great conquered all of Akkad and Sumer after making himself king of Kish. During his 50 year rule, inscriptions in the Akkadian language took their place side by side with those in Sumeric, but there were hardly any changes in religion or customs. Sargon's empire and influence reached far into Iran. Cuneiform writing was adopted by Hurrians and Elamites; trade relations extended to the Indus civilizations of Harappa and Mohenjodaro.

In 2230 the Sargonic empire collapsed under the continuous pressures of the neighboring mountain and desert peoples from without and of the drive for independence by the cities within. In the ensuing chaotic interregnum, much of Sumer and Akkad was ravaged and dominated by the Gutian invaders from the east. About a hundred years later the *ensi* of Uruk gathered an army and, helped by other cities, threw off the Gutian rule. In 2113 BC Ur-Nammu, king of Ur, the Biblical home of Abraham, became "King of Sumer and Akkad" and re-established Sumerian rule. Mesopotamia prospered under a Sumerian renaissance for about a hundred years. But towards the end of the 3rd millennium the empire fell again to invaders, this time the Amorites, Semitic tribes from the Syrian desert. Sumerian rule was not to return.

From the beginning of the 2nd millennium, Mesopotamia was dominated most of the time by speakers of Semitic languages who easily adapted to the Akkadian language and script. But the Sumerian religion myths, literature, and learning survived. Although most writings had been translated into Akkadian, the Sumeric texts continued to be studied, and even new literary works were still being composed in Sumeric a thousand years after it had disappeared as a spoken language. Mesopotamia was successively ruled by Babylonians for most of the 2nd millennium with Hittite, Kassite and Elamite interludes, and then by Assyrians from the 9th century BC until the Persian conquest in the 6th.

Thus, the history of the Sumerian civilization presents not only the first, but a most innovative, economically successful, influential, and durable urban civilization which survived and assimilated all its invaders and conquerors.

Its driving force seems to have been a relatively small literate elite centered on an important institution, the *edubba*, the scribal school. The following discussion, mainly based on Samuel Kramer's work,[2] will show how literacy, born of economic necessity, took on an intellectual life of its own and raised the cognitive processes of its practitioners to a higher level.

Almost from the beginning, Sumeric pictorial writing and the cuneiform Sumeric, Akkadian, Babylonian, and Assyrian scripts into which it developed were a mixture of ideographic and syllabic phonetic writing and remained so until their final development into a purely phonetic system, the late Assyrian syllabary in the 7th century. The great number of signs, in excess of 900, the inexactitude of the phonetic renderings with many homonyms and homophones, and the confusion created by the fact that the same sign often could be read either as an ideogram or as a phonetic syllable, made the learning process lengthy and difficult. Consequently, writing and reading remained the province of highly trained specialists, the professional scribes. Scribal schools came into existence early in the third millennium, as attested by word lists found in Uruk dating from about 3000 BC. Many such "lexical" texts from around 2500 were found in Shurupak. During the reign of Sargon the Great, (2370-2316) the first "dictionaries"- bilingual lexical texts appear, which list the Sumeric signs together with their pronunciation and their meaning in Akkadian. It was these tablets that made the decipherment of the Sumeric language possible. The importance of the *edubba*, the scribal school, cannot be overestimated. We know much about its operation. In addition to many lexical texts and thousands of students' practice tablets, we have accounts by teachers and alumni of their school activities.

The training lasted from childhood to early adulthood. The pupil spent all day in school. He began with practice of the syllabic characters, such as *tu ta ti, nu na ni, bu ba bi,* etc. Then he had to learn a repertory of some 900 signs with their pronunciations. This was followed by hundreds of words represented by groups of more than one character. After memorization and practice of these fundamentals the student was confronted with lists of thousands of items arranged by subject matter-- for instance, parts of animals and the human body, names of domestic animals, of birds and fishes, of plants, of implements made from wood, kinds of food and beverages, place names, and on and on. Such a system of categorization is a kind of mental exercise which is a hallmark of literacy and totally foreign to members of illiterate societies.[3]

Only when the student had mastered the cuneiform signs and the complex vocabulary in writing and reading did he begin to copy short sentences, proverbs, fables, and model contracts-- a most important part of his practical training. This curriculum reveals a pedagogical plan and a considerable effort at systematization by the teachers, and much greater mental efforts and discipline by the students than those demanded in nonliterate pursuits. The categorization reflected in the various word-lists and sample contracts shows a significant step towards abstraction. After all, classification is a prerequisite of systematic logic and scientific thought.

The advance in abstract thought fostered by literacy manifests itself also in the mathematical achievements of the *edubbas*. Like the linguistic training, the teaching of mathematics began with the copying and memorization of tables- tables of multiplication, of reciprocals, and the study of metrological tables showing the equivalences of measures of capacity, length and weight. There were tables of squares and cubes, of square roots and cube roots, and tables of exponential functions for the calculation of compound interest. Later the student progressed to solving practical problems dealing with wages, canal-digging, and construction work.

We can judge the mathematical knowledge of the scribes from school texts dating only as early as the Old Babylonian era, ca. 1800 BC, since no older readable mathematical texts are in existence. Although Neugebauer,[4] our foremost authority on cuneiform mathematics, doubts it, it seems reasonable to assume a gradual preceding development. Not only is it unlikely that the high degree of mathematical sophistication revealed by the cuneiform texts could have come overnight, but the very raison d'etre of the oldest written notations was the need for acccounting. And indeed, as Neugebauer states two pages later, "the mathematical tables must have developed together with the economical texts." Even in the undeciphered texts of the fourth millennium BC we can distinguish the numerical entries. An accurate calendar was developed at an early stage.

In the Babylonian texts number-notation was far advanced. Although no zero sign existed, the principle of place value was used;

for zero values the position was simply left empty. Both the decimal and the sexagesimal systems were used side by side, with the sexagesimal system deemed more useful for large values and small subdivisions, such as those used in astronomic angle measurements. As a numerical base, 60 has also the advantage of being divisible by 2, 3, 4, 5, 6, 10, 12, 15, 20 and 30. Neugebauer[5] cites an example in which the scribe used both systems on the same tablet. The number 225 is expressed sexagesimally by 3 45 (three times 60 plus 45), and in decimals by 2 2 5, for the dating of his own signature.

Two types of "problem texts" for teaching purposes have been found. On one kind of tablet step by step instructions are given outlining the procedure for solving different specific problems such as various equations. The second type gives problems only, without answers, but arranged in an instructional sequence. Each sequence starts with a problem stated in its most simple form: e.g., two numbers are to be found if their sum and product are given. Each successive question restates the problem in a more complex polynomial form requiring the student to transform and reduce the equation to its basic form. The numerical values of the unknowns are the same in each series of problems; this shows that the specific values were of little importance. It was the pedagogic procedure that counted. The Pythagorean theorem in its application to specific numbers was well known. Neugebauer,[6] however, points out that no attempt was ever made at what we would call mathematical proof. The formulas are empirically derived, some are only approximations (for instance the constant *pi* in the calculation of circles is sometimes stated as 3, at other times as 3 and 1/8). Procedures for the solutions of problems were handed down like cooking recipes. Thus Mesopotamian mathematics never reached the level of scientific mathematics. Their usefulness and relative sophistication, however, could not have been reached without writing and literacy, and remained unsurpassed until the advent of Greek scientific mathematics, for which they had provided the starting point.

Although the basic function of the schools was the teaching of writing in Sumeric and later the Semitic languages in order to fill the needs of the temple and palace administrations, we can see that the teachers and scribes branched out far beyond the purely practical pursuits. In literature they committed the religious traditions and oral epics to writing and created a variety of original literature of their own. They wrote love poetry, hymns, lamentations, epics, proverbs and essays of various kinds. Composition in Sumeric continued in the *eddubas* during the Sargonic dynasty in the third millennium, even while Akkadian became the prevalent spoken language. After the Sumeric renaissance during the last century of the 3rd millennium, in Babylonian times in the second millennium new compositions were mainly in the Semitic languages, but the scribes continued to study, translate, and copy the Sumeric texts. The mythical epics, such as the creation myth, the flood story, and the legends of Gilgamesh and other heroes, were copied and re-copied and edited with literary understanding. Most literary tablets have been recovered from three principal libraries in Nippur in Sumer, and in Assyrian Assur and Nineveh. Although the earliest Sumerian literary texts date from 2400 BC, and many are Babylonian and Assyrian copies or adaptations, there is no doubt that the dates of their composition in many instances go back to the beginning of the third millennium. Visual representations on much earlier artifacts, such as cylinder seals, indicate that some of the themes were already part of the oral and the protoliterate tradition.[7]

Like their literary and linguistic accomplishments, the mathematical and astronomical achievements of the scribal schools far exceeded the practical and bureaucratic needs. The schools used literacy to develop an unprecedented comprehensive system of education which would never have been possible in an oral society and through it created an intellectual elite. As many of the thousands of surviving tablets give the names of the scribes and sometimes the names and occupations of their fathers, we can draw some conclusions about their status in society. As is to be expected, the scribes came from the important and wealthy families and many went on to high office in the administrative buraucracies.[8] Although it is true that the religious establishment exerted an influence of varying degrees on the economic and political life of the cities, the evidence indicates considerable independence of the scribal schools. They supported themselves through tuition paid by the pupils' families. The training included all the secular, legal and commercial aspects of writing, and many of the alumni assumed positions outside of the temple hierarchy.

The fact that the schooling became bilingual added to its complexities. Translation requires analysis of the grammatical and syntactic structures of both languages as well as of the linguistic phonology, an analysis for which no need existed in the purely oral use of language. The mathematical texts show a parallel development of abstract reasoning to derive general rules from specific cases. Written notation makes possible the prolonged and repeated contemplation of linguistic and mathematical problems. Thus literacy has the effect of raising cognitive processes from the specific and momentary to the abstract and permanent, We can follow the same phenomenon in the legal texts. From the recording of specific judicial decisions writing progresses to the formulation of laws. To do this, the writer must anticipate and categorize possible future cases. Written law codes, which made their first known appearance in the third millennium, are a giant step towards theoretical thought. The projection of the principles of codified law from the human to the cosmic sphere brought with it the concepts of divine and natural laws. Even in the field of religion, writing raised the myths to a more abstract symbolic level. In religious literature the mythical tradition was not only written down, it was creatively transformed. Just as Herodotus said that Homer and Hesiod gave the Greeks their gods, the Sumerian scribes gave to the Babylonians, the Assyrians, the Canaanites, and the Hebrews the stories of the creation, of paradise, and of the great flood. The Gilgamesh epic developed from a series of adventure legends into the search for an understanding of the human condition. It was translated not only into the Semitic languages, but also into Hurrian and Hittite. In fact we know one of its sections only through the Hittite version. The Assyrian king Ashurbanipal in the 7th century boasted of his literacy and scholarship in the ancient language and literature. He collected old texts and had them copied, and the remnants of his library are the source of much of our information.

Beginning urbanization may have created the need for writing. But when literacy became a system of education and the full time occupation from early youth of a class of people exclusively devoted to cognitive activities, it became one of the most important milestones in history providing to an elite the intellectual foundation for the intricate social and cultural complex we call civilization.

As literacy was the monopoly of the scribal establishment and assured its members a privileged position, they had a vested interest in the status quo and no incentive to simplify the writing system whose intricacy protected their positions. In addition, the scribes' employment in the service of the palace or the temple demanded a conservatism that discouraged innovations. Therefore, like other cultures in which literacy and the dispensation of knowledge are restricted to a small educated minority, Mesopotamian civilization, after its initial thrust, reached a plateau and remained static for many centuries.

As Samuel Kramer[9] notes, the most important legacy of Sumerian literate civilization was the institution of the more or less autonomous city-state, After the growth of the Sumerian cities in the second half of the 4th millennium BC, cities sprang up all through the Near East from the Indus to the Aegean. Within their complex political and socio-economic structures, procedures of government and usually written laws regulated the relationship of the free citizens with the nobles and priests above them and with clients and slaves below. In view of the Sumerians' and their successors' direct relations with most of the neighboring areas and their manifest technological and cultural influence in so many fields, they probably can be credited with being directly instrumental in the urbanization of the Near East although other urban societies (such as China and Pre-Columbian America) developed independently in other regions. Self-governing cities became the focal points of successive civilizations in the West.

Notes

1. Henri Frankfort in *Cambridge Ancient History* I, Chapter 12, p. 44

2. S.N. Kramer, *The Sumerians: Their History, Culture, and Character* (Chicago 1963), 229-248

3. E. A. Havelock, *The Muse Learns to Write* (New Haven and London 1986), 38-39

4. Otto Neugebauer, *The Exact Sciences in Antiquity* (Princeton 1952), 28

5. Neugebauer, 17

6. Neugebauer, 42-45

7. George Roux, *Ancient Iraq* (London 1964), 79-80

8. Kramer, 230-231

9. Kramer, 289

3

The Aegean Bronze Age

The third millennium saw the rise of other civilizations in the Near East and the Aegean region. Although these societies profited from the Mesopotamian technological innovations, such as wheeled vehicles and potter's wheels, and from such abstract concepts as the ideas of writing and the astronomic calendar, every civilization developed its own different characteristics and evolved in a distinct and individual style.

Egyptian civilization, in the long Nile valley, protected by deserts on both sides, was not as much exposed to the continual inroads of warrior tribes as Mesopotamia. Unified into one empire at an early stage, the Egyptians enjoyed a much more sheltered existence. Even the river Nile was more docile and predictable than the Euphrates and the Tigris. Perhaps because of these circumstances, Egyptian society showed fewer of the militaristic characteristics so dominant in Mesopotamia and developed along considerably more peaceful lines under the firm control of a monolithic hierarchic establishment. Literacy was a monopoly of the priesthood and the scribes who administered the day to day affairs. Three forms of writing had evolved from early protoliterate pictographic inscriptions: the formal hieroglyphic system for monumental inscriptions, cursive hieratic for official records and cursive demotic for other uses. The Egyptian scribes overcame the problems of ambiguity inherent in a mixed syllabic and ideographic system by providing a great amount of redundancy. They attached determinants to signs indicating the class to which the entity denoted by the sign belonged. Besides its utilitarian functions, Egyptian literacy produced also various types of literature, such as religious and "wisdom literature" and long narratives of travels and adventure. Egyptian writing, as stylized as Egyptian art, changed little after its first development. With a rigid caste system and an ubiquitous hieratic and scribal bureaucracy keeping continuous watch over most activities Egyptian civilization, like its art and its writing system, remained static for two millennia with minor interruptions.

After a somewhat later beginning, the Minoan civilization evolved on the island of Crete. Although it showed influences of Mesopotamia, Egypt and Anatolia in its architecture and art, it had its roots in the maritime cultures of the Aegean and developed an individuality quite different from that of its neighbors. The influence of the Minoan civilization on Greece, and thus eventually on European culture, was so important that it merits more detailed consideration. Although the *Iliad* and the *Odyssey* had depicted a highly developed aristocratic Bronze Age society, the skepticism of the early 19th century discounted the epic tradition as a mixture of myth, folktale and fiction. The disbelief extended to the Greek efforts in classical times to distill kernels of historical fact from the traditional stories. Even Thucydides' judicious examination of the legendary material was rejected. The very possibility of the existence of an "Achaean" civilization as described by Homer, of a city like Troy, or of Cretan seapower, hundreds of years before recorded history, encountered general disbelief.

The Homeric epics present a panoramic view of the purported history and unfold a background of an advanced society with very specific characteristics. The force before Troy consists of contingents from many regions of Greece and the islands, each led by its own ruler, who offers more or less voluntary allegiance to the supreme leader of the expedition, Agamemnon, king of Mycenae. Agamemnon's authority rests on his superior prestige, wealth and military power, but depends to a large degree on the consent of the other leaders. When Achilles, wounded in his honor by Agamemnon's high-handed action, withdraws his troop from the fighting, Agamemnon has no recourse and eventually must make apologies and amends beyond the return of the captive girl who was the object of their quarrel. The organization of the army before Troy apparently is representative of the political situation in Bronze Age

Greece. The "Catalogue of Ships" in the second book of the *Iliad* not only lists all the regional contingents and their leaders but, by giving the numbers of their contributions in ships and men, shows the relative importance of the various centers of power. Archaeological investigations have confirmed the evidence of Mycenaean settlements at all the sites mentioned in the Catalogue which could be located.[1]

With the noticeable nostalgia of a poorer age, the Homeric epics describe an affluent society surrounded by beautiful possessions. Skilled craftsmen provide golden goblets, silverstudded swords, and armor with elaborate inlay work. Iron is known but still a rare metal, not used for practical purposes. Teams of fine horses are the pride of their owners. Troy is a walled city of great wealth, apparently not too different from the major Greek centers. In the royal houses guests and strangers enjoy lavish hospitality; they are bathed upon arrival, wined and dined, and sent off with valuable presents. Singers and acrobats provide entertainment. The nobles are always conscious of their obligation to live up to the glory of their ancestors and to leave their own fame to be remembered by future generations. To pass the time they engage in martial and athletic contests, "sing the glory of men" to the lyre, or listen to a professional reciter. Their wives are great ladies, at ease in the company of men and treated by them with great respect, and often preside over social gatherings. The epics frequently mention Crete in a favorable light. Homer calls it "golden Crete" and "the island of a hundred cities." The Cretans are an important contingent in the expeditionary force, and the island is famous for its prosperity and gracious way of living. There is no indication of any cultural or linguistic differences between the Achaean leaders from Crete and the mainland. Thus we are offered a picture of a uniform Aegean culture governed by a chivalrous court society not too different from those of other legendary heroic ages. This, of course, is not surprising since, at least in the western world, the Homeric poems remained the prototypes of all future epic narratives.

In historical Greece, notwithstanding some early skepticism and attempts at rationalization, the Greeks generally accepted the

Homeric epics as their ancestral history, albeit poetically embellished, somewhat as the Bible in its greater outline is by and large accepted as history in the Judaeo-Christian orbit. Similarly, the Homeric poems were considered a storehouse of ethical wisdom and were used as a manual for education of the young. Therefore it can be said that the epics were the greatest single formative influence and unifying factor that shaped the world view of the Greeks in the historical era. The pervasive force of the Homeric mythology, which comprises in nuclear form practically all the known myths of the Greeks, is reflected in most of classical art from vase painting to sculpture to tragedy.

One myth most significant for Aegean history, the story of Theseus, is mentioned only briefly by Homer. At first glance the plot consists of many archetypal mythical themes. Theseus' mission to kill the Minotaur, half-man-- half-bull, takes him into the Labyrinth, home of the monster, whence no one who has entered can return. Images of such hybrid creatures are frequent motives in representation art of the near-Eastern cultural area. This Labyrinth theme is generally considered by mythologists to symbolize a descent into the underworld or death while the protagonist's return represents resurrection. The visit to the land of the dead is performed by every self-respecting hero from Gilgamesh, Heracles, Odysseus, and Aeneas to Jesus. The modern student has the choice between various interpretations: the mystical belief that one has to die in order to know the truth as it can be grasped only by a soul freed of its mortal body; or the Freudian view of the myth as a subconscious wish to return to the womb; or the structuralists' explanation as an attempt to mediate the conflict between life and death and thus to alleviate one's fear of death. Theseus, however, was not aware of any such subtleties.

Besides the underworld theme the Theseus myth contains many other traditional, much used motifs. Minos' daughter Ariadne, like Medea, Atalante and other such maidens, takes the part of her suitor against her father who tries to send him to his death by giving Theseus the skein of thread as a lifeline. The use of a device to find the way back is common in fairy tales-- e.g., Hansel and Gretel, etc. Thus it is no wonder that the Theseus legend, like others, was considered as folktale or fiction devoid of historical interest.

But then new windows were opened on the prehistoric period. From 1875 to 1884 Heinrich Schliemann published three books on the results of his excavations at Troy. In 1878 he gave an account of his discoveries at Mycenae; a report on his excavations in Tiryns followed in 1886. Schliemann's successes spurred intensive and increasingly more scientific archaeological activity throughout the Aegean area. In 1897 Sir Arthur Evans surveyed the site of Knossos and began his excavations in 1900; he continued them, with an interruption caused by World War I, until 1932. Evans presented his findings between 1921 and 1935 in the four monumental volumes of his *The Palace of Minos*.

Evans' discovery of a civilization that flourished during the second millennium BC, comprising the Middle and Late Minoan periods, came as a great surprise. His excavations at Knossos unearthed a large palace. Exploration of other sites at Phaistos, Mallia, Hagia Triada, Gournia, and Zakros followed. The palaces and cities were built around 2000 BC with some rebuilding later after earthquake damage. There is no evidence of fortifications at any time. This indication of the Cretans' confidence in their security seemed to confirm the Greek tradition of "King Minos'" superior seapower and domination of the Aegean. Many other facets of the mythic tradition seemed to find equal confirmation. The archaeological investigations produced evidence of great material wealth, large centers of population, and great aesthetic achievements in a unique style of building, pottery, metal work, painting, dress, and-- significantly-- writing.

The palace of Knossos was a sprawling structure of several stories with many rooms, stairways, passages, courtyards, light and air-shafts, galleries, and water and drainage conduits. It housed not only the rulers, but also a multitude of officials, craftsmen, and servants. To any stranger it must have appeared as a "labyrinth," but there was a deeper meaning to this name. *Labrys* in Greek signifies a double-axe. The symbol of the double axe was everywhere in the Palace of Knossos, the actual tool as well as replicas in jewelry and decoration, topping large upright standards, or appearing in the many wall frescoes. We do not know its significance but there is little doubt that it played a part in some cult. The Labyrinth was the house of the *labrys*, the double axe, and this name is also found in writing on a Linear B tablet from Knossos. There were other reminiscences of the myth: the bull was a frequent subject of paintings and sculptures. Several representations depict a scene in which a human figure grasps an onrushing bull by the horns and vaults over its back to land behind him where a catcher is waiting to receive him or her. Whether this was just an acrobatic game, a religious ritual, or a spectator sport, we do not know, but it may have been the source of the Minotaur story. Other frescoes show great masses of spectators, elaborately dressed and made-up women and men crowding the galleries, apparently watching some spectacle. Similar throngs of both sexes associating freely can be seen participating in processions and dances, something quite unthinkable in the male-dominated Greek society of historic times. A memory is preserved in the charming vignette Homer paints in his description of the dancing place of Ariadne at Knossos on the shield of Achilles (*Il.* 18. 690-605)

If archaeology seemed to confirm some of the memories embedded in myth, it vindicated also the more sober speculations of the classical Greek historians. Herodotus mentions in passing that Minos of Knossos was the first to establish a seapower. Thucydides, trying to peel historical facts out of myth, wrote: "The first person known to us by tradition as having established a seapower is Minos. He made himself master of what now is called the Hellenic sea, and ruled over the Cyclades." Although to date no evidence for the existence of the person or the name of Minos has been found, the maritime focus of the Minoan civilization seems confirmed. As mentioned above, fortifications were absent from the palaces from the beginning of the second millennium BC. According to the palace frescoes Cretan men did not wear arms except decorative daggers, as described by Homer. The wealth of Crete came from maritime trade, especially the export of oil (mostly scented cosmetic oil) and the excellent products of Minoan craftsmanship.

Ample evidence of this export has been found in Egypt and around the rim of the eastern Mediterranean. Conversely many imports from Egypt and Asia, such as ivory, alabaster, gold and gems tones, have been found in Crete in addition to imported artifacts. Egyptian flora and fauna provided many motifs for Minoan decorative designs. The Theseus myth seems to imply that Athens was tributary to Knossos. The archaeological finds on the Greek peninsula and some of the islands indicate a pervasive Minoan influence; the palace culture, mode of womens' dress, pottery and jewelry styles, and metalwork show, if not Cretan provenience, Cretan models. Consequently, Evans concluded that the mainland was colonized by Cretans, and he considered the mainland "Mycenaean" civilization an offshoot and subdivision of the Minoan. There was still no clue to the linguistic or ethnic affiliation of either the Minoan population of Crete or the Mycenaean inhabitants of the mainland. Finally a partial answer was provided in 1952 by Ventris' decipherment of one of the Cretan scripts, Linear B.[2]

To many, especially the followers of Evans, it came as a real shock that the language of the tablets was an early form of Greek. There was no indication in the Greek tradition, either in the myths or in the historians, of any knowledge that the Greeks had ever had any kind of writing other than the alphabet borrowed from the Phoenicians. Although all the tablets turned out to be accounting records of one kind or another, they still shed considerable light on various aspects of cultural life.

Evans had encountered writing from the inception of his excavations. Some specimens were sun-dried clay tablets with incised lines of quasi-geometric signs separated by horizontal dividing lines. Groups of signs were separated within the line by vertical dividers. The signs were written by drawing a pointed instrument over the wet clay surface (in contrast to the jabbing motion by which cuneiform signs were imprinted into the clay). Therefore Evans called the script "linear." He surmised correctly that the writing consisted of ideograms and syllabic signs. He also recognized that the tablets contained two different but closely related types of scripts with some signs common to both, and that the two systems probably served to represent two different languages. To distinguish the two scripts from each other, Evans named them Linear A and Linear B. Two earlier types of notation had also been found. The Phaistos Disk, named after the palace of its provenience, is a clay disk with a diameter of six and a half inches. On each side a spiral with five convolutions was drawn. Within this spiral from the outside in towards the center, from right to left, characters were inscribed in groups of two to seven, separated by dividers. On one side there are 31 groups (words?) totaling 123 signs; on the other face, 30 groups with a total of 118 signs. The disk contains 45 different signs, some of them recurring, representing mostly recognizable objects. The most remarkable feature is that each sign was impressed by a stamp and that thus we are faced with the first example of "printing". The disk was hardened by baking. From the dress of a woman among the signs and a man's headdress on another symbol, it appears that the disk might be a local product. That is also borne out by the fact that other spiral inscriptions of Cretan provenience have been found, and similar signs on a double axe from a sacred cave at Arkalokhori.[3] In addition, Evans found types of signs which he termed hieroglyphic. Today the "hieroglyphic" signs are believed to be syllabic; Evans may have been right to see in them the antecedents of the linear scripts.

Even before the decipherment of the Linear B tablets and the identification of their language as an early form of Greek, serious questions had arisen concerning Evan's views on the relationship between the Minoan-Cretan and the Mycenaean-Mainland civilization (later termed "Helladic"). Such scholars as Nilsson, Wace, and Blegen had been able to shed considerable light on the Mycenaean chronology and the differences between the two cultures. The theory of a Minoan colonization of Greece was doubted because some changes of style in Knossos had been anticipated on the mainland. Homer's Catalogue of Ships listed Knossos as a Greek city. Finds in Mycenae and Pylos in the late 1930's and the 1940's confirmed the suspicion that at least from 1500 BC on, influence extended from Mycenae to Knossos rather than in the opposite direction. These assumptions were strikingly confirmed by the decipherment of the

Linear B tablets as Greek.[4] The language of Linear A is still unknown and is apparently the language of the Pre-Greek Minoan population of Crete. Linear B seems to be an adaptation of Linear A to the Greek language which occurred when the Greeks established themselves in Knossos.

Today approximately 3,000 Linear B tablets from Knossos, 1,000 from Pylos, 60 from Mycenae, and scattered small quantities from other Helladic sites are in existence. The tablets are horizontally ruled and words are separated by vertical dividers. The script consists of about 80 syllabic characters and a great number of ideograms. Each of the syllabic signs represents either a vowel or a consonant followed by a vowel. As mentioned earlier, such a writing system can accurately represent only open syllables and is very unsuited to a language like Greek, with its many consonant clusters and consonant word endings. It was clearly derived from Linear A, with which it had quite a few signs in common and which was certainly used to write a different language.

Despite their limited economic content the tablets shed considerable light on the social and political conditions in the Bronze Age. They vindicate some Homeric descriptions of life, contradict others, and reveal totally unexpected features. Besides confirming the occupation of Knossos by mainland Greeks, they show the cultural if not political unity of the Mycenaean settlements. The names of most of the Homeric gods appear on the tablets in the context of commodity allocations to the various sanctuaries-- the word for sanctuary is *temenos*, the term used by Homer for a religious precinct. The names of many heroes of the epics appear on the tablets as common proper names. Some objects described by Homer are listed in the inventories with descriptions of the same types of decorative features mentioned in the poems. Certain minor but characteristic details in Homer are confirmed by the tablets, e.g., that the wheels and bodies of chariots were stored separately. Many words that had disappeared from the spoken language in classical times are common to Homer and the tablets (e.g. *laos*, *wanax*, etc.)

One completely unexpected feature of Mycenaean society, however, was its centralized, pyramidal, bureaucratic structure, of which there is no hint in the epics. The scribes, it seems, kept track of every man, woman and child in the territory and of their trades, work assignments, rations, taxes in kind or work, and allocations of land and materials to them and to the religious entities. Records are maintained on animals large and small, keeping track of cattle even by name. There are inventory and disbursement lists of wheat, barley, oil, wool, textiles, copper, chariot wheels, all kinds of implements, pots and vessels with detailed descriptions Another unsuspected facet revealed by the tablets was a high degree of "industrialization" in the Mycenaean society, which to some extent explains the need for a great amount of accounting control. For instance, there were some 400 bronzesmiths in the employ of the palace in Pylos. The palace also fed 750 women and as many children, most of whom seem to have been engaged in the production of textiles.[5] The extent of Minoan and Mycenaean export of aromatic oil and unguents to the shorelands of the Mediterranean as far west as Sicily had been previously deduced from archaeological finds of the typical Minoan and Mycenaean containers. Just as in classical Athens, oil was a major source of wealth because it was not only an important factor in the diet, but also the fuel for interior lighting, and the base of cleansing agents for personal hygiene. One Knossos tablet lists 1,800 so-called stirrup-jars, normally used as containers for oil.[6] All in all, about 26 different trades controlled by several layers of functionaries in the palace administration are identified in the tablets. Thus the bureaucratization appears as a consequence of the production system which supported the maritime trade and generated the wealth of the ruling nobility.

Although the tablets offered a great amount of information, it was a disappointment that Mycenaean writing did not provide any texts of a literary, historical, or religious nature. In the absence of a single specimen of non-economic writing, scholars have drawn the conclusion that the Linear B writing system was used exclusively for bookkeeping and administrative purposes. They have further supported this view by pointing to the absence of any reference to a scribal establishment in the tablets themselves, which mention 26 different trades or craft people but no scribes. There is no evidence for scribal schools: no word lists, no practice tablets have been found as in Mesopotamia or Egypt. These scholars also cite the Homeric poems as depicting an illiterate society while discounting the evidence of the Bellerophon passage (about which more later). It is further asserted that Linear B is so clumsy and unsuited to the Greek language that it was inadequate for literary use.[7]

I believe that the dogmatism with which these assertions are being made and widely accepted goes far beyond the justification of arguments *ex absentia*. It will, of course, be impossible to prove a literary use of Linear B until an actual sample has been found. There is very little hope for such a discovery for the same reasons that none has occurred so far. The following factors have to be considered:

1] Unbaked clay tablets are apt to dissolve in contact with moisture and are unlikely to have lasted for centuries in the Greek climate. The main hoards of tablets were apparently preserved because they were baked in the fires that destroyed the buildings which housed them, possibly connected with the events which marked the ends of these Mycenaean power centers. Whatever the cause, the baking and survival of the tablets was purely accidental. Other contemporary writing materials such as papyrus or leather have been preserved only in the absolute dryness of places like the Dead Sea caves, Egyptian tombs or similar desert locations. Although we know from literary sources that these materials were used in historical Greece, none have survived and we would have to deny their use then just as in Mycenaean times if we had to rely on archaeological evidence alone. The preservation of three lots of tablets, one from each of three sites where the script had been in use at least for two centuries, is more in the nature of a freak accident than a sample of any kind of validity.

2] Generally the parts of the buildings where the tablets were found were the storerooms for the commodity to which the tablets pertained. What documents can be expected to be found in an oil-storage place other than store records for oil? Actually Bennett in

Pylos and Olivier in Knossos, by examination of different handwriting and content of the tablets, have been able to relate specific
scribes to the administration of specific commodities.[8]   Thus
Olivier was able to identify by their "hands" ten scribes engaged in
the administration of sheep and wool, fifteen concerned with textiles, three with vessels, fifteen with chariots, etc. In spite of this
degree of specialization, it might still be possible that there was a
poet among the oil clerks, but it appears unrealistic to expect to
find his poem among the oil records-- or for that matter, any type
of literature in our hoards of tablets.

3] In the remains of comparable contemporaneous Near Eastern
civilizations only a small fraction of the preserved texts are literary;
as we have seen, less than 5 percent in cuneiform. All the rest are
economic Thus, *ipso facto*, the probability of finding literary texts is
infinitely smaller than that of finding commercial ones. Yet there is
no parallel among any of the contemporary societies, with all of
whom the Mycenaeans maintained contacts and trade relationships, of not using their script for literary, religious and legal purposes (e.g., Hittites, Mesopotamians, Egyptians). The Mycenaeans
would have constituted an improbable exception in view of all the
interchange of ideas that took place as attested by the communality
of motifs in art, and themes in mythology (papyrus plants, sphinxes,
griffins, composite figures like the Minotaur, etc.).[9]

4] As we have seen, writing came into being to satisfy administrative and economic needs, and that remained its most wide-spread
function. Correspondence between distant localities was part of
this function. The exchange of letters was intensive between all of
the trading partners of the Mycenaeans as attested by the finds of
the far-flung Egyptian correspondence at Tell el Amarna, at Ugarit
(Ras Shamra on the Phoenician coast where a Mycenaean trading
colony existed), and at Bogazkoi in Anatolia where Hittite correspondence with *Ahaiawassa* whom some scholars identify with the
Achaeans has been found. Are we to assume that the Mycenaeans
traded with these peoples without the benefit of written communications, letters, contracts and receipts? There is the well-known
passage in the *Iliad* (6. 168-9) in which Bellerophon is sent to the

king of Lycia to deliver a tablet with "death-bringing signs" which tell the king to kill the bearer-- a clear reference to a letter. Scholars have tried to discount this passage as a later insertion, but Tritsch has conclusively disproved this suggestion.[10] Furthermore there is the internal evidence of the Linear B tablets themselves. The difficulty of representing the Greek phonology required consistent conformance with a rigorous "spelling" system to hold ambiguities to a minimum. Actually, the language, the signs, the format and the writing system on the tablets from more than three widely separated centers, besides the natural variations between different hands, show virtually no differences in modes of writing or dialect. This uniformity can only be explained by continuous communication between the distant settlements-- i.e., correspondence. We know that the sites were connected by roads. We also know that on occasions, such as the Trojan war, the tribes acted in concert. Thus all indications point to a use of Linear B at least for the writing of letters.

5] Generally in archaeology arguments from silence are very deceptive. A good example is the description of body armor in Homer, which for many decades was considered a total anachronism for the bronze age; no such armor could have existed before the 8th century. In 1960 a cist-grave dating to the 15th century was excavated at Dendra in northern Greece. It contained the interment of a warrior with a complete bronze corselet consisting of front and back plates tied with thongs on the sides. Attached to it were shoulderguards, a high collar, and a short skirt, all of bronze and matching Homer's description.[11] Just a few years ago the archaeological record failed to show any Northwest Semitic inscriptions between 1300 and 1000 BC. Today, through revisions in dating and new finds the gap has disappeared. On the island of Cyprus and at Ugarit on the Canaanite coast across from Cyprus three versions of a script clearly derived from Linear A and Linear B have been found. The inscriptions on various objects and tablets date from the 16th to the 11th centuries. Although they share many signs with the Linear scripts and with the classical Cypriot syllabary, their languages are unknown, none have been deciphered and they are lumped under the name of Cypro-Minoan scripts. The classical Greek Cypriot syllabary, however, has been deciphered with the help of an inscription written in both the syllabary and the Greek alphabet. The signs are clearly derived from the Linear scripts by way of the Cypro-Minoan syllabary and the communality of some characters furnished one of the keys for the decipherment of Linear B. The interesting point is that no texts in the classical Cypriot syllabary dating from earlier than the 7th century BC have been found while the latest Cypro-Minoan inscription from Enkomi dates to the 11th century. Thus there exists a 400-year gap in the archaeological record in what we know must have been an unbroken line of transmission. This is a good indication how deceptive the argument *ex silentio* can be when it is based on the archaeological record alone. The Cypriot script also defeats the argument that Linear B was inadequate for literary writing because in spite of the same shortcomings, the Cypriot syllabary was used for poetry.[12] Finally, the ease with which the Greeks adapted the alphabet to their own language indicates some previous familiarity with the mechanics of writing.

Like Greece in historical times, Mycenaean Greece consisted of individual city-states without any central unifying structure. There was no Greek Sargon or Hammurabi and no Greek empire before Alexander the Great although a particularly strong city could take a position of leadership for a time by prestige and power. Mycenae apparently held such a position, as Athens or Sparta did in classical times. There seems to have been a strong bond of common language, religion and tradition which made some common enterprises possible. Classical Greece had a strong consciousness of being heir to Bronze Age Greece. The Mycenaean civilization had been successful for more than three centuries dominating the Greek mainland, most of the Aegean islands, Knossos, and some locations on the coast of Asia Minor. During that time the Greeks controlled the sea and the maritime trade. They developed high skills in architecture, shipbuilding, pottery, metallurgy, and other crafts, and a refined aesthetic sense.

Notwithstanding its limitations, literacy was at the heart of the Mycenaean civilization. The Myceaean palace communities like the earlier Mesopotamian city-states, rested on a complex economic base. Specialization in agriculture, in the culture of the vine and the olive tree in the Aegean complex, and division of labor in manufacturing had been carried to great length. Exchange of goods and commodities through foreign trade provided the wealth for a prestigious and sophisticated lifestyle of the elite in control of the upper layers of the distribution system. Literacy was a prerequisite and the foundation for the administration of the intricate economic structure. Without a monetary medium the exchange of materials, goods and labor between individuals and economic entities had to be centrally planned and controlled by a system of written records. Although the existence of literary activity beyond the accounting functions of the scribes as we have seen is still an open question, there are implications of cognitive and mental processes that go deeper than the few accounting records that have come down to us. These prerequisite thought processes fall into several categories.

The Minoan and Mycenaean Linear signs differ so much in shape and writing technique from earlier and other contemporary scripts that a borrowing from foreign sources (such as Egyptian or cuneiform) can be ruled out. The native origin of the scripts on Crete seems confirmed by the antecedent experimentation in writing and the probable derivation from the earlier "hieroglyphs" as proposed by Evans. "Idea-transmission," however, the suggestion that the Minoans learned the concept of writing or received the idea of written notation from a foreign source, is quite possible. Linear B must have been adapted from Minoan Linear A for Greek use after the occupation of Knossos. This, as G. S. Kirk points out,[13] opens the door to many interesting speculations. The people who converted the script from Minoan to Mycenaean must have known both languages. Thus we again find bilingualism associated with literacy in the creation of a civilization.

The assumption that bilingualism may have been quite common is believable if we consider the continuous interplay between the

Minoan and Mycenaean cultures. Whether the Minoans dominated the mainland at one time, as Evans proposed, or not, their influence there was pervasive: Minoan styles in women's dress, in pottery, furniture, jewelry, metallurgy, etc. were adopted by the Mycenaeans. Either Greeks employed Cretan craftsmen or else Greek artisans had served their apprenticeship in Crete. In either case a considerable extent of communication and association must be assumed, which would have been impossible without a certain prevalence of bilingualism on both sides. Around or after 1450 BC, Mycenaean Greeks occupied Knossos and ruled over Minoans, an event which certainly fostered the spread of bilingualism. It was during that time that Greek Linear B was developed from Minoan Linear A presupposing a literate bilingual group of people. Kirk suggests that the Mycenaeans simply took over the palace of Knossos and its economy and had no reason to change the clerical control system. It would seem that in this case the Minoan scribes might just as well have continued the bookkeeping in their own language and script unless the Greek masters wanted to be able to read the records so that they could take control of the operations. Thus the change of the language and consequently the change of the script imply an expansion of literacy, or at least of the ability to read, to include the governing elite in addition to the record clerks. And indeed it is hard to imagine that the rulers in Pylos as well as in Knossos, whose total wealth and power depended on the palace economy, would take so little interest in the stocks and movements of their goods and commodities, that they would leave the accounting an arcane secret in the hands of their scribes. The destination of the tablets for eyes other than those of the scribes alone is also indicated by their format which seems designed to facilitate their being read by not fully literate persons. In fact it is the simplicity of their standard format which made modern decipherment possible. The tablets usually contain an ideogram, recognizable in most cases as the pertinent commodity or article, followed by a few easily learned numerals, short descriptive remarks, and the destination or provenience in form of a personal name or place name or some other identification of the provider or recipient.

On the other hand, if the content of the tablets was easy to read for someone fully conversant with the language (which modern scholars are far from), such a person habitually reading the signs would have eventually learned to write them. Thus, literacy may not have been as narrowly confined as it is made out to have been. The standardization of the language points towards the same direction of an attempt to assure readability by an audience larger than the group of scribes themselves. Some scholars believe the language of the tablets is an artificial amalgam of various dialects somewhat like the later poetic language of the Homeric epics, a sort of Mycenaean *koine*.[14] This would explain its uniformity from place to place and the absence of change over several centuries. There is then a possibility that literacy may have been spread throughout the governing class in a situation analogous to that in the Near Eastern kingdoms, as Webster has suggested, where a literate and bilingual elite was the incubator of cultural advance.

Towards the end of the second millennium the Mycenaean palace complexes were successively destroyed. There are still disputes of plus or minus 50 years concerning the exact dates, but general agreement exists that by thousand BC the Mycenaean and Minoan civilizations and a large part of the population had disappeared. Various theories have been advanced to explain the collapse. None of them has found wide acceptance, and any one of them alone or in combination with others might offer adequate explanations.

An invasion by new tribes, the Dorians coming from the north, was for a long time generally accepted as cause of the fall. In the latter part of the 13th century BC a wall was built across the Isthmus of Corinth with the apparent intent to protect the Peloponnesos against an enemy descending from the north. Around the same time Mycenae, Tiryns, Argos, and Athens improved their fortifications and water supplies. Shortly thereafter occurred the destruction of the palaces at Pylos, Tiryns, and Mycenae, followed by a general decline of population and abandonment of as many as 90 percent of the inhabited sites. But there is no archaeological evidence for arrival of a new population group or of re-occupation of the abandoned Mycenaean sites. The Dorian dialect is now believed to have evolved by gradual linguistic change.[15] V.R. d'A. Desborough thinks that the Greek tradition of the coming of the Dorians and a series of migrations continuing after the Trojan war can well be reconciled with the archaeological evidence if one assumes not a sudden invasion, but rather a continuous pressure from the north which caused a chain-reaction of tribes migrating south and displacing others on the way. This steady movement of populations eventually reached the Peloponnesos in the 13th and 12th centuries. He believes the Dorians spread out much later in the Dark Age.[16]

Another hypothesis is that the Mycenaean power-centers were destroyed by internal revolt. Because violent destruction is undeniable and as there is no evidence of foreign invaders or of any new cultural elements, it is argued the attack must have come from within. There is some support for this possibility in the Greek epic tradition: in the *Nostoi* we find many stories of violence at the reception of the homecomers: Agamemnon killed by Clytaemestra and Aegisthus, Odysseus' bout with Penelope's suitors, the fate of old Peleus, the murder of Neoptolemus, etc. Thucydides tells us that a period of factional strife followed the Trojan war (1.12.2). Hesiod says that the age of heroes ended because they killed off each other (*Works and Days* 152).

Rhys Carpenter has advanced the thesis that a sudden climatic change may have caused prolonged drought and crop failures leading to famine, emigration, and possibly internal conflict. Soil studies and pollen analyses, however, have given no indication of a radical climatic change at that time. Another study points out analogies between the mediaeval period in western Europe and the Post-Mycenaean period in Greece. It finds some close parallels between the Mycenaean palace economy of the 14th century BC, as depicted in the Linear B tablets, and the economy of mediaeval estates in the 12th century AD. During both periods of material and cultural prosperity, populations increased, and previously untilled lands were put into production furthering. more population increase. Since in the primitive agriculture only a small surplus is available to feed the nonagrarian part of the population, it would take only two or three bad harvests in succession caused by the exhaustion of the marginal lands, once the original nutrients were used up, to cause famine conditions. Estate records show that this is what happened in mediaeval Europe. Hutchinson sees in the Pylos grain tablets the reflection of a very similar economic situation of prosperity and population increase in the 15th and 14th centuries BC, resulting in an inevitable decline in the 13th.[17] J. Chadwick, an early interpreter of the Linear B tablets, also notes the parallels between the Mycenaean and mediaeval economies.[18]

I suggest that there is probably some truth in all these theories. No sudden climatic catastrophe may have occurred, but rather a gradual destruction of the ecological balance by the inhabitants. The Homeric poems, the representations in Bronze Age art, and the records reflect a much greater fertility of Greece in the second millennium BC than existed in classical or modern times. There is evidence of an abundance of cattle wild or tame (e.g. the Vapheio cups). From Homer we hear of hecatombs, i.e. one hundred oxen sacrificed at one time. Meat was the mainstay of the Achaean diet.[19] Stories and pictures of lions are common. Their representations in Mycenaean art, such as on the inlaid dagger blades from the shaft graves of Mycenae, are most lifelike. It is clear that the artists knew lions from their own experience. By the classical period lions were certainly extinct on the Greek peninsula;[20] their images in art had become conventionalized and unrealistic. Lions can exist only in an environment able to support large grazing animals. Such conditions no longer existed in historical Greece. It cannot be proven that the Mycenaeans were responsible, but Homer's Achaeans were lavish in their use of wood. In the *Iliad*, they denude a whole mountain for Achilles' funeral pyre. Even allowing for Homer's heroic scale it is easy to imagine the effect of the unrestricted use of timber for building, shipbuilding, and the use of wood as the only known fuel for heating and cooking on perpetual hearthfires. Centuries of relentless deforestation, overgrazing and primitive farming methods must have led to a loss of topsoil, which, overlaying a permeable limestone as in Greece, is a thin and precarious cover anyway. When the vegetation no longer was able to support cattle, the proliferation of goats and sheep accelerated the soil erosion. The Knossos tablets show almost a hundred thousand sheep at one time.[21] We know that in historical times the same process of denudation took place on the Italian penninsula and on the Dalmatian coast where similar conditions prevailed. The depletion of the agricultural resources may have impelled the Mycenaeans to undertake the ill-fated expeditions to Troy and Egypt. Resentment over costly wars abroad and famine at home would have led to internal strife, dislocation of populations, attacks on the centers of wealth and power with their storehouses, and overthrow of the establishment. This picture is consistent with the archaeological evidence which reflects a long period of deterioration and decline rather than a sudden catastrophe. The same process is now under way in Sub-Saharan Africa.

Notes

1. R. Hope Simpson and J. F. Lazenby, *Catalogue of Ships in Homer's Iliad* (Oxford 1970)

2. Michael Ventris and John Chadwick, *Documents In Mycenaean Greek* (Cambridge 1956)

3. R. F. Willets, *The Civilization of Ancient Crete* (Berkeley and Los Angeles 1977), 95

4. Emily Vermeule, *Greece in the Bronze Age* (Chicago 1964), 137-9; G. S. Kirk, *The Songs of Homer* (Cambridge 1962), 7-9

5. T.B.L. Webster, *From Mycenae to Homer* (London 1964), 110; J.V. Luce, *Homer and the Heroic Age* (New York and London 1975), 85

6. Vermeule, *Greece in the Bronze Age*, 138

7. Rudolf Pfeiffer, *The History of Classical Scholarship from the Beginnings to the End of the Hellenistic Age* (Oxford 1968), 21

8. J.P. Olivier, *Les Scribes de Cnossos* (Rome 1967), 8, 108; E.L. Bennett Jr., *Mycenaean Studies*, (Madison 1964)

9. Webster, 284; C.H. Gordon, *The Commom Background of the Greek and Hebrew Civilizations* (Toronto 1964), 52, 143 and *passim*

10. F. J. Tritsch, "Bellerophon's Letter" in *Atti e Memorie del 1º Congresso Internationale di Micenologia* v.l (Rome 1968), 1223-1230

11. Vermeule, 135

12. Olivier Masson, *Les inscriptions Chypriotes syllabiques* (Paris 1961), 40-41, 138, 284

13. Kirk, 26-29

14. V. Georgiev, "Mycenaean among the other Greek Dialects" in E. L .Bennett, *Mycenaean Studies* (Madison 1964)

15. A.M. Snodgrass, *The Dark Age of Greece* (Edinburgh 1971),   385-386.

16. V.R. d'A. Desborough, *The Greek Dark Ages* (London 1972), 324 and *passim*

17. J.S. Hutchinson *Historia* 26 (1977), 1-23

18. John Chadwick, *The Mycenaean World* (Cambridge 1976), 111 f. and *passim*

19. Snodgrass, 378

20. Snodgrass, 435)

21. J.T. Killen, *BSA* 59 (1964), 5, n.23

4

Dark Age and Rebirth

After the fall of Mycenae, just as after the fall of Rome, an era of advanced civilization gave way to upheavals, widespread population movements, general regression in the arts, insecurity, and especially a loss or near-loss of literacy lasting several centuries. During both periods there were areas of continuity and lingering remembrance of the past, so that recovery when it eventually arrived could be viewed as a renascence rather than a new beginning. The comparison, however, should not be pushed too far. In both cases the term Dark Age has been hotly disputed.

Essentially two meanings are implied in this designation: first, a timespan of which little is known as a result of the total absence or a low level of literacy; second, a period of material and cultural depression, perhaps caused by as well as resulting in a loss of literacy. Because much more archaeological information has come to light since the term Dark Age was first applied to the Post-Mycenaean period, a great amount of effort has been expended by scholars to re-valuate our knowledge and opinions about it. Thorough study of the archaeological evidence leads Snodgrass, Desborough, Chadwick, and others to the conclusion that the term Dark Age truly fits Greek history from 1200 to 900 BC. This judgment is based on the following characteristics: a devastating decline in population, a decline or loss of technological skills and arts (most strikingly the loss of the art of writing) a loss of communications, a decline in living standards, and general insecurity. The evidence of burials, grave gifts, building remnants, and pottery attests to these conditions.

A decline in craftsmanship in pottery, beginning in the 12th century and accelerating in the 11th, is paralleled by a loss of skill in the other arts. Monumental architecture and building on a large scale have ceased; mudbrick takes the place of stone as building material. Sculpture, painting and gem-cutting have disappeared. The art of writing is generally said to have been completely forgotten, but this point will be discussed more extensively below. All these manifestations indicate a material collapse that goes much deeper. At its base is a tremendous decline in population. For instance, of 320 sites known to have been occupied in the 13th century BC, only about 40 were occupied in the 11th.[1] Desborough estimates that the population had been reduced by 90 percent.[2] Since these conditions applied also to the islands and Asia Minor, emigration cannot have been the reason for the depopulation. Except around Athens and in the Argolid, the occupation of traditional sites seems to have been totally interrupted. Everywhere we find poverty, insecurity and isolation. Most settlements along the coast have been abandoned, probably out of fear of piracy. Inland settlements are often in remote, inaccessible locations. Elaborate tombs have given way to simple wood-lined cist graves, pithos burial, or cremation. Burial, especially of children, is often intramural under floors. Imported materials such as ivory, gold, gems, faience and even copper or tin are no longer available, and where some have been found they were obtained from melted down old Mycenaean objects and the workmanship is primitive. There is even a return to obsidian for implements. The only attempts at plastic art are in clay, and even in jewelry baked clay and bone take the place of precious materials. Communications with most of the outside world seem lacking between 1025 and 950 BC.[3]

Athens appears to have been the only major Mycenaean population center which weathered the storm. Thucydides says in his *Histories* that among all the Greeks, the Athenians were the only ones who were still dwelling where they had originated, and that in the upheavals after the Trojan War so many people took refuge in Athens that they eventually had to send colonists to Ionia (1.2,12; 2.36). This tradition is corroborated by the archaeological finds. At the end of the 13th or the beginning of the 12th century the Athenians had strengthened the defenses of the Acropolis, added an emergency water supply and abandoned the houses outside the walls.[4] The use of the burial grounds and the pottery sequence in Athens show no break. Athens not only survived but became a shelter for refugees from other areas. The migration from Athens to Ionia began in the 11th century and gathered momentum in the 10th. Another center of continuity was in the Argolid, which supported emigration to Cyprus, where Mycenaean settlement had begun in the 13th century. Cyprus and Arcadia shared linguistic features that are thought to have originated in the Bronze Age and which characterized the Arcado-Cyprian dialect in the 5th century BC. Recent archaeological finds of Mycenaean IIIC1, supposedly Arcadian, pottery at old Paphos lend credence to the legendary connection between the Argolid and Cyprus.[5] Maritime communications between Athens, Ionia, Cyprus, and the Argolid seem never to have been completely interrupted. It is probable that the most important innovation of the Dark Age, the technology of iron-working, came to Greece from Cyprus. The late tenth century marks the beginning of the Iron Age in Greece. Significantly, when gradual recovery began in the 9th century, it originated in Athens, Ionia, the Argolid and Cyprus.

One of the most startling aspects of the collapse of the Mycenaean civilization is the loss of the art of writing. Some scholars have refused to accept the possibility that literacy, once established, could be forgotten again. Their arguments are similar to those quoted above in defense of the assumption that Linear B might have been put to literary use. In his introduction to Michael Ventris' and John Chadwick's pioneering work,[6] A.J.B. Wace stated that the decipherment of Linear B removed the last excuse for the notion of an illiterate age in Greece. If one assumes that the Greeks learned the Phoenician letters around 1100 BC, no gap would exist and such a date used to be widely accepted.[7] But Rhys Carpenter from a comparison of Phoenician and Greek letter-forms argued for a date in the last quarter of the 8th century.[8] The debate has continued ever since. Recent opinion favors the middle of the 8th century for introduction of the alphabet, but the controversy has by no means ended. Semiticists generally advocate the 10th or 11th centuries because they see in the Greek letters the earlier Semitic lapidary style rather than the later cursive writing.[9] There are other arguments that have been adduced by scholars who do not believe in the Greek "literacy gap." But this is not the place to try to decide this controversy; I do not think its import on this study is of a crucial nature: it would seem that if any form of literacy existed during the Dark Age, outside of Cyprus, from where it had no apparent influence on the rest of Greece, it was so thinly spread and so isolated that it did not affect developments at all until the alphabet was widely diffused from the 8th century on- wards. Thus cultural regression seems as inextricably connected with regression of literacy as cultural advance is connected with ad- vances in literacy. At least this appears as applicable to the Greek Dark Age as to the European Dark Age after the fall of Rome, when indeed a few oases of literacy survived in western Europe.

Similarly, in prehistoric Greece a few localities managed to pre- serve relative security and material well-being in comparison with the surrounding depression and disruption. To these centers must be attributed what memories and cultural continuity survived the dark 11th and 10th centuries. When recovery slowly began in the 9th, it radiated outward from these places: Geometric pottery styles from Athens, use of iron from Cyprus, and eventually maritime trade from Athens, Ionia, and newly important Corinth. A gradual increase in population resulted in re-occupation of abandoned Mycenaean sites and settlement of new locations, and culminated in a veritable population explosion in the 8th century BC, which gave impetus to large scale emigration - the colonization of Sicily and Southern Italy, and to a lesser movement along the Black Sea. The increasing contacts with the outside world, notably Egypt and Phoenicia, manifested their influence in Greek orientalizing art and especially in the adoption and adaptation of the Phoenician al- phabet. Writing in the new Greek alphabet proliferated through- out the Greek lands in the 7th century and marked the beginning of the Greek renascence.

For most of Greece the period from the 12th to the 9th century had been a true dark age, but it incubated several social and cul- tural developments that prepared the way for an unprecedented success of literacy when the alphabet finally reached the Greeks. Some of the most important of these developments were: Geometric pottery, emancipation from feudal aristocratic and theocratic establishments, emergence of the *polis*, and the evolution and perfection of oral poetry.

Pottery had developed a new aesthetic sense based on geometric perception, symmetry, balance and proportion. In mathematics empirical and intuitive recognition of relationships almost always precedes logical derivation and theoretical formulation.[10] Familiarity with the shapes and abstract designs of Geometric pottery prepared the Greeks for their encounter with applied and theoretical mathematics.

The Mycenaean kingdoms, if we draw conclusions from the analogy of other contemporary empires, had rested on a strong theocratic foundation; this is confirmed by the evidence of the Linear B tablets. We learn of large quantities of different commodities delivered to various religious entities. The tablets mention considerable numbers of slaves or servants of the gods (*hierodouloi*), owned by the sanctuaries. The word *basileus*, which in the Linear B tablets had designated subordinates of the *wanax*, meant "king" in the Homeric poems, but as used by Hesiod, presumably at the end of the 8th century BC, it was the title of the petty princes or aristocrats who ruled collectively in the cities. In Athens, where nine *archontes* held the executive power, one of them charged with the supervision of religious rituals and practices held the title *basileus*, indicating the former hieratic power of the king. A recent study confirms that the title *basileus* in post-heroic Greece designated certain magistracies, rather than kingship.[11] Furthermore, the epics and myths preserve the memory of the authority once held by powerful priests and professional seers, such as Calchas, Chryses, and Tiresias. When the religious and royal hierarchies disappeared in the upheavals which left the palaces in ruins, even the title of the ruler (*wanax*) vanished from the post-Homeric colloquial language. In archaic Greece after the Dark Age no hierocratic establishment controlled the lives of men; there is no sign of the crushing weight of religious fear that lay so heavily over most

Near Eastern empires. What theocratic institutions may have existed in Mycenaean Greece had been swept away with the palaces. Only Delphi retained a measure of prestige. This prestige was probably well founded: since the oracle was consulted by travellers, traders and politicians from far and wide, the priests there would have been better informed about the world situation and in a better position than anyone else to judge the consequences of different courses of action.

Homer's poetry, as Nilsson has pointed out, shows an unprecedented emancipation from superstition. Anthropomorphism has been carried to its logical conclusions. The gods, except for their greater power and immortality, are in every respect like humans with all their foibles. In the *Iliad* all the comic relief is provided by the frailties and lapses of the gods. Gods, like men, are subject to fate and to an extent to the laws of nature. They show great strength, but hardly any magical powers. They do not create something *ex nihilo*, or cause something to happen by just willing it. They must use physical means of some kind to accomplish their intent. If they want to displace themselves, they might leap or fly or ride a chariot over water or through the air, but they cannot simply wish themselves to their destination instantly; they have to use some kind of transportation consuming a certain amount of time. When a god desires to heal a wounded human, he cannot do it by an act of will or even by the laying on of hands; he has to apply some powerful herb or ointment to the wound. Even Zeus is not all-knowing and can be deceived by Hera. The gods represent the forces of nature and the externalized forces within human beings. Homer does not hesitate to create his own abstractions, to personify these as gods, and to use religion as allegory. We encounter such deities as Anger, Rumor, Panic, and the Prayers: daughters of Zeus, slow of foot, always behind fast moving Delusion (*Ate*).

Thus for the first time in history we find a religious climate in which man does not cringe before the gods, because he is able to understand them and free to form his own image of them, free also from a priesthood with the power to enforce its orthodoxy. And when literacy arrives it will be accessible to all instead of being a jealously guarded monopoly of priests who use writing as holy writ to ensure their own power.

Religious emancipation was paralleled by political and social change. The breakup of central authority, the isolation of settlements in a hostile environment and the collective enterprises of emigration and colonization had fostered a greater sense of community in the cities. Changes in military tactics had shifted the balance from the aristocratic chariot warriors to massed heavily armed infantry. The citizen soldiers, training and fighting together as *hoplitai* in close order formation, had become the decisive factor in warfare and were beginning to assert their weight in city governance. Although the cities were still largely under the control of the aristocratic families by virtue of their wealth and prestige, a greater sense of cohesion and responsibility for the city, as well as competition for power, had initiated the evolution of the city towards the *polis* as communal association of all freeborn male citizens. There never had been a rigid caste system in Greece, as for instance in Egypt. Privilege of birth, of landownership, of wealth had been and always remained important in Greek politics, but as the consent of the governed continued to become more and more indispensable in the administration of the evolving *polis*, class differences were on the way to becoming less of an unbridgeable gulf than they had been in any of the surrounding empires.

Thus an environment of relative equality existed in archaic Greece and much greater intellectual freedom than in any previous or contemporary political entity-- with the possible exception of the earliest Sumerian city-states, which had provided a receptive soil for the first growth of a literate civilization.

During the Dark Age, as Milman Parry has demonstrated, the Greeks had developed the highly refined and versatile art form of oral poetry that resulted in the Homeric epics, which needed only the *litterae* to become literature. The intellectual climate was ready for literacy when the alphabet arrived.

The problem of the actual date of the introduction of the alphabet into Greek territories has been briefly noted in the foregoing. Today the most generally accepted opinion is that the Greek alphabet originated close to the middle of the 8th century B.C. This is also the opinion of L.J. Jeffery, whose monumental work, *The Local Scripts of Ancient Greece*, is internationally considered the most authoritative work on early Greek literacy. The exact place of transmission is unknown.

There is, however, no question concerning the source of the alphabet. The Greeks themselves called their letters the "Phoenicians." The Greek name for a book was *biblion* after the Phoenician city of Byblos, which was apparently their source of papyrus rolls. As Byblos is the source of the earliest cuneiform "alphabetic" inscriptions, it might be the place where the Greeks first became acquainted with the Semitic alphabet. But there are other places along the Syrian-Palestinian coast where the Greeks had contact with Phoenicians-- such as Al Mina, where a Greek trading colony existed, or off-shore Cyprus, where Greeks and Phoenicians lived side by side. In the Bible (note *biblion*), the Phoenician area was called Canaan and its inhabitants Canaanites. Linguistically they belonged to the West Semitic language family, which also includes Hebrew and Aramaic. There is a consensus that the West Semitic alphabet gradually evolved over several centuries until it was fully developed in about 1000 B.C, the approximate date of the first inscriptions. It consisted of 22 letters expressing consonants only, and was written from right to left. The Greeks, however, adapted the Phoenician alphabet to their own language by using five characters whose Semitic sounds had no equivalent in Greek to represent the five vowels a, e, i, o, and y. Thus, the Greek alphabet of 22 letters came closest to the ideal relationship of one letter for each sound in the language and was subsequently adopted by all western countries, with slight modifications. The Greeks later added the consonants *Chi, Phi, Psi,* and *Xi,* and differentiated between the long and short o and the long and short e. At first the Greeks, following the Semitic example, had been writing from right to left and this tradition continued in one-line inscriptions for some time. But soon, when need arose for several lines, the writers, at the end of each line, reversed direction, making the individual letters about face at the same time. In this way writing as the plowing ox turns at the end of each furrow (*boustrophedon*) became a popular style. Vase painters, labeling the characters in painted scenes, wrote in either direction so as to begin the name as close as possible to the depicted character. Thus the direction of writing became loose and optional for a time until it was eventually standardized from left to right.

This account is an oversimplification because there were many local variants, especially between eastern and western Greeks, and different uses of some of the Semitic letters in various localities, but it depicts the essential outline of the developments which eventually ended with the adoption of the "Ionian" alphabet by the Athenians in their official inscriptions in 403 B.C. The Ionian alphabet and orthography became the standard for all of Greece. It must be emphasized that from the beginning all the variants of Greek writing reflected the same principle of unambiguous phonetic presentation of the spoken language with a great economy in the number of signs realized, to a degree seldom equaled afterwards. It was the first time anywhere in the world that reading and writing could be learned easily by practically everyone, including children.

From the first appearance of Greek writing in the archaeological record, inscriptions and graffiti proliferated at a steady rate in all areas inhabited by Greeks; the rapid dissemination of the alphabet was not restricted by any social barriers. Literacy reached all classes of the population, including stonemasons, potters and mercenary soldiers. Many of the earliest preserved inscriptions are casual graffiti. To be sure, writing was generally confined to personal names such as the labeling of characters on painted pottery, or to simple statements identifying the creators or the owners of artifacts, the donors or recipients of votive gifts, or the "Kilroy was here" type of graffiti. Inscriptions containing more than a personal name frequently are in the form of an utterance of the inscribed object, e.g. "X made me", "X dedicated me to Athena", "I am (property) of K", "I am the gravestone (sema) of X, daughter of Y." Although such statements are no evidence of great literary articulateness, their shortness is probably attributable in part to the limitations of avail-

able space on the inscribed surfaces and to the fact that anyone
writing on stone with hammer and chisel will not tend to verbosity.
And as primitive as some of the epigraphic specimens may appear,
they imply an important assumption, namely the author's or his
client's expectation that the inscription can be and will be read by
its viewers.

Inscriptions on grave steles and votary objects soon expanded
into metric epigrams of one or more lines. The supposition of a
reading citizenry is also indicated by the appearance of law codes
on temple walls on Crete, the earliest in Dreros from the 7th century B.C., followed by another one at Gortyn. Parts of law codes
have been found on walls of buildings in eight Cretan cities. As we
have tried to show in our discussion of Mesopotamian literature,
the formulation of written laws is a most important step towards
abstract thought. Once the concept of the rule of law has been established in human society, it is a short step to transferring the
same principle to an anthropomorphic view of nature and to visualize the sequence of physical events as following predetermined
laws. Scientific thought originated from the attempt to ascertain
these "natural laws." Literacy is a prerequisite for the formulation
of both concepts, human as well as natural law. Mosaic law began
with ten inscribed tablets.

It is historically significant that the first preserved law codes are
found on Crete. In the Greek tradition, king Minos of Crete and
another Minoan, Radamanthys, were considered the first lawgivers
and consequently the judges of the dead in the underworld. Just as
Mycenaean literacy had originated in Minoan Crete, archaic Crete
was possibly one of the first if not the first Greek area to attain alphabetic literacy and to use it almost immediately to codify laws.
Plato viewed the Spartan constitution and laws as derived from
Crete and directly descended from the kingdom of Minos. Plato
made the Minoan constitution, as he conceived it, the model of his
ideal state in the *Republic*.

During the 6th century law codes were promulgated in Athens
and other Greek cities. It was a time of social unrest throughout
Greece. The pressures of population increase and the resulting re-

peated division of small farms, in the absence of a law of primo-geniture, and the competition for small farmers and artisans from an increasing number of slave-operated larger estates caused great hardships. At the same time the introduction of coinage and a money economy based on expanding trade created a new wealthy class in addition to the older landed aristocratic families who mo-nopolized the political and judicial powers. The political and social tension caused revolts or the threat of revolts in many cities. "Tyrants" used the discontent of the underprivileged and the ambi-tions of the newly rich to seize power and to establish autocratic governments. In almost every case, the first demand of the com-mon people, the *demos*, was the promulgation and public display of written laws. The insistence on written law codes shows not only that a relatively great number of people must have been able to read, but also the close relationship between written law and the concept of legality and legitimacy in government. Our language still reflects this concept, as the words legality and legitimacy come from the Latin root *leg*, meaning law.

In addition to its function in epigraphy and law, writing began to play its part in literature. The Homeric poems were written down, probably in one of the cities of Ionia, soon after the alphabet be-came known. There is general agreement that Hesiod was ap-proximately contemporary with the first written texts of Homer. Al-though Hesiod's work has many of the earmarks of oral formulaic poetry, and is considered such by some scholars, his *Theogony* and *Works and Days* appear to be in an entirely different class. They clearly show the original imprint of an individual author. As Hes-iod's foremost commentator M.L. West remarks, "And they (viz. Hesiod's poems) belonged to him, inalienably, more than any oral poet's work has ever done."[12] West further believes that Hesiod wrote his poems down.

Some scholars try to erect an artificial dividing line between oral and written poetry and have tried to classify Hesiod as an oral poet on the basis of his use of some of the formulaic language of oral poetry. I believe the question is moot because in the last analysis all poetry is to an extent oral. One cannot write a line of poetry without first sounding it out, if not aloud, then at least silently to one's internal ear. It makes no difference whether it is written down afterwards or not. The oral technique comes into play mostly when the poet improvises before an audience, drawing on his repertory of memorized formulas. But even a literate poet steeped in the Homeric language will tend to express himself in its terms, as the dramatists so frequently do. There is, however, a difference between Hesiod and the reciter of oral poetry that goes much deeper, a difference that might already to a lesser extent set Homer apart from the singers of the true oral tradition. This difference is the poet's consciousness of how he is using his art.

In the *Theogony* Hesiod deliberately tries to use literally or allegorically all the traditional myths of the gods and the creation to construct a connected rational history of the world-- rational, that is, on the basis of the available knowledge. It is a natural history and also a history of civilization, with the gods acting as personifications of natural forces as well as of abstract concepts. There is still no differentiation between the concrete and the abstract. His creation story, beginning with the *gamos* of Sky and Earth, is a continuing process of separation and proliferation of every conceivable divine, natural, and human entity, force, and idea, evolving towards order, intelligence and civilization.

The *Works and Days*, ostensibly giving instructions to Hesiod's brother on how to become a good farmer and citizen, is a manual on social ethics that could well have been issued by New England puritans. As a fitting counterpart to the Homeric aristocratic ethical value system, it presents the aspirations of the small subsistence farmer and incidentally depicts the economic and social class conflict in the Greek cities. While Hesiod uses the traditional stories, he shapes them to suit his purpose.

In Hesiod we find a consciousness not only of his work, but also of himself as an individual. He tells us who he is and how he received his inspiration for poetry, and he is never reluctant to present his view of the world as his own. The poet's awareness of his own personal feelings becomes an important part of literate lyric poetry, which appeared at the same time or shortly after Hesiod.

Greek lyric poetry as we know it, like epic, must have been the culmination of a long oral tradition. The earliest preserved written examples show already a variety of well developed meters. It is clear that among the Greeks, as in all other cultures, songs for many occasions were customary, such as marching songs, work-songs, hymns and prayers, and songs accompanying weddings, funerals and other rituals. Pictorial representations of musicians, dancers, and groups of people singing in unison go back to Minoan times (e.g. the famous "Harvester Vase"). Greek tradition preserves the names of ancient legendary singers, such as Orpheus, Amphion and Arion. Some of the poets of the 7th and 6th centuries B.C. stayed within the Homeric tradition. Callinus and Tyrtaeus applied the heroic aristocratic ideals of conduct to the citizen soldiers of their *polis*. Epic had been concerned with the past and the conventional view. These themes were now reshaped to fit changed social conditions, and to convince every common defender of his city that he was another Achilles obliged to live up to the heroic code.

But even Archilochus, the first lyric poet whose work was preserved in classical times and is known to us, put himself deliberately into opposition to the conventional wisdom and values. Hesiod had been a shepherd. Archilochus tells us that he was a mercenary soldier: " I serve Ares, the lord, yet know well the lovely gift of the Muses... By the spear my bread is won, by the spear my Ismaric wine, and I drink it leaning on my spear." The traditional sentiment about the fallen hero is expressed by the martial poet Tyrtaeus: "young and old equally lament him, the whole city mourns him, his grave and his children are famous, and his children's children and their future generations. His glory and his name never die and, although beneath the earth, he is immortal." Realistic Archilochus is not afraid to sing a different tune: "No man by dying gains respect and fame among his fellow citizens. We all who are alive seek the favor of the living. The dead will always have the worst of it" (quotations from the translation by Richard Lattimore, *Greek Lyrics* [2nd ed. Chicago and London 1960]).

The greatest hindrance to a fleeing warrior was his heavy shield and thus it was apt to be thrown away. Consequently loss of the shield in battle was the symbol of cowardice and disgrace. The famous Spartan maxim was: A soldier returns either with his shield or on it. Archilochus flouted the convention:

> Some Thracian gloats over my shield now; reluctantly I left this flawless implement under a bush, but I saved myself. What do I care about that shield? Let it be damned; I'll buy one just as good.

The 7th and the 6th centuries BC have been called the age of Greek lyric. They mark the beginning of literary self-assertion of the individual, sparked by the spread of literacy. The tendency to oppose the poet's own feelings to the traditional view appears not only in other poems of Archilochus, but throughout Greek lyric poetry. Sappho begins one of her poems: "Some say the most beautiful sight on earth is a parade of men on horseback, others of men on foot, still others a line of ships, but I say the one I love." Solon, lawgiver, statesman and poet, in a similar vein contradicts popular belief:

> Our city will never be destroyed by Zeus' allotted fate nor the intent of the felicitous immortal gods... The citizens themselves in their folly want to overthrow their great city, driven by greed. (my trl.)

This statement is typical for its era, as it states original thought while reshaping a passage in Homer (*Odyssey* 1.32) and adapting it to the economic-political power struggle of its own time. Without a doubt, in the 7th and 6th centuries lyric poetry, like epic, was composed to be recited and heard rather than read. This is especially true for choral poetry, the martial songs of Callinus and Tyrtaeus. It seems equally clear that some of the intimately personal lyrics such as Sappho's love poems cannot have been meant for public recitation, at least not by the poets themselves and probably not during their lifetimes. That written copies existed and were circulated is attested by several facts. The poets were familiar with each other's work. Simonides quoted poems by two other poets and then opposed their content. Pindar celebrating a victor in the Nemaean games, says "my poem will go out from Aegina in the hold of every ship." (*Nemaean* 5.1-3). Collections of poems survived over several centuries and some of them eventually wound up in the library of Alexandria.

As Hesiod stood at the beginning of literate self-conscious poetry, so he can also be considered the forerunner of Greek cosmological speculation. According to Aristotle "philosophy" began in Ionia, and its first representative was Thales of Miletus. The term *philosophia*, "love of wisdom", was coined much later(probably by Socrates or Plato) to designate all search for knowledge and wisdom, which still were an indivisible whole, including religion, cosmology, ethics, and the beginnings of what were to become the different branches of science. Philosophy in this sense began not with a rejection of the mythical tradition but rather with attempts to understand and confirm it on the basis of rationality and observation. It is no coincidence that the search for reasoned knowledge started in Ionia, where literacy had gained a strong early foothold. In Ionia the Homeric poems had been first written down. Archilochus, too, wrote his poetry in Ionia. The later Greeks often mentioned him together with Homer and Hesiod as one of their poetic founding fathers. Ionic poetry displayed the same daring questioning spirit which we will find among the first philosophers. Many factors may have contributed to a climate of intellectual independence in the Ionian cities. It was there that the cities had developed early in the direction of the *polis*. The Ionians at an early stage developed extensive trade relations and became prosperous. Miletus and offshore Samos were the first Greek cities to establish a trading colony in the Nile delta, the city of Naucratis; thus they had an early opportunity to become familiar with Egyptian mathematical knowledge. Even more advanced Babylonian mathematics and astronomy might have reached Ionia by the overland trade routes.

On Samos, the home of Pythagoras, Egyptian influence was very prominent. Herodotus tells of the friendship between Polycrates, the tyrant of Samos, and the Egyptian king Amasis. Many Egyptian artifacts have been found on Samos, as well as local products that show strong Egyptian influence. Polycrates built one of the first monumental temples in Greece and a one-kilometer-long tunnel. The tunnel was dug through a mountain from both ends simultaneously to an almost perfect juncture at the center. Both projects, still visible today, show the use of Egyptian technical knowledge. The unit of measurement used was the Egyptian cubit. According to the tradition, the architect of the Hera temple on Samos invented the carpenter's square and the plumb line level. Both instruments, essential for large scale building projects, had been in use in Egypt for many centuries. Thus, it is not unreasonable to assume that the Samians took over the Egyptian mathematical procedures together with the Egyptian measurement system and the measuring instruments.

It comes then as no surprise that the Greeks considered Pythagoras of Samos the first mathematician and credited him with the formulation of the theorem that bears his name in its generalized form. In the specific form of a triangle with sides of 3, 4, and 5 units of measurement, the theorem had been used for centuries by the Egyptian surveyors ("ropestretchers") to lay out right angles in the field. The derivation of a generally valid theorem from a special case that had been empirically found may have been Pythagoras' achievement, which would make him indeed the founder of theoretical mathematics. He was also aware of the equal ratios between the sides of similar triangles. Pythagoras is further said to have discovered that the intervals between musical notes produced by a stringed instrument can be expressed in ratios of the numbers from one to four based on the length of the chords. Thus consonance (harmony) in music could be reduced to numerical ratios. From this observation Pythagoras seems to have concluded that all the opposing forces in the cosmos were kept in "harmony" by the right numerical proportions, and that the whole world-order (cosmos) was a function of numbers and their ratios. Pythagoras may have been the first to sense that the physical world might be expressible in quantitative terms. His philosophy was a strange mixture of mathematics and mysticism. He founded his "school" as a religious society. We are told that the Pythagoreans believed in transmigra-

tion of the soul and the kinship of all living things and therefore re-
frained from eating meat. At one time they became a political
power in southern Italy. Some of their ideas had lasting influence
throughout antiquity.

The Greek tradition generally considered Egypt a source of ancient knowledge and wisdom and credited the 6th century sages
with learning periods in Egypt. Thus Thales of Miletus is supposed
to have visited there. This is quite possible in view of Miletus' connection with Naucratis, but there is no evidence for it. Several important geometric and astronomic discoveries are ascribed to
Thales. He is said to have calculated the distance of a ship at sea by
triangulation from two points on shore, and to have measured the
height of the great pyramid by measuring its shadow. He first established the ratio between the length of a pole he had planted in
the ground and the length of its shadow. The same ratio applied to
the shadow of the pyramid gave him its height. We notice that
Thales' calculations, like those ascribed to Pythagoras, are all based
on the proportionality of corresponding sides in similar triangles,
the beginnings of a primitive trigonometry. Thales is also credited
with having predicted an eclipse and with having calculated the
precession of the solstices. These types of calculations, however,
originated and were practiced in Babylonia, not in Egypt.

Anaximander, Thales' younger fellow-citizen, introduced the
gnomon, another Mesopotamian invention, into Greece. In its simplest form the gnomon is a stick planted vertically into the ground.
By empirically marking the length of its shadow on the ground at
certain times of the day and certain dates of the year, the gnomon
can be made to function as sundial and a calendar. Anaximander
applied a geometric perspective to the world as a whole; according
to later testimony he drew the first map of the world. Anaximander
had the boldness to visualize a cosmos in which a cylindrical Earth
was suspended at the center, kept in equilibrium by being equidis-
tant from the other parts of the universe. This is a long step from
the mythological story in which the Titan Atlas supported the
world on his shoulders. Thales had expressed the view, probably
derived from Egyptian beliefs, that the (supposedly flat) Earth

floats on water. He saw evidence for this in earthquakes, which he thought were caused by wave-motion in the supporting water. This theory, however, as Aristotle pointed out, raises the immediate question: "What supports the water?" Anaximander's concept of an Earth kept in balance by its relationship to the other parts of the universe was perhaps too far ahead of its time, for his younger compatriot Anaximenes reverted to the more primitive notion that the Earth floated on air because of its flatness.

The eclipse which Thales is said to have predicted occurred on May 28, 585 BC according to modern calculations. Miletus was destroyed by the Persians in 494. Thus the overlapping lifespans of the three Milesians extended approximately over the length of the 6th century. Characteristically, all three started their speculations from two premises that were deeply rooted in mythology. 1) All existing things have evolved from a single material source. This is essentially the same belief as the one expressed in Hesiod's *Theogony*, which saw creation as a continuous process of differentiation and separation from the original *chaos*. 2) The world itself is somehow a living organism.

For Thales the primary material constituent of the world was water, an idea we find already expressed in mythological terms by Homer (*Iliad* 14.200, 14.244). According to Aristotle - and this may well be Aristotle's own attempt to reconstruct Thales' thought processes - Thales reasoned that "the nurture of all things is moist and that the warm (sc. life), having come into being from the moist, lives by it... and the sperms of all things have a moist nature." Aristotle further tells us that Thales considered the soul the moving force, and that there must be soul even in seemingly inanimate objects, since the magnetic stone has the power to move iron; he further quotes Thales as teaching that "the world is full of gods." This may be interpreted to mean that the whole world is animated. In the mythological belief, life was the source of motion and soul was the source of life. Soul was equated with breath, the most obvious characteristic of living things. The primary meaning of all the ancient words for soul was breath: *psyche, thymos, pneuma* in Greek, *anima, spiritus* in Latin. In the Semitic myths, Enkidu and Adam were brought to life by a god breathing into their nostrils. In Homer, the stricken warrior dies when his soul in the form of his last breath escapes "through the fence of his teeth." Our language still reflects the same notion when we differentiate between "animate" and "inanimate" objects.

It was this identification of breath with soul and life which caused Anaximenes, the third and youngest of the Milesians, to substitute air for Thales' water as the primal material. Air, always in motion, is the breath of the world. Aetius quotes him as follows: "As our soul, being air, controls us, so breath and air enfold the cosmos." Therefore air is not only the constituent of all existing things, it is also the divine life-force of the universe. In addition, Anaximenes offered an explanation for the change of air into other substances: the process of condensation and rarefaction. Condensed air becomes clouds and water, and still further condensed it solidifies. Fire is rarefied air. The different states keep changing into each other in a continuous cycle.

Anaximander had started from the same mythical assumption of a common material element, but in this respect, too, his view was wider in scope and more imaginative. He visualized a primordial substance unlimited in extent and undifferentiated in quality. Since all the different materials with their opposite properties had to be generated from it, it could not be one of the visible elements with its specific characteristics, but rather must be a substrate in which all the opposites were present and neutralized each other. The prime matter had to be limitless (*apeiron*) to be able to supply all possible forms of existence. But if one of the known elements were limitless, its properties would have overwhelmed all the others: water would have drowned out or dissolved the dry, fire would have consumed everything, etc. In Anaximander's cyclic scheme the different elements might become predominant at different times but would eventually again be submerged into the indestructible and divine *apeiron* because "they pay penalty and compensation to each other for their injustices according to the assessment of time." The last phrase is almost certainly a direct quotation and fits in well with the mythical view that any arrogation of excessive power calls down the retribution of the gods. It is the typical anthropomorphic transfer of human ethics to the physical world. In the cycles of nature-- dark of the night followed by light of the day, heat of summer, cold of winter, dry season and wet season-- balance, equaling justice (*dike*), is still maintained over the long run. Anaximander thought that life had originated in water heated by the sun and emerged later onto land. Humans came into being inside fish and came forth fully grown; otherwise they would not have been able to survive because of their long growing up process. Thus Anaximander speculated on the origin of man and formulated a primitive "theory of evolution."

From Colophon, another city in Ionia, came Xenophanes whose life span of about one hundred years (570 - 470 BC ?) encompassed a good part of the 6th century and the beginning of the 5th. He typifies the transition from the oral-mythical to the literate-logical age: he was both poet and philosopher. In one of his poems he tells us that he was in the 67th year of his wanderings through all of Greece, which he had begun when he was 25 years old. He seems to have earned his living as an itinerant reciter of Homeric poetry. Xenophanes acknowledged that "from the beginning all have learned from Homer," but later in his own poetry he became severely critical of the traditional Homeric world view. His speculations seem to have begun in the Ionic tradition with inquiries into the physical universe. From fossils of marine animals found in limestone quarries on various islands he drew the conclusion that the Earth goes through wet and dry cycles, being dissolved in water and then drying and becoming land again. Earth and water are the constituents of everything. But from these inquiries, which had become more or less commonplace at that time, he struck out into entirely new directions. The anthropomorphic view of the gods no longer satisfied him:

> All that is blameworthy and shameful among men, Homer and Hesiod imputed to the gods stealing, adultery, and deceiving each other.

...but humans believe that the gods are born, wear human clothing and have human bodies. The Ethiopians believe their gods to be snubnosed and dark, the Thracians blue-eyed and redhaired. If oxen, horses, and lions had hands and could draw with their hands, and do what men can do, the horses would draw their gods like horses, and oxen like oxen; each would draw their gods' faces and bodies in their own likeness.

One god, the greatest among gods and men, neither in body nor mind like mortals...
Always he remains in the same place not moving at all; nor does it behoove him to go now here, now there, but effortless, by the thought of his mind, he shakes all.

All of him sees, all thinks, all hears.

Thus Xenophanes takes a giant step from the oral mythical past into a new literate rational present. He recognizes the traditional gods as man's primitive projection of himself. The anthropomorphic gods can no longer satisfy civilized morality. In their place he proposes a moral, omnipotent, all-pervading god who is all mind. Whether this god is also non-material is impossible to tell. After Xenophanes anthropomorphic mythology was dead as religion among intellectual Greeks, although it remained a powerful poetic symbolic language.

Even more important for the development of philosophic thought were his speculations on the possibilities and limitations of human knowledge:

No man knows, nor will anyone know clear certainty about the gods and what I am saying about all other things; for, even if anyone happened to tell the perfect truth, he would not know it himself. Only conjecture is formed in regard to everything. (My translations after Kirk and Raven, *The Presocratic Philosophers*, [Cambridge 1957].)

Xenophanes thus was the first to raise the fundamental issue of epistemology: how do we know that we know what we think we know? He knew that perceptions can be deceiving: "If god had not brought forth yellow honey, figs would be thought much sweeter."

Since sense perception may be deceiving, and our opinions are based on conjecture, he can only say, "let these things be considered as resembling the truth." But even if human knowledge can be only tentative, Xenophanes has confidence in reason: "The gods have not from the beginning revealed everything to mortals, but by seeking, in time they will find out better."

Thus Xenophanes, the reciter of the mythical collective wisdom, through literacy has found his own individual voice. Early philosophy originated soon after the beginnings of literate poetry. Both started with the traditional views of the world and submitted them to critical examination. Each generation grows up in the beliefs of its predecessors and the image of the world as it is received may never be questioned as long as it is not blatantly contradicted by experience. In oral society the tradition is continuously being revised to conform to the present. The storyteller or oral poet, never reciting his tales twice in the same words, composing the familiar stories each time anew, subconsciously reflects his own environment. Sensitive to the tastes of his audience, he may add or omit details or shift emphasis between different aspects of his themes. In these subtle and unconscious ways the oral tradition keeps adjusting to changing conditions, never contradicting current perceptions. But once it is written down it becomes fixed and loses the capability to adapt. With the passage of time, gaps develop between things as they are told and as they are seen, and shed doubt on some of the traditional verities. Thus literacy itself eventually invites critical reexamination of the traditional heritage.[13] Therefore, it is no coincidence that critical thought began to assert itself, as we have seen, a few generations after the advent of literacy and the writing down of the oral poems. Enough had changed in the intervening period to make many of the Homeric perspectives and values questionable. Since the *polis* began to develop towards government by written law the heroic assertion of the right of the stronger, no matter how tempered by the code of chivalry and the spirit of *noblesse oblige*, had lost much of its moral appeal. Tribal obligation for blood vengeance had become incompatible with the administration of objective justice by courts of law. The gods as ruling forces of the cosmos could no longer be viewed as acting in an arbitrary or unethical fashion. Man begins to look for order and justice in the universe just as he does in his *polis*. Later, when drama will become the dominant form of poetic expression, much of its subject matter will be the conflict between the new and the old morality. In the light of the new insights gained from geometry and astronomy the old cosmology has lost its credibility.

Notes

1. A. M. Snodgrass, *The Dark Age of Greece*, 364

2. V. R. d'A. Desborough, *The Greek Dark Age*, 18

3. Snodgrass, *Dark Age*, 246-249

4. Snodgrass, 361; Emily Vermeule, *Greece in the Bronze Age* 265-9

5. M. E. Voyatzis, "Arcadia and Cyprus", *Report of the Department of Antiquities* (Cyprus 1985); Vassos Karageorghis, *View from the Bronze Age: Mycenaean and Phoenician Discoveries at Kition* (New York 1976), 58-94

6. *Documents in Mycenaean Greek* (Cambridge 1956)

7. E.g.: B. L. Ullman, "How old is the Greek Alphabet?", *AJA* 38 (1934), 359-381

8. "The Antiquity of the Greek Alphabet", *AJA* 37 (1933), 27

9. E.g.: Joseph Naveh, "Some Semitic Epigraphical Considerations on the Antiquity of the Greek Alphabet", *AJA* 77 (1973), 1-8

I0. S.P. Zervos, "On the Development of Mathematical Intuition: On the Genesis of Geometry", *Tensor* 26 (1972), 397-467

11. Robert Drews, *Basileus: The Evidence for Kingship In Geometric Greece* (New Haven 1983), 129

12. M. L. West, *Hesiod Theogony* (Oxford 1966), 40,47-48; cf. also E.A. Havelock, *The Muse Learns to Write* (New Haven and London 1986), 79, 82

13. Jack Goody and Jan Watt, "The Consequences of Literacy", in *Literacy in Traditional Societies*, ed. J. Goody (Cambridge 1968) 27-68

5

The Fifth Century

For centuries oral poetry had been the medium perpetuating the national tradition of the Greeks. It had created a common language which through its rhythms and images provided an aesthetic pleasure and transcended the boundaries of tribal dialects. Homeric poetry provided the Greeks with a collective identity. When the alphabet arrived in Greece, it was used not only to record the poetic tradition but, since no establishment controlled the oral heritage or the new literacy, it stimulated the creation of new poetry and the expression of personal sentiments and individual identities. It was only natural for the writers to compose in the existing poetic language which had conditioned their development and to which their audience was attuned. Thus literature remained initially poetic. Yet, because the alphabet had also the capability to give an exact rendering of everyday speech, its "prose" use spread immediately and widely for simple statements addressed to other individuals or to public audiences, such as epitaphs, dedicatory inscriptions, lawcodes, lists of names, etc. How much private written communication there was we do not know because of the perishable nature of the writing materials, such as leather. Since early Ionian inscriptions show some letter-forms which seem patterned after cursive script, there may have been more than generally suspected.

The 5th century BC brought to their full maturation all the developments that had their beginnings in the 6th. The Western world has venerated this "Golden Age of Athens," the "Greek miracle" ever since and has acknowledged classical Greece as its spiritual ancestor. Even discounting the rampant idealizations and recognizing the negative aspects of ancient Hellenic life, such as the incessant internecine warfare, slavery, the oppression of women, general callousness and cruelty, the fact remains that some fundamental conceptual changes occurred in that period. The efforts of historians to characterize the nature of this intellectual revolution are reflected in such book titles as *From Religion to Philosophy* (Cornford),[1] *From Mythos to Logos*,[2] (Nestle), *The Discovery of the Mind*, (Snell),[3] etc. Fifth century Athens produced the masterpieces of classical drama, art and architecture, and developed democratic government. But most important, the Greeks gained unprecedented confidence in the human intellect and created a language capable of expressing precise logical thought. The transition from mythical to logical expression is the very essence of the cognitive break-through which changed the human perspective on the world. Different reasons have been offered why this unique phenomenon occurred in that particular place at that particular time.

For generations, historians accepted the Greek accomplishments as a special Hellenic genius or racial endowment. Among more attractive and more plausible explanations various geographic, economic and cultural factors have been suggested. While the other ancient civilizations at an early stage had been unified into centralized empires, Greece from Mycenaean times onward had remained a loose confederation of more or less independent cities and tribal areas. The free inhabitants of the *poleis* enjoyed more freedom and control over their lives than did any of their contemporaries. The development of close-order infantry warfare had made the *hoplitai*, the heavily armed well trained citizen-soldiers, a decisive factor in war and internal confrontations, and had built up their self-confidence, especially after their successful defense against the superior forces of the Persian empire. The Greeks' free money economy and reliance on foreign trade had brought them prosperity and a wider horizon. All these and probably still other factors played a part.

But the primary catalyst, as E.A. Havelock[4] has pointed out, was literacy. For the first time in history an entire population had access to the arts of reading and writing. By the fifth century at least a basic functional literacy had begun to spread throughout the citizenship of Ionia, Athens and most Greek cities. It was the advance in literacy that brought about the transition from an oral-mythical mode of thought to a more formal literate-logical way of thinking. When we use the terms mythical and logical, we are not implying a strict dichotomy. We are only trying to distinguish between two ways of reasoning which have always existed side by side. After all, as Albright observed, it took logical reasoning to invent a fishhook. On the other hand a lot of mythical thinking exists today. The transition was a gradual shift in frequency from one to the other, obviously more pronounced among the urban elite than in the rural backwater. When we talk about a change from an oral to a literate culture, it never can mean more than a quantitative increase of literates and a qualitative improvement of their literacy. Therefore one must beware of some of the unqualified generalizations that have been made and which will be discussed below. But first a clarification of the terms mythical and logical seems in order.

The mythical tradition and its associated rituals and religious practices have many functions. While offering entertainment and aesthetic pleasure, the mythical story expresses the common consciousness of a community and provides a collective identity to its members. Mythology satisfies the individual's need for security through belief in protecting deities and a life after death. Myth preserves the customs and sets standards of behavior; it socializes the young, and perpetuates tribal integrity by subordinating the welfare of the individual to that of the tribe. Sociobiologists suggest that the predisposition to mythical thought may be rooted in genetics. Societies held together by strong mythic bonds and an altruistic code of individual subservience to the common good would have a better chance of surviving and of passing on their genes than those with a less dominant mythic orientation and less tribal coherence. If mythical thought is indeed inborn, as its instinctive subconscious nature seems to indicate, this would explain why literacy, logic, and science have never been able to displace myth and why even the most authoritarian regimes have never been able to "abolish" religion. Myth usually tells an objective story of concrete people and events; it makes its points through analogy rather than through explicit explanations. The subjective motivations of the actors, the causal relationships, are tacitly implied by the reciter and subconsciously felt by the audience. The mythic language has few of the particles and connectors which bring out the causal connections. Often profound insights are conveyed through a comparison or a striking word picture aided by sound and rhythm. The image is received whole and grasped instantly by the audience; its appeal is affective and emotional. The medium is at least part of the message, in McLuhan's sense.[5]

Logical thought, as we use the term, is different in that it is conscious of its rational consistency. Logical thought, in the words of Werner Jaeger,[6] is based on the principle that, "nothing is correct but that which I can explain to myself on conclusive grounds, that for which my thought can reasonably account." To this we might add with Aristotle that nothing can be true that is totally contrary to human experience. While the truth of the mythical image is "felt," the truth of logical thought, in the words of Snell,[7] "is something that requires to be sought, to be investigated, pondered; it is the unknown element in a problem which must be solved with due consideration of the law of contradiction; the result must be accepted by all." One could agree with this statement except that its last part requires some qualification. Very few pronouncements are accepted "by all;" all that can be expected is that a statement be accepted by those who reason in a similar fashion. This presupposes some mutually agreed upon rules that determine what makes a statement valid - in other words, rules of logic. These rules may later turn out to be invalid, but the important point is that they provide a common ground for thinking about thinking. This process was impossible before the literate era. While the faculty for mythical thought is inherited, the ability for logical thought must be acquired by each individual in a learning process. Literacy and written communications made the learning and the acceptance of common rules possible.

As mentioned before, Eric Havelock played a leading role in pointing out the significance of literacy as the most important moving force in the Greek intellectual breakthrough. The evidence for widespread literacy from the beginning of the 5th century on is found in the numerous inscriptions, vase paintings, references in the historians and dramatists, and especially in Plato. It is strikingly confirmed by the procedures and practices of political life in the Athenian democracy. Since Cleisthenes' constitutional reforms at the end of the 6th century Athenian government relied heavily on the functional literacy of its citizens. The system required ordinary citizens to maintain membership lists, voters' rolls, and military records on three levels of government. The five hundred members of the Council (*boule*), chosen by lot, drafted and proposed laws, state treaties and other communications with foreign powers, and acted as law courts in certain cases. They took turns in groups of fifty in the administration of the day-to-day tasks of government, writing contract specifications for construction projects, reviewing financial records and issuing and receiving reports. They served on various commissions and committees, and those chosen by lot as secretaries, recorded proceedings and documented in writing the actions and decisions of the various government bodies. Laws and decrees often contained the stipulation that their text was to be engraved in stone and publicly displayed "so that everybody who wished could see" (*skopein toi boulomenoi*), thus implying that the public was able to read. In sum, all the government housekeeping functions, what we would call paper-work, that in most ancient and modern states are performed by lifetime bureaucracies, were the responsibility of ordinary citizens selected by vote or lot for short terms in office. General functional literacy was a prerequisite for such a system of constitutional government.

At the beginning of the 5th century BC new centers of philosophic speculation began to spring up. Pythagoras had left his native Samos around 520 BC and had gathered a following in southern Italy which eventually developed into a religious society and gained considerable influence in politics. The increasing encroachment of the Persians on the independent Greek cities in Ionia caused many of their inhabitants to migrate to other Greek locations. Anaxagoras of Clazomenae, a thinker in the Ionian tradition, went to Athens and joined the intellectual circle which Pericles was gathering around himself. His considerable influence will be discussed later. Xenophanes went to Elea in southern Italy. There may well be truth in the tradition that his teaching influenced Parmenides of Elea and the so-called Eleatic school of philosophy.

According to Plato, Socrates met Parmenides some time around the middle of the fifth century. Parmenides' ideas were to have a profound influence on Plato. Parmenides carried Xenophanes' thinking to the most unexpected conclusions. The concept that nothing can come from nothing seems not particularly startling and seems always to have been implied in the mythological as well as in the early philosophical views. When the Milesians tried to determine the original material from which everything was formed, the assumption seems to have been that this material had always existed. When Xenophanes said that his god was not born, he must have meant that god had always existed. When Parmenides stated the principle that something cannot come from nothing, he made it the foundation stone of his whole construction of a world view. Starting from the obvious semantic meaning, he asserts that what is, or "being," exists and what is not, or "non-being," cannot exist. Non-being can never change into being or being into non-being since non-being simply does not exist. Thus generation or destruction is impossible. But since the only thing that could separate one part of being from another part of being would be non-being, or void, which by definition is nothing and cannot exist, all being must be a continuous oneness-- continuous in time because it has always existed and continuous in space since nothing exists that can separate being from being. But Parmenides went even further. Because, like his predecessors, he made no distinction between concrete objects and their abstract qualities such as whiteness or other colors, size, shape, wetness or dryness, etc, these properties seem to have been included in being. (The Greek word "to be," like its English equivalent, can be a verb meaning to exist as in "God is," or a connector as in "God is immortal"). By endowing the properties of things with the same characteristic of "being" as the things they qualify, he made any change in an existing object impossible since none of its qualities could have a beginning or an end-- just like the object itself. Thus any change in an existing thing is as impossible as its generation or destruction. Furthermore, as the world is fully packed with continuous being, no movement is possible within it. Therefore the world of being is eternal, indestructible, unchangeable, and motionless. Consequently the visible world of continual change and motion must be an illusion, a deception of the senses-- a world of "seeming" which hides the true world, the world of "being", from us.

Parmenides was the first in the western world to form a theory based purely on abstract reasoning, building relentlessly one speculation on top of another, leaving sense-perception and experience far behind-- in fact, totally denying their validity. It is just as paradoxical as Parmenides' mental edifice itself that this construct became an important contribution to the advance of logical thought. By denying the possibility of change and motion, Parmenides pointed out the shortcomings of the Milesians' attempt to derive a world of diversity out of a single prime matter, be it air, water or the *apeiron*. Any future cosmological system which proposed generation or change would have to provide an explanation of the cause or moving force (in Aristotle's terminology, an efficient cause) which brought the change about.

By declaring the world we see and live in a sham and making an invisible unverifiable speculative structure the "true world", he introduced dualism and transcendentalism, a two-world system that was to haunt philosophy forever after. Plato followed in Parmenides' footsteps and carried his thoughts further. As no truth can be found in this ever-changing world of seeming, Plato had recourse to devising a non-material ideal world of changeless pure forms or ideas, separate from our world with its pollution by perishable ever-changing matter. By denying the existence of the observable phenomena Parmenides raised the fundamental question of "being," *to eon*, of existence itself, of ontology, which is still at the heart of philosophy in the modern sense.

In the most immediate context Parmenides had introduced a deductive reasoning which his contemporaries were unable to refute in the current state of logic. His follower Zeno tried in his famous paradoxes to prove mathematically the impossibility of motion and incidentally established the concept of infinite divisibility which led to integral calculus. Contemporary mathematics was as unable to deal with Zeno's reasoning as logic was to deal with Parmenides' assertions.

The search for a common single origin of the world was rooted in the mythological tradition. It apparently satisfies a human psychological need to find some unity in a world of bewildering variety. Einstein was still looking for the all-encompassing field formula when he died. Although none of their observations of nature could have suggested such a thing, the Ionian philosophers had taken for granted the inherited concept of a single material source of all existence. Parmenides' reasoning exploded the assumption of a single primary material and, as Kirk and Raven[8] have pointed out, established certain principles with which subsequent cosmologists had to deal:

1. Being must not be allowed to spring from not-being: anything that is claimed as real must also be ultimate.

2. The void, being sheer non-existence, can find no place in reality.

3. Plurality cannot come from an original unity: if there is to be plurality, it too, like reality, must be ultimate.

4. Motion is no longer to be taken for granted, an explanation must be given for its existence-- which also involved an explanation and justification of sense-perception.

The influence of Parmenides showed itself clearly in the work of his successors. It also illustrates the effects of literacy. As Parmenides had reacted to the theories of his Ionian predecessors, so Empedocles and Anaxagoras reacted to his. Such a discourse over distance and time would have been impossible in an oral society.

Empedocles of Acragas in Sicily, acknowledging the principles laid down by Parmenides, accepted some and rejected others. He echoes the statement that nothing that exists can have come from non-being or can be destroyed into nothingness. He also denies the existence of void, which would be non-being. He insists, however, on the validity of sense-perception, while conceding that deceptions may occur. To avoid errors, the findings of one sense are to be checked by those of another and the truth must be found by critical evaluation of the results of sense-perception. In his view everything in the world consists of various mixtures of the four elements earth, water, air and fire. Coming into existence consists in the combining and mixing of the four elements, ceasing to exist in their separation. The elements themselves have always existed and always will; their sum total is eternally constant. Empedocles is thus the first to formulate the "law of the conservation of matter." Generation, i.e., mixture of the elements, and destruction, i.e., separation, take place in two cycles and are caused by two forces: Love and Strife. Combination occurs under the rule of Love. Living things form at random, among them many monstrosities; the ones properly constituted survive, the unfit die out. During the opposite cycle the elements separate, each element joins its own kind and the world changes into four concentric spheres with earth forming the innermost layer, water the next, then air, and fire the outermost. We apparently live in the transition phase when Love and Strife balance each other. As the theory is described in poetic form and language, it is impossible to tell whether the personifications of Love and Strife are simply poetic images representing physical attraction and repulsion for which Empedocles had no technical terms available, or whether he visualized them as divine powers. When he talks about the four elements he alternates between names of the deities representing each element, such as Zeus for air and Hera for earth, etc.; at other times he mentions the elements only by their prosaic names. Within his poetic framework it seems quite possible that he uses the personifications of Love and Strife simply to designate attraction and repulsion, for which he had no specific vocabulary, especially since he never resorts to their established mythological identifications as Aphrodite and Ares. However that may be, Empedocles introduced a pluralistic theory of a primitive "chemical" formation of all types of matter which was defensible in the light of Parmenides' strictures. In other respects he followed Xenophanes and the Italian school of Pythagoras. He proposes a deity or world-soul that is coextensive with his spherical world. The human soul is part of this divine substance, but has become separated from it as punishment for the original sin of shedding the blood of other living creatures for food. Polluted by blood-guilt the soul must migrate through recurring incarnations in all kinds of animals and humans until it is purified and allowed to return into the world-soul.

Empedocles was followed almost immediately by Anaxagoras, who reacted to Parmenides in the rational demythologizing fashion of Ionia. He reached for a fully mechanistic model of the universe. It should have become obvious very soon that no matter how you mix earth, water and air, you still will wind up with mud. To derive such specific materials as gold or bone, etc. from the four Empedoclean elements would still constitute a total change in kind incompatible with the principles established by Parmenides. Four elements were simply insufficient to create the diversity in the world. Therefore Anaxagoras proposed an infinite number of constituents infinitely divisible and retaining their characteristics into the most minute parts. Each constituent itself contained parts of all the other constituents and received its appearance and properties from its most prevalent component. Thus there was no fundamental change in kind, since all the materials were present from the beginning. Anaxagoras followed in the footsteps of the Milesians by assuming that in the beginning everything was mixed together in an undifferentiated neutral mass like Anaximander's *apeiron*. The original mixture began to rotate in a vortex motion which started a process of sifting, separation and aggregation which formed and is still forming the materials of the world. It formed the earth and the heavenly bodies out of similar materials and put them into their circular motions. In this rotation new worlds continue to be generated while older ones are being dissolved in a purely mechanical process. As Anaxagoras' rotation moves only in one direction, not in two opposite cycles like Empedocles', he needed only one moving force. For Anaxagoras the moving force was Mind (*Nous*).

Nous implies knowledge, foresight, planning and was different from Xenophanes' god, who continually directed the course of events in the world. *Nous* had only started the chain of events by putting the original primeval mass into rotation. He did not have to direct the creation process, as he knew in advance what the consequences and results would be. Anaxagoras seems to have had a notion of inertia: once the circular motion had started it would continue by its own momentum. This is in marked contrast with Aristotle's later but more primitive view, in which a continuous movement depended on a continuously acting force.

Later, Plato's Socrates and Aristotle never were able to understand Anaxagoras, for they repeatedly complained about what they considered Anaxagoras' inconsistency: he makes mind the controlling power in the universe, but then, instead of showing how the intelligent mind arranges every detail of the world for the best, he turns things over to blind mechanical forces. Yet Anaxagoras had been more scientific in the modern sense of the word because he had tried to understand the workings of the world as the function of cause-effect relationships rather than the result of the teleological action of a supernatural entity. Since no concept of natural forces or energy existed Anaxagoras was unable to manage entirely without a transcendental agent, but he tried at least to reduce its intervention to a minimum. Mind only pushed the starter button; from then on natural laws did the rest to keep the world going. It is interesting to note that most Greek thinkers had apparently no problem in accepting that matter had always existed, but had up to that time not been able to visualize that in the same way motion had always been there. Anaxagoras explained the world still within the confines of Parmenides' stipulations. There was no void. Diversity was brought about through various combinations of unchanging eternal constituents. Motion was supposedly explained.

In the mid-fifth century Anaxagoras came to Athens, which by then had become the cultural center of the Greek world. There he became a member of Pericles' entourage. When the opposition to Pericles' leadership gathered strength, but was not able to attack Pericles in person because of his control of the popular assembly, his foes directed their attacks in the law-courts against his close associates. Anaxagoras was accused of blasphemy because he had written that the moon consisted of earth and that the sun was just molten rock. He was convicted and banished. Later, when Socrates was confronted with the same accusation, he challenged his accuser in court in these words: "Do you think you are accusing Anaxagoras? Do you hold the jurors in such contempt and do you consider them so illiterate that they don't know that the books of Anaxagoras are full of such statements?... [books] which can be bought for about one drachma near the theater..." (Plato, *Apology*, 26c20). As there were 500 jurors, all chosen by lot, Socrates' words, as reported by Plato, are an important testimony not only to Anaxagoras' theories but also to the state of general literacy in Athens.

It remained for the atomists, Leucippus and Democritus, to break out of the restraints set by Parmenides, and also to remove the last vestiges of the supernatural from the physical world. It is nearly impossible to distinguish between their individual contributions, since the ancient sources always name them together and only the barest shreds remain of their writings. Neither do we know how they arrived at their theories except that they built on Anaxagoras' thoughts. But instead of his infinitely divisible constituents of matter, Democritus proposed unsplittable (*atoma*) smallest particles. The whole universe is composed only of atoms and void. Atoms exist in an infinite variety of shapes. Their shapes and their density, i.e., the amount of void between atoms, determine the consistency of any material: a solid material encloses less void than a liquid, and air has more void between its atoms than the liquid. The atoms are always in motion, even in seemingly solid matter. As in Anaxagoras' view, the atoms spin through the void, colliding, deflecting each other, cohering and separating again. In the process innumerable worlds are formed through aggregations of atoms and eventually destroyed through their dissociation. The infinite void, the atoms, and the vortex motion are eternal, without beginning or end. Democritus' lifespan (about 465-370) made him contemporary with Plato. His influence, however, did not make itself felt until later periods. His totally mechanistic universe without interference by the supernatural made his theory an ideal base of the Epicurean philosophy. Atomism and the Epicurean philosophy were restated by the Roman poet Lucretius in the first century BC and rediscovered in the French age of enlightenment, but atomism had to await the advent of chemistry in the 18th century to become a viable scientific theory.

Even this sketchy review of protoscientific and philosophic thought should show clearly the line of continuity in the evolution towards logical thought through literacy. The interplay of ideas, the direct reactions of some thinkers to the views of others, the continuation of certain trends by successive writers, show a steady progression towards the point where logic and science could begin. Although the Greeks traveled widely, and some of the thinkers undoubtedly had personal contacts, it seems obvious that in their wide dispersion from the Asiatic coast to Sicily, the mutual exchanges and influences would not have been possible without the benefits of literacy. Complex ideas of a nature such as those discussed could have been neither formulated nor communicated except in writing. If literacy was a prerequisite for the development of the ideas, the ideas in turn stimulated the interest in literacy.

While the Ionian inquiries into nature and the Pythagorean mathematical tradition in Italy may be said to have anticipated the natural or exact sciences, Athens incubated the social sciences and the humanities, although nobody would have been aware yet of such a distinction. In our discussion of the Presocratic philosophers we have found little concern with the role of humanity in the world. Yet the awakening of man's awareness of himself was at the heart of the Greek intellectual revolution. In 5th century Athens internal and external events gave impetus to introspective and self-conscious speculations. When at the beginning of the century the small city-state of Athens had defeated the military might of the great Persian empire, every citizen, as part of his democratic community and its armed force under leaders elected out of their midst, could claim credit for their victory. Man had replaced the gods at the center of the stage. In classical art even the statues of the gods were glorifications of the human body. Unavoidably the question presented itself: "What made our achievement possible? What qualities of body and mind made us superior?" The question became even more compelling when the Athenians had made themselves the leading power of Greece. The great dramatists tried to cope with this question. Thucydides, the historian, gave an answer in Pericles' funeral oration. Whether or not the text or even the content of the speech is authentic, there can be no doubt that it depicted the collective image the Athenians had of themselves. The following are some excerpts:

> We live under a constitution that does not have to be envious of anybody else's. We set an example to others rather than imitate them. Ours is called a democracy because it serves the interests not of the few, but of the majority. According to law, the same opportunities are open to all regardless of individual differences. According to public judgment, a person is valued highly more for his ability than his inherited position, nor if someone can make a good contribution to the community, is he hindered by the lack of means or reputation. We are just as liberal towards each other in our private life as we are in our political affairs. We hold no suspicion or grudge against our neighbor if he does as he pleases...

> It is up to the same people to carry on their private business and to make public policy, and up to those occupied with their labors to have adequate knowledge about public affairs...

> In sum, I say that Athens as a whole is the educator of Greece and I believe that our citizens, man for man, each by himself, among their other gifts in every respect show the most versatile and self-reliant personality. And that this is no idle boastful talk, but the factual truth, is proven by the power of our city...   (Thucydides, *Histories*, 2.37, author's translation)

This was how the Athenians saw themselves in the period of their greatest successes. But just as in the tragedies the occasion of the speech, the funeral of the first victims of the Peloponnesian war, already foreshadowed Athens' approaching catastrophe. Soon the self-searching questions would project themselves in the opposite light: "How was such a disaster possible? How did we go wrong? Which of our character traits and actions brought us down?" These questions were to echo through Socrates' and Plato's speculations. Athens' ascent to power and collapse all within one century offered indeed food for introspective thought. Under the democracy in its final form no man could escape responsibility for success or failure of the city. The problem of man's responsibility for his actions was central to Greek drama throughout the century.

The work of the three great dramatists, Aeschylus, Sophocles, and Euripides, typifies the transition from blind acceptance of the mythical tradition to its use in conscious artistic creation. It seems significant that the time span of their activity, from 490 to 406 BC, coincides with the Athenian rise and fall from power. Greek drama, like philosophy, had its beginnings in myth; it apparently evolved out of choral songs and enactment of mythical stories as part of religious ritual. Yet within a generation from the inception of Athenian democracy Greek tragedy developed from its tentative beginnings into a mature art form. The tragic concept of *Ate* had been dominant in mythic belief at least as early as the Homeric epics: human beings favored by outstanding gifts of the gods, such as excessive power, wealth, physical strength or beauty, etc., tend to overreach themselves. They lose touch with reality and in overbearing arrogance they incur the wrath of the gods. In retribution a god or fate will strike them with blind delusion (*Ate*): failing to recognize their human limitations, they will take the fateful step which brings them to their doom. These beliefs underly the central themes of most tragedies. Originally drama represented the interactions of humans and gods, but gradually the dramatists moved the human protagonists to the foreground and relegated the gods more and more to a symbolic or allegorical role. In Aristotle's analysis of Greek tragedy in his *Poetics*, an error of judgment by the tragic hero takes the place of *Ate*, delusion sent by the gods, as cause of his downfall. The free choices of men began to displace fate as the moving force in human life. With ever deepening psychological insight Greek tragedy sublimated every conceivable religious, ethical, and personal dilemma. The tragedies probably more than any other influence awakened men's awareness of themselves and their capabilities.

The effect of tragedy on Greek self-consciousness was complemented by Old Comedy. Aristophanes' biting humor satirized the politicians and warmongers, ridiculed the petty foibles of the average citizens, and castigated greed and corruption. Social criticism had been part of Greek literate poetry since its beginnings. We find it in Hesiod's *Works and Days* and in lyric poetry from Archilochus onward, but it remained for old comedy to arm it with the sharp rapier of satirical humor. Aristophanes developed the technique, still frequently used today in humorous writing, of setting up an impossible situation and carrying it to its logical conclusion. Once the imaginary premises are accepted by the audience, the course of events proceeds in a perfectly consistent fashion to reduce some common conceit *ad absurdum*. Typical examples of such phantasies are the bird-city in Cloud Cuckoo-Land (*The Birds*), the confederation and sex-strike of the women in *Lysistrata*, and the poetry contest of the dead Euripides and Aeschylus in the underworld (*The Frogs*). In the last-named play Aristophanes also offered early examples of explicit literary criticism and parody as a means of criticism. Aristophanes' caricature of Euripides was part of his continuous spoof of pretentious intellectualism by which he also victimized Socrates. Thus he held up an unflattering mirror to almost every social group or clique in Athens from politicians to philosophers and sophists, to playwrights, to professional war veterans, profiteers and ordinary citizens. We are told that there were two inscriptions over the entrance to the Delphic sanctuary which proclaimed: "Nothing to excess," and "Know thyself." Tragedy and comedy equally served these mottoes.

When in the midddle of the 5th century BC Athens had become the center of Greek political and cultural life, it was only natural that the various strands of inquiry should be drawn together there. Pericles deliberately tried to attract the best minds of Greece to his side, and many, such as Anaxagoras, the city-planner Hippodamus, and the sophist Protagoras, joined his circle. Eventually most of the sophists who found the financial and intellectual climate of Athens stimulating appeared for more or less prolonged visits in Athens. They were to make a considerable contribution to literacy and to give the human-centered concerns a more purposeful direction. They elevated some of their anthropological and sociological speculations to a sort of secondary education curriculum.

As Werner Jaeger[9] points out, the sophists' most important contribution to literacy was their theory of education and culture. They were the first to make a formal statement of the nature/nurture problem. In the aristocratic tradition, which had found its most vigorous expression in the poetry of Theognis and Pindar, excellence, (*arete*) was a quality inherited through noble birth and ancestry; it could be neither acquired nor taught. But the inquiries into nature (*physis*) by the Ionian thinkers, the "physicists" and the medical writers, the physicians, had established man as a product of nature with a *physis* of his own, and thus subject to physical inquiry. The nature of his body could be improved through physical exercise and through the ministrations of a physician. The sophists extended the concept to include the human mind and its motivations-- human nature in our sense of the word. The natural endowment, the quality of the *physis* of each individual, was important, but to attain its full potential it had to be developed through the proper education. Without education a gifted nature might go to waste while a less well endowed nature under the right educational care might reach a higher level of accomplishment. Plutarch later on, probably drawing on a sophistic source, gave the classical analogy taken from farming: a good harvest requires a good soil, a good seed, and a good farmer. In education the *physis* of the pupil is the soil, the teacher is the farmer, the instruction is the seed. The image was taken up by the Romans: *agri cultura*, the tilling of the soil, inspired the metaphor of *animi cultura*, the tilling of the mind, and also influenced Cicero's combination of *natura et doctrina*. The sophists promised to produce "cultured" individuals. Literate culture soon became an ideal of society.

Essentially the sophists were teachers of rhetoric. With the development of democracy, the prestige of aristocratic birth and inherited wealth alone was no longer enough to assure one a commanding position in the political life of the city. The ability to direct the decisions of the assembly or Council through eloquence became a prerequisite for leadership and power. The sophists attracted pupils by the promise to teach them for a fee how to gain success in public life through the art of convincing oratory. The sophists developed their professional skill through the study of the existing literature and by analysing the use of words and the techniques of logical argument -- or at least convincing arguments hard to refute. In the process they laid the foundation for the study of semantics and stylistics, and raised the use of language to a more conscious level. To provide their students with an arsenal of analogies in support of their arguments they tried to impart a knowledge of literature and the current scientific and philosophic ideas. They concentrated, however, on the practical aspects of daily life and human nature and thus inaugurated what we would call sociology. They were well aware that the play on the emotions of the audience at political and judicial forums was at least as important as the logic of the arguments. In debating, their favorite technique consisted in inducing their opponent to agree to a seemingly innocuous non-controversial statement. Once he conceded the truth of that statement, they tried to show that whatever proposition they were advancing followed inescapably from the statement that had been conceded. The procedure might involve several syllogistic steps, sometimes based either on acceptable logic or, more often, on dubious analogies or equivocation, i.e. manipulations of different meanings of the same word. It is no wonder that the Athenians considered Socrates just another sophist since the examples of Socratic debating which Plato gives us in his dialogues generally use the same technique. It was precisely this practice which made the study of semantics so important to the sophists, not only to sharpen their own skill but also to recognize their opponents' attempts at equivocation. The sophists introduced the practice of preparing speeches in writing and thus made oratory a literary activity.

The sophists prided themselves on their ability to argue successfully on either side of a question. Today, we expect this ability of any lawyer, but this is probably the reason most people distrust

lawyers and why the sophists were accused of insincerity and un-
scrupulousness. Aristotle used the method of arguing both sides as
a method to determine the probability of propositions that could
be neither proven nor disproven. Still later, Cicero followed the
Skeptics in denying that any truth could ever be positively established and made the argument from either side (*argumentum in
utramque partem*) the only touchstone of probability. In any event,
the ability to look at a question from both sides was an important
step on the road to rationality and logic. By distributing written
sample speeches to their pupils and by encouraging them to read
the existing works of literature the sophists helped the propagation
of literacy.

On the other hand, because of the sophists' concern with human
relations and practical matters they had little regard for the abstract theories of the philosophers. With the exception of Hippias,
who was an important mathematician in his own right, the sophists
considered mathematics irrevelant because it dealt with concepts
that did not exist in real life, such as the perfect circle, infinite divisibility, etc. Similarly they turned away from the search for universal truths which did not help to solve particular problems that
required practical action. Gorgias expressed his disdain for the abstract and universal in his dissertation *On nature and the not-being*:
Nothing exists. If it existed, it would be incomprehensible. If it
could be comprehended, it could not be communicated. What
counts in life is the right action at the right time (*kairos*); to do
what is required to the thing requiring it (*to deon toi deonti*). From
the sophistic point of view, what difference did Parmenides' "world
of being" make to someone living in this supposedly illusory "world
of seeming?"

Protagoras' famous statement that "man is the measure of all
things" was probably a reaction against such "other world" concepts.
To be successful in life a man had to deal with his immediate world,
his human environment. For the sophists the various cosmic theories were interesting because they sharpened one's reasoning powers and skeptical outlook. But because the theories often contradicted each other and there was no way of proving one against the

other it was up to each individual to form his own opinions. In this sense too, man was the measure of all things. But Protagoras' statement has been interpreted by some of his contemporaries and ever since as a denial of all ethical standards and the assertion of a totally subjective morality. There may be some truth in this interpretation in the case of some of the later sophists, but probably not for Protagoras himself. The Greeks had become familiar through their colonizing and trading activities with many different peoples and tribes and their various customs. It also had become customary for travelers and geographers such as Hecataeus and Herodotus to describe other lands in their writings and public lectures. Herodotus' *Histories* are full of accounts of diverse ethnic traditions, customs and practices, some of them totally incompatible with the Greek sense of propriety and morality. Herodotus, for instance, reports that in Egypt the roles of men and women in many respects were reversed according to the Greek perspective. Conversely, the Greek practice of performing athletics publicly in the nude was considered most shameful by the Persians-- and there are many other such examples. The recognition of the diversity of moral notions from country to country led to the conclusion that ethics were a matter of convention and that absolute standards did not exist. This view was in keeping with the sophists' theories of social evolution. Man was a part of nature. Since humans lacked the speed, strength and natural defenses of other animals they had to band together and cooperate in order to survive. But living together for mutual protection required certain rules of behavior. Laws had to be created to enforce a tolerable communal way of life. Thus laws and ethical standards were not god-given but a matter of convention, the result of a natural evolution. If we believe Plato some of the later sophists, such as Callicles and Thrasymachus, held the view that the laws were devised by the stronger and more intelligent individuals to dominate the weaker. Such leaders by virtue of their superiority had a right to domination and what was right for them was morally right. But such a subjective morality which amounted to advocating that might makes right was not part of the doctrine of Protagoras or Gorgias. They distinguished between "natural" ethical imperatives which are common to all people, and without which civilized life is not possible, and mere conventions which might vary from place to place. In this sense, too, that man recognizes certain laws of morality, he is the measure of all things. If the sophists had not respected the time-honored ethical precepts they could not have plied their lucrative trade of teaching the sons of the rich and therefore conservative families who still considered instruction in the traditional morality the most important part of education.

The sophists were products of literacy themselves, and in turn were instrumental in making articulate eloquence in speech and writing the foundation of intellectual life. Their influence was all-pervasive. They were the first to present a case for the need for an education beyond the customary primary curriculum of music, gymnastics, and basic instruction in reading and writing. Although their approaches were different and haphazard, they pointed out the effectiveness of education and led the way toward the establishment of more systematic schooling. The study of language initiated by the sophists developed eventually into the disciplines of grammar, syntax and stylistics.

The study of rhetoric set the pattern for education throughout Greek and Roman antiquity. Effective oratory was not only a prerequisite for success in public life, it had a profound effect on literature. Many of the speeches in later drama, especially in Euripides, are composed according to the rules of rhetoric. Thucydides, writing history, presented the viewpoints of the opposing parties by putting rhetorical speeches into the mouths of the leading personalities. The sophistic techniques of debating pointed out the need for formalized rules of logic.

The anthropological and sociological speculations of the sophists made human motivations and behavior, until then an intuitive concern of the dramatists, a subject of protoscientific inquiry, and in turn influenced the dramatists and historians. Thus literacy assured the continuous interaction between the exponents of all branches of intellectual endeavor.

The last third of the 5th century also produced the first extensive connected works of historiography written from unifying perspectives. Some accounts of events had been written in the older literate empires, but they usually had consisted in the enumeration of their glorious deeds by some kings or pharaohs. Since the 6th century, some local chronicles had been written in Greece by prose-writers whom Pindar called the *logioi* to distinguish them from the poets who reported the mythical history in verse. Some travelers who wrote descriptions of their voyages included the historical traditions of the places they had visited. But the histories of Herodotus and Thucydides were of an entirely different nature.

The Persian wars of the early fifth century were the critical turning point in the ascendancy of Greece. Herodotus saw in them the climax of a continuing struggle between Europe and Asia that had its beginning in the legendary times of the Trojan war. Although he viewed the wars through the mythical lens of the tragic concepts he approached the legends with typical Ionic detachment, rationalizing them whenever he could, debunking them without hesitation when they contradicted what he considered more reliable information or when supernatural events strained rational credibility. He tried to provide all the geographic and historical background possible, although often more concerned with the entertainment value of his stories than their veracity or even probability. In spite of all digressions, he imposed an overall unity on his work. Herodotus saw the Persian war in a perspective not too different from Homer's or Aeschylus'. The Persian king corrupted by his unlimited power, had striven for more than human status and thus called the jealousy of fate upon himself. When in his *hybris* he overreached himself the Athenians became the instrument of divine retribution and therefore able to to defeat the "hundredfold" superior Persian force.

If Herodotus' history was the tragedy of Persian despotism, Thucydides' was the tragedy of the Athenian democracy. The Peloponnesian war began in 431, lasted for almost thirty years and ended with the utter defeat of Athens. It involved all of Greece and drained much of her manpower and resources before it was over. Thucydides, too, saw the war in tragic terms. For him the tragedy lay in the relentless way in which both sides stumbled into a war nobody wanted and missed many opportunities for peace during the war through the ineptitude and ambitions of their leaders and the greed of the Athenian populace. He stated specifically that he wrote for posterity so that a similar catastrophe could be avoided in the future. In the same vein he described in great detail the symptoms of the plague that hit Athens so that future generations would be able to recognize it if it ever recurred. Thucydides was the first critical historian who, within the limits set for every human being by subconscious bias, strove for the greatest attainable objectivity and truth. He describes how he searched for the most reliable sources and checked one report against another, sometimes finding even eyewitness accounts contradicting each other. In his introduction, where he attempted to reconstruct the dim past, he tried to extract every kernel of historic fact out of the mythical legends and even anticipated archaeology by speculating about the misleading impressions an examination of ancient ruins can convey. Thucydides tried to analyze the characters of the main actors, and tried to represent them in their speeches. We have quoted earlier from his rendition of Pericles' view of the Athenians and their self-image in his funeral oration. But Thucydides looked beyond personalities for the political, geographic and economic causes of the course of events. His standards of objectivity and historiographic excellence were not reached again until modern times. Herodotus and Thucydides, each from the vantage point of his own philosophy, tried to discern the patterns and forces which shape the relentless stream of human history. In their works, prose literature had reached the high level of perfection where it could become the main medium of intellectual discourse. The stage was set for the philosophic and scientific works of Plato and Aristotle and their successors.

Henceforth the poetic genres, besides their use as school texts, essentially provided aesthetic enjoyment, while prose became the vehicle and storehouse of knowledge. Literacy had reached the point where logical thought took its place side by side with mythical thought. Still, we should remind ourselves that the two modes never obtained a valid formal divorce, that there is rationality in mythopoeic activity and that affective intuitive recognition underlies most great discoveries of the mind before they are worked out by the painstaking methods of logic and science.

By the end of the fifth century the Greek city-states had become fully literate societies. The terms "full" or "universal" literacy have to be taken with caution. Generally most modern European countries, the members of the British Commonwealth, the United States, and Japan are considered fully literate. At the same time residues of illiteracy exist in all these countries and even larger percentages fall short of effortless, near-automatic reading and writing abilities. The U.S. Navy, for example, routinely rejects about thirty percent of its would-be recruits because of "functional illiteracy." Obviously there must have been great differences in ancient Greece in the level of literacy from place to place, between countryside and city, and between social strata of free male citizens. Only a few women and fewer slaves received a literate education. But books seem to have been freely available and the workings of society were based on the assumption of at least functional literacy of its citizens. Apparently almost all children received some schooling. And it is perhaps significant that Athens adopted the Ionic alphabet for its official inscriptions. This step not only standardized the letter forms, but also had the effect of standardizing the orthography. The Athenian standard soon became the standard throughout the Greek-speaking world. The written word had created a new type of civilization that was to last for the next one thousand years.

Notes

1. F. M. Cornford, *From Religion to Philosophy: A Study in the Origins of Western Speculation* (New York 1957)

2. Wilhelm Nestle, *Vom Mythos zum Logos* (Stuttgart 1942)

3. Bruno Snell, *The Discovery of the Mind* (Cambridge, Mass. 1953)

4. E. A. Havelock, *Preface to Plato* (Cambridge, Mass. 1963); *The Literate Revolution in Greece and its Consequences* (Princeton 1982); *The Muse Learns to Write* (New Haven 1986)

5. Marshall McLuhan, *The Gutenberg Galaxy: The Making of Typographical Man* (Toronto 1962); *Understanding Media: The Extensions of Man* (New York 1965)

6. Werner Jaeger, *Paideia: The Ideals of Greek Culture* I (New York 1939), 144

7. B. Snell, 224

8. G. S. Kirk & J. E. Raven, *The Presocratic Philosophers* (Cambridge 1957), 319

9. Jaeger, *Paideia*, 305-311

6

The Fourth Century - Plato
and Aristotle

Plato

Plato started his speculations as a follower of Socrates, who never wrote anything himself. Whatever we know of Socrates we know from Plato, a few remarks by Aristotle and Xenophon's *Memorabilia*. Aristotle tells us (*Metaphysics* 987b) that "when Socrates, disregarding the physical universe and confining his studies to moral questions, sought in this sphere for the universal and was the first to concentrate on definitions, Plato followed him..." That Socrates concentrated on the definition of ethical terms and values seems confirmed by Xenophon. There is no hint in either Xenophon or Aristotle that Socrates held all the beliefs ascribed to him by Plato, such as transmigration of the soul or the theory of recollection and the theory of ideas. In his Socratic dialogues, however, Plato puts all his own thoughts into Socrates' mouth, probably out of reverence for his friend and teacher but also as a convenient literary device. Therefore it is difficult in reading Plato to decide where Socrates ends and Plato begins. It is safe to assume that "Socratic" opinions presented by Plato, but unconfirmed by Xenophon or Aristotle, are probably Plato's own, at least in their final formulation. The fundamental concept of the duality of a mortal body and an immortal soul in humans might well stem from Socrates. That the theory of forms or ideas was created by Plato we are specifically told by Aristotle. When in the following discussion of the Platonic system Socrates' words are quoted, it is always to be understood that the reference is to the Socrates of the Platonic dialogues.

Socrates' and Plato's philosophies seem to have had their beginnings as a reaction against the relativity of the sophistic ethics and in their own search for absolute universal standards of morality. The sophists claimed that they could teach *arete*. The most basic meaning of this word is "goodness" or excellence, and it usually meant being good at something. In Homer it had meant being a good warrior. For the sophists it meant being good in the arena of public life, being an effective leader. But for Socrates and Plato *arete* meant moral goodness and has usually been translated by the unfortunate term virtue. In most of Plato's earlier dialogues the question is raised "what is virtue?" or more specifically "what is piety, or courage, or justice?" or some other kind or aspect of virtue. Under questioning by Socrates it always turns out that the person claiming a certain virtue is unable to define what it is. Socrates, disclaiming any knowledge of the answer, then would prove that his interlocutor did not know what he was talking about, but would always leave him with the implication that virtue in general or the virtue under discussion were somehow aspects of one supreme goodness or "the good." Plato's most elaborate effort to provide an explanation of the supreme good is in his *Republic*.

The dialogue begins with the usual discussion, an attempt to define the meaning of "justice." The sophist Thrasymachus proposes that whatever is advantageous for a person is just or right for that individual and that it is just for the stronger to dominate the weaker. Socrates proposes his own view that just or unjust must be defined in the social context of the community. Right and wrong must be judged by their effect on the well-being of the citizens. Therefore he suggests that the problem might be solved more easily by examining it in terms of the state rather than in terms of the individual. Since the state is the sum total of its citizens, the answer to the problem thus magnified would be more clearly discernible. Socrates then develops the utopia of the ideal state. Only those best prepared by character and education can be qualified to govern. A state will be best ordered if every citizen does what he is best fitted for. In Plato's state the population will be divided into three classes selected and trained for three tasks essential to the working of any community: (1) farmers, craftsmen and other laborers; (2) "guardians" or watchmen to defend the state and to protect the other citizens; (3) rulers who must be motivated only by desire for the good of the state; therefore they must be searchers for wisdom and the knowledge of the "good"-- that is, philosophers. The division into the three classes is apparently not meant to be a hereditary caste system, although selective breeding is proposed to bring out the best quality in each individual. The rulers will observe the character and talents of the children and assign them accordingly to be educated as either workers or guardians. The most promising among guardians eventually will be chosen for more studies to become philosophers. During the education process individuals may still be promoted or demoted between classes.

The farmers and workers will follow the normal pattern of life, receiving a primary education, including reading and writing, and learning their trade-- typically literacy is given equal status with apprenticeship. When they have finished their schooling, they will receive compensation for their work or product and will be free to acquire property. The principal virtue for which they are trained is moderation or self-restraint (*sophrosyne*), which presumably means that they stick to their trade and leave politics, warfare and government to their betters.

Both males and females may be selected to be trained as guardians. They will be treated equally except that the actual hand-to-hand fighting will be left to the males. As their training is mainly directed towards military duty, the cardinal virtue for which they are educated is "spirit" (*thymos*). Perhaps the term might be translated as strength of character. For Plato it includes courage, a fierce drive to excel, the determination to face hardships and labor, and a strong sense of honor. Since the guardians must not have any ambition or interest other than the protection of the community, they are not allowed any exposure to distracting influences. They may not own any private property and must live in a garrison-type commune sharing possessions, wives and families. They may mate with other guardians, but children will be taken from their mothers at birth and raised in communal nurseries so that no one will know his or her own children nor will children know their parents. Thus, the children will be common to all guardians, who will consider all children their own without any distracting family ties. The training of guardians begins with learning while playing and moral instruction, followed by systematic education in reading and writing, epic, gymnastics and "music" in the Greek sense, which includes all the pursuits of the Muses: poetry recital, music in our sense, dance, and mathematics. Plato's literary emphasis is on heroic poetry meant to set a pattern of example and inspiration for the future guardians. All literature will be heavily censored to remove any model which might set a bad example, such as for self-indulgence, fear, dishonesty, etc. This education continues until age 17 or 18. The next two years will be exclusively devoted to military training.

Those among the guardians most gifted with intelligence and character will be selected for the schooling that may make them eventually true philosophers and fit to rule the ideal state. Only a few of those selected will be able to attain this final objective after 35 more years of study: ten years (until age 30) devoted to the study of mathematics, five years to what Plato calls dialectics, and the last 15 years until they reach the age of 50 in subordinate government positions for practice and more abstract study. In his description of the education of the philosopher-rulers Socrates presents the essential features of the Platonic system of philosophy which will be discussed later. The pre-eminent virtue of the philosopher is philosophy in the literal Greek meaning of the word: "love of wisdom." His goal is to gain as much knowledge of the "supreme good" as is humanly possible and the ability to provide for the good of the state. Thus in Plato's state each class acts in accord with its own *arete* or virtue.

Plato's scheme has been used by every totalitarian regime ever since as justification for the complete subordination of the individual to the state and the rule of an elite who alone knows what is best for all. It may be said in Plato's defense that he never expected that such a state could become reality and that his imaginary structure was only meant to illustrate his point in the discussion of the universal "good" and the need for total selflessness.

After the good of the state has thus been defined, Socrates proceeds to apply to the individual the lesson learned on the larger scale of the state. Since the state is the sum of its citizens, the same three elements essential for the functioning of the state should also be present in the individuals. He proposes that every human soul has indeed three analogous components. One part of the soul serves the natural needs and urges of the body; it corresponds to the working class. He calls it the "appetitive element," which has to be controlled by self-restraint (*sophrosyne*). Another part is the rational element, which will often be in conflict with the appetitive part. For instance, thirst might urge a person to drink from a pool, but reason warns against it since the water might be polluted. If the appetite is strong, reason (the ruler) might not prevail without the help of a third part-- the spirited element, which corresponds to the virtue of the guardians. Thus reason in the individual must be supported against the appetites by strength of character like the ruler in the state by the guardians. Freud has resurrected the tripartite psyche with his *id*, the *ego* and *superego*. Plato assumes that the soul of every individual contains all three elements, but in different proportions. Based on observation of early childhood play and education, children would be assigned to the three different classes in the state. It is important to note that Plato has fully accepted the nature/nurture theory of the sophists. Every child is born with a natural endowment that must be strengthened by the appropriate education. That all education begins with instruction in reading and writing-- universal literacy-- is taken for granted by Plato.

The twin pillars of the Platonic system of philosophic education, or (as he called it) dialectics, were his theory of recollection and his theory of ideas or forms. Earlier, in the *Phaedo* (74a-74b), he used the concept of equality as an example to explain the two theories as follows: we might call two sticks or two stones equal, but on close examination we will find that no two things are ever perfectly equal. Although there are no instances of complete equality in the physical world, we judge the degree of equality against an absolute standard of perfect equality which seems to be common to all people. Since no such ideal equality exists in our world of sense-perception, we cannot have acquired the concept through our experience in the physical world. Therefore, our souls must have contained the knowledge of absolute equality when they entered this world. When we see two, albeit imperfectly, equal objects, our soul is "reminded" of the idea or form of perfect equality which it has known in another transcendental world before birth. All learning is such recollection. The same holds true for the perception of beauty; nothing in this world is absolutely and perfectly beautiful. A thing may seem to a person beautiful at one time and ugly at another, or the same thing may seem beautiful to one person or ugly to another. Yet, as in the case of equality, when we judge the beauty of an object, we compare it to a standard of beauty which is not attainable in this world. Furthermore the idea of perfect beauty cannot change, since anything changing from perfection can only change for the worse. What is true of equality or beauty holds true for all other qualities, such as whiteness, roundness, goodness etc. There must exist then a realm of perfect "ideas" or "forms" (*eide*) which the soul has once known.

Our world, however, is a world of matter, and matter is never perfect and is constantly changing. Thus the qualities found in our material world can never achieve the perfection of the ideas in the transcendental world which they dimly reflect. When the human soul at birth is imprisoned in a mortal material body, it loses its knowledge of the perfect forms. From a world of continuous change and imperfection no real knowledge can be gained, since what is true in one moment might not be true the next. Therefore, the soul can acquire an approximation of knowledge only through remembrance or a mental return to the world of unchanging ideas, the only reliable source of truth and knowledge. The mental process of reasoning by which this return is accomplished, the only path to wisdom, Plato calls dialectics.

The first step towards an understanding of the ideas is the study of mathematics. The geometric figures and solids are also ideas which do not exist in the physical world. No one can draw a truly one-dimensional line or a perfect circle. When the mathematicians draw a line, it will still have a certain width; yet they formulate theorems based on the concept of an ideal one-dimensional line. Based on imperfect figures drawn in the sand, mathematicians derive universal formulas that pertain to perfect squares or perfect circles.

Thus mathematics is the first step in dialectics, which is reasoning not on the basis of physical objects, but from ideas using the physical objects as aids in visualizing the ideas, as the figures in the sand helped to visualize the ideal mathematical concepts. There is, however a difference between mathematics and dialectics. Mathematicians start with first principles (axioms) and develop their theorems, proofs and corollaries based on these first principles. Since they consider their first principles as self-evident, they never feel obligated to prove them. Therefore if the axioms are wrong, their whole structure of theorems and corollaries will be wrong. In dialectics, on the other hand, the first assumptions must be treated not as proven principles, but merely as hypotheses. Conclusions drawn from them remain purely hypothetical. The philosopher builds hypothesis on hypothesis without reference to the physical world, working with ideas alone until he is able to catch a fleeting glimpse of the idea of the supreme good, the real first principle of everything. When this happens, and only then, will he consider proven all the assumptions and hypotheses which led to this point.

Mathematical concepts are the lowest and most easily conceived ideas or forms, while the idea of the supreme good is the highest and most difficult to grasp. In between is a hierarchy of all the other ideas. Every object and quality in the physical world has its corresponding idea in the transcendental world of forms. To learn the truth about any object one has to know the idea of which the object is only an imperfect approximation. The idea is the cause of being of each object and also the source of knowledge about it. Thus the theory of ideas combines ontology with epistemology and, since many of the ideas are ethical concepts, also with ethics.

Much of Plato's reasoning is based on analogy, for instance his simile of the sun. The sun is the only light by which we can see clearly. Just as the sun is the source of our ability to see, the supreme good is the source of our ability to know. But the sun is also the cause of the natural things which we can see. As the sun makes things visible and is also the cause of their existence in the physical world, thus in the world of ideas the supreme good makes things knowable and is also the cause of being of all knowable things. The supreme good is the highest idea, the truth, the source of all being-- the deity. It is for this reason that the all-consuming purpose, the ultimate objective of the philosopher, must be to gain the clearest possible perception of the supreme good.

There is, however, a great obstacle. As long as the soul is prisoner in a material mortal body it can never attain full knowledge of the supreme good. In other words, one has to die to learn the truth. This is an old mythical theme. Ishtar, Odysseus, and later Aeneas must descend into the underworld to have the truth revealed to them. The concept re-appeared in the Christian view of heaven, where the reward of the blessed souls consists in being able to see God. And God is the truth. But according to Plato even if the soul is unable in this life to grasp fully the idea of the supreme good, it may sometimes get a brief dim glimpse of it by devoting itself wholly to the philosophic life, in which the rational soul reigns supreme over the body and the appetitive soul and dedicates itself wholly to dialectic inquiry.

Plato concludes this section with the famous simile of the cave, which is not only an illustration of the philosopher's intellectual ascent from the world of the senses to the world of ideas and eventually to the sunlight of the supreme good, but also an obvious reference to the trial and execution of Socrates by the Athenians.

Plato seems acutely aware of the conflict between abstract reasoning and the concrete imagery of the poetic tradition-- in other words, between logical and mythical thought. In his works he tried to reconcile the two. The *Republic* itself is a mixture of logical argument and reasoning by analogy, and image-- e.g., the just-mentioned similes of the sun and the cave. Whenever logic failed him, Plato tried to convey his meaning through a myth, either traditional or invented for the occasion. It is typical that he ends the essentially logical structure of the *Republic* with the grandiose apocalyptic myth of Er:

Er, a soldier killed in battle, after twelve days came back to life and reported what his soul had seen in the other world. Judges held court over the newly arrived souls. The just were directed to the right and into an upwards passage, the wrongdoers to the left and downwards. They were each to be respectively rewarded or punished during the next one thousand years for their deeds on earth. Processions of souls who had completed their terms emerged from the passages. Not all the souls had been permitted to return. The totally corrupt had been thrown into Tartarus where they suffered eternal torture. The returning souls had been shown the structure of the universe, its central axis and the rotation of the heavenly spheres around it. When the returning souls had congregated, they were allowed to choose lots for their next life on earth. Then they drank from the river of forgetfulness and each was turned over to his guardian spirit to be launched on his rebirth into the sensible world. Er, however, was ordered not to drink and to report what he had seen upon his return to earth.

The influence of this myth, in all its details, on Christian beliefs and on literature from Vergil to Dante to Milton is obvious: the immortality of the soul, its judgment after death, heaven, hell and purgatory, the segregation to the right and left, the concept of free will which makes individuals responsible for their choices, the protective spirit or guardian angel-- all have become permanent fixtures of Western mythology.

Plato was an extremely prolific writer and later changed some of his ideas. The reason this discussion was limited to the *Republic* is that of all his works it has had the most pervasive and lasting influence on Western thought, surviving into our own time.

Besides his influence on philosphy and religion, Plato set a new standard for literacy and education when he established the Academy, the first institution of higher learning. The sophists had pioneered a kind of secondary education which had been further developed in the rhetorical schools, but Plato was the first to gather a staff of outstanding specialists as teachers in his school, among them the mathematician and astronomer Eudoxus and Aristotle, probably chosen for his studies in biology. Although the first library attested by the ancient sources (Strabo 13.608) was that of Aristotle, it is clear from Plato's thorough knowledge of the existing literature and also from the preservation of almost all of his own writings that he must have collected a sizeable library in the Academy. Plato's Academy set the pattern for similar institutions, such as Aristotle's Peripatos, Epicurus' "Garden," and Zeno's Stoa.

The culture of the mind had become a universal ideal, the mark of civilized man. General literacy was taken for granted. Even political campaigning and propaganda were conducted through the written rather than the spoken word. Isocrates never made his "speeches"in public; they were written pamphlets. Although he was a fervent proponent of the Athenian Panhellenic movement, he expressed sentiments that became typical for the Hellenistic age:

> In thought and expression our city has left other people so far behind that our pupils have become the teachers of others, and has brought it about that the name Greek seems no longer to refer to descent but to reasoning power, so that those who share our education are to be called Greeks rather than those who share our common ancestry.

Aristotle

Plato's great pupil, Aristotle, was born in 384 BC as the son of the court physician to the Macedonian king. In 368, at the age of 17, he went to Athens and joined Plato's Academy. He remained there until Plato's death in 348/7. Then he went to Assos in Asia Minor, where he seems to have taught and studied; he later pursued his activities on Lesbos. In 343 he was invited back to the Macedonian court in Pella to become the tutor of Philip's son Alexander. He stayed there until 340. Philip completed his conquest of Greece in 338 with the battle of Chaeroneia. After Philip's death in 336 the Greek cities rose up against Macedonian rule, but their resistance collapsed quickly when young Alexander, immediately after his succession to the throne, marched south into Greece and re-established the Macedonian hegemony. A year later, in 335, Aristotle returned to Athens and founded his school in the Lyceum. In the following decade Alexander conquered the Near East from the Nile to the Indus. After Alexander's death in 323 Aristotle's life became endangered in Athens because of his connection with the Macedonians, and he went to Euboea where he died in the same year.

Aristotle's first studies, perhaps influenced by his father, were apparently in the fields of biology and zoology. We are told that during his stay in Lesbos he collected all kinds of specimens. From the beginning he seems to have considered all scientific knowledge an interconnected whole in the service of a total unified worldview, a teleological philosophy. In this he was undoubtedly influenced by Plato. Aristotle was a product of the new literate culture. He collected all information that he was able to obtain in written form and systematized the existing body of knowledge. He sifted its dialectics, its thought processes, through the fine mesh of a critical logic and imposed on it the discipline of a scientific methodology. Aristotle's work became the foundation of all subsequent scientific thought and provided its language. No matter how often Aristotelian rationality was misinterpreted, swept away by mysticism, starved by illiteracy, and buried under unreason, it was always rediscovered and has become stronger with each renascence. There is obviously no room here to do justice to all the achievements of Aristotle's mind. Nevertheless it will be necessary to touch on some of his theories in order to explore his influence on literate civilization, our civilization.

One fundamental difference between Plato and Aristotle was their attitude towards language and the written word. We have seen that Plato, like Gorgias and Socrates before him, was still doubtful whether knowledge could be transmitted from one person to another. Socrates' method had consisted in refuting all preconceived notions of his interlocutors in order to force them to search for the truth by their own reflections. Plato had elaborated on that approach with his theory of recollection and by offering his system of dialectics as an aid to the individual to find knowledge and truth within himself. Plato habitually resorted to symbolism and myth to illuminate problems rather than giving succinct explanations. He held even stronger reservations about the effectiveness of the un-aided written word. Plato still considered face-to-face dialogue the only way, if not of teaching at least of directing the pupil towards learning. His attitude towards the book seems to have been some-what like that of the Indian philosophers who considered the book of little value without the guru to explain its meaning. Therefore he was not afraid of vagueness and ambiguities in his writings, as they would only stimulate the reader to ask further questions.

Aristotle, on the other hand, wanted to fix and transmit his doc-trines in writing in incontrovertible terms that precluded any possi-bility of misunderstanding. His paramount objective was to present his findings and theories in precise form and to support them by in-escapable conclusions based on previously proven or obvious ax-iomatic premises. The study of rhetoric had made him keenly aware of the dangers of equivocation inherent in the different meanings and connotations of commonly used words. Therefore, beginning with an examination of the semantics and sentence structure of the Greek language he proceeded to the creation of his "tool," the *organon*, an analytic outline of systematic logic. In the process he created the terminology and language of science that is still spoken around the world, no matter how modified through borrowing and translation between languages and artificial derivatives and cre-ations. Aristotle established the rules for the definition of terms, the testing of the validity of statements, inductive and deductive reasoning, and separation of the abstract from the concrete. We owe the very concept as well as the vocabulary of formal logic to Aristotle.

For Plato, knowledge of the truth which he considered eternally unchanging cannot be gained from observation of the ever-chang-ing world of sense perception; and particular objects or phenom-ena can be understood only through study of the permanent uni-versal principles of which they are reflections. Aristotle's view was diametrically opposed. Although he agreed with Plato that scien-tific and philosophical knowledge is the knowledge of universals, he considered sense perception the starting point from which every inquiry must proceed. He insisted that inquiry must always progress from the particular to the general. Only the individual material objects and specimens that we perceive are "first substance," i.e., have primary existence. First substances consist of the matter and the form, as a coin consists of the metal and the imprint. Because matter and form are inseparable except by mental abstraction, disembodied forms cannot have any existence of their own. Neither can any quality or property exist separate from the substance of which it is a quality or property. Obviously, Plato's forms or ideas which are essentially qualities, such as beauty or goodness or whiteness, etc., cannot exist separate from a substance which is beautiful or good or white. The study of the qualities and properties of a substance, however, is necessary for the understanding of the nature of the substance. The species or class to which objects belong exists only in the individuals which make up the species or class. While science and philosophy consist in the knowledge of universal characteristics of species and classes of substances, this knowledge must be gained by study of individual specimens. The species itself and higher classes are products of mental abstraction and do not exist in the same immediate sense the individual exists. Although we can say that man exists as a species, man does not beget man; only an individual man can beget an individual child, as Peleus begot Achilles. Thus the species exists, but not in the full sense in which the individual or primary substance exists. Aristotle called the species secondary substances.

According to Aristotle the beginning and end of any inquiry is clear definition. The best definition is the one that tells us most about its subject. A good definition indicates the next higher class to which the substance belongs and the most characteristic properties that differentiate it from all the other members of the next higher classification. Thus in Aristotle's definition, man is an animal with the capability of theoretical thought, since in Aristotle's opinion the capability of theoretical thought is the one characteristic that among all the animals is possessed by man alone and therefore distinguishes man most clearly from the other animals. The most significant characteristic which differentiates an individual or a species from all others in its class Aristotle calls its essence. Thus the capability for theoretical thought is the essence of man.

Similarly, "soul" is the property of all living organisms. For Aristotle soul is a property of the living body and includes all the capabilities which are associated with the life of an organism, such as self-nutrition, self-motion, sense perception, emotions, and some thought processes (although not all these capabilities are necessarily present in every class of living being). He says that life is the essence of the whole living body as seeing is the essence of the eye. Function, essence and final purpose (*telos*) in Aristotle's definition are almost identical. Since the soul is what distinguishes animate from inanimate bodies it is the most important property, the essence, of the living body. The body is primary substance, and the soul, as one of the properties of that substance, cannot be separated from it except by mental abstraction, and consequently dies with the body. At this point, however, Aristotle was never able to make up his mind whether the capability of theoretical thought, which is one of the aspects of the human soul, also dies with it. He suggested at various times that theoretical thought might be something divine since it was the only capability that man shared with the deity and thus possibly immortal. Otherwise body and soul are indivisible. This, Aristotle finds, is confirmed by experience, as everything that affects the body also affects the soul (e.g., fatigue, illness, drunkenness, etc.), and similarly all affections of the soul also involve the body (e.g., anger and fear, and other emotions affect the heartbeat, breathing, etc.). Thus in spite of his quandary concerning abstract thought he was the first to formulate a mind-body identity theory.

Aristotle insists repeatedly that no results of theoretical speculations which contradict experience can have any validity. Experience is gained from particulars, from observation of first substance. Nature, which is made up by first substances of every kind, is in a state of continuous motion and change. That was the reason Plato, who was fully aware of the physical studies of his contemporaries, had disdained the pursuit of natural science. Following Heraclitus' view that everything is in flux, Plato thought the truth could not be learned through the observation of nature, as what was true one moment would not be true the next, and therefore that the truth had to be sought in an ideal realm of pure forms outside the physical world. For Aristotle, on the other hand, change and motion were the very essence of nature, a fact confirmed by every observation. Therefore science was the knowledge of the causes of change and motion. He posited his famous four causes thus:

1. The matter without which no first substance can exist: the material cause.

2. The form which makes the first substance what it is, sometimes identifiable with the essence: the formal cause.

3. The agent of change, inherent in every natural object: the cause of motion or efficient cause.

4. The end or purpose: the final cause (*telos*).

The final cause is the most important for Aristotle. He says repeatedly: "Nature acts as if it did nothing without a purpose." The final cause often determines and shapes the other three. At the basis of Aristotle's natural science is the observation that in physical substances changes are repetitive and predictable.

Aristotle, like his predecessors, had no concept of physical forces. Ever since Parmenides on purely theoretical and semantic grounds had "disproved" the possibility of change and motion the Greek physicists had had to resort to the assumption of some transcendental agency to explain the obvious phenomena of change and motion in the natural world. Empedocles had seen the forces of Love and Strife as the causes of natural processes. Anaxagoras had suggested "Mind" as the originator of the vortex motion from which he thought all movements derived. Aristotle made nature itself the moving force. Every natural object had the "cause of motion" within itself, and thus moved "naturally" from its potential to actuality. By this sleight of hand he disposed of the need for an external force acting directly on nature (although, as will be seen, there remained a transcendental agency acting indirectly). As the cause of motion was inherent in every natural entity it was accessible to physical inquiry and human understanding. Every substance was endowed with its own natural motion. Aristotle defined motion as quantitative and qualitative change as well as locomotion. Fire by nature moves upwards while everything else, if unhindered, moves down towards the center of the earth at a speed proportional to its weight (that weight controlled the speed of free-falling objects became a dogma for 1800 years until it was refuted by Galileo). Each living thing has the potential to develop in one direction only, towards its mature form; when it reaches that, it has achieved its actuality, its *telos*. The only mechanical forces Aristotle knew were a physical push or pull, and he thought that natural motion of inanimate objects usually proceeds along a straight line.

Aristotle's views on nature, however, applied only to physics on earth; the cosmos was subject to entirely different laws. Like most of his predecessors he was convinced of the perfection and eternity of the heavenly bodies. Therefore celestial bodies had to be different from terrestrial matter -- imperishable, unchanging and eternal. They were spherical and moved in circles because the sphere and the circle were the most perfect geometrical forms. Furthermore, only circular motions could be sustained eternally, since in a finite universe any rectilinear move would eventually have to reach a terminus. This assumption Aristotle considered confirmed by observation of the fixed-star heaven moving continuously in a perfect circle. On the whole he shared his astronomic concepts with Plato. These were based on the system devised by the mathematician and astronomer Eudoxus, a member and teacher at Plato's Academy, and later refined by Callippus. The universe was finite, a sphere bounded by the fixed-star heaven. Since the fixed stars never changed their relative positions and distances to each other, they were visualized as being held in place by the rotating sphere of the outer heaven. Nested within this sphere were the successively smaller concentric spheres of the planets, including sun and moon.

To define the motion of each planet mathematically it was conceived as the resultant of several circular movements at different speeds and angles. Aristotle modified this system to fit it into his unified metaphysical scheme. As he considered the outermost sphere of the fixed stars as the origin of all motion he believed that it transmitted its own movement successively to all the inner (planetary) spheres. The outermost planetary sphere (of Saturn) rotated in a motion compounded from the revolution of the fixed-star heaven and its own rotation. Each successive sphere towards the center moved at its own speed and angle compounded with the motion of its outer neighbor. At the center of it all was the stationary motionless earth.

Aristotle knew that Eudoxus' and Callippus' systems were purely mathematical constructs. It is to be noted that neither Aristotle nor Ptolemy after him actually believed in the physical existence of solid "crystalline" spheres. This myth has no foundation whatsoever in their original writings and is actually refuted by their own words, as Edward Rosen has so conclusively demonstrated.[1] The assertion of Aristotle's belief in solid spheres emerged with the rediscovery of his astronomy in late mediaeval scholasticism and is still being repeated by many historians of science.

With the improvement of instruments and more systematic observations during the next two centuries, discrepancies between the Eudoxan or Aristotelian models and the observed data led Hipparchus to correct the system by adding eccentricities and epicycles. With these features it eventually became known as the Ptolemaic model, named after the author of the most successful ancient work on astronomy (see Appendix, 322 ff.). The simpler Aristotelian system, however, misinterpreted by mediaeval commentators, held such appeal for the scholasticists that it became almost a dogma, and even affected adversely the understanding of the Ptolemaic and later the Copernican system.

The eternal movement of the outer heaven as the cause of the perfection of the celestial region, as well as the indirect cause of the workings of the imperfect material sub-lunar world, is the cornerstone of Aristotle's theology. Aristotle tried to deal with the fundamental question of any teleological philosophy or religion--viz., why an omnipotent, omniscient, moral deity would ever create an imperfect world in which immorality, injustice and suffering could exist. Plato had tried to resolve the problem in two ways: 1. The world consists of matter. All matter is inherently flawed and corruptible. Therefore the creator fashioning the world-order out of matter was only able to make it "as good as possible." 2. For the world to be as nearly perfect as possible it had to contain everything that existed and possibly could exist; this included imperfect and flawed beings. Aristotle took the question a step further: Why would a perfect supreme being, a being by definition totally independent and self-sufficient, create any kind of a world at all, even a perfect world? Aristotle's answer was that there cannot possibly be any conceivable reason for doing so. If the world was not created, it must have always existed. Aristotle further supports this assumption: Time must have always existed, for, what could there have been before the beginning of time except more time? But time is inseparable from movement. Without movement there would be no passage of time. (We still say when there has not been any movement that time has stood still). Therefore the motion of heaven, which defines time, must have always existed and, like time, will always exist. Thus the universe exists eternally and was never created. Since all of Aristotle's predecessors had assumed that matter in some form had always existed, and that the process of creation had consisted in introducing order (*cosmos*) into the mixture or chaos or elements or atoms, or whatever there was, Aristotle's concept that not only the matter but also its arrangement had always existed, was really not a radical departure. Still, Aristotle could not dispense and probably did not want to dispense with a transcendental agency.

Since in Aristotle's view motion could be caused only by a force acting on the object moved, and the motion would end when the force ceased to act, the question arose: what caused the eternal rotation of the fixed-star heaven? He reasoned as follows: whatever moves something else must itself be in motion and consequently moved by still something else and so *ad infinitum*. To avoid this infinite regress we must assume an entity which causes motion without moving itself. This "unmoved mover" is God. Since God is immaterial pure abstract thought and self-sufficiency, he could not and would not act directly on the world. But he acts indirectly by his mere existence as the universal object of love. What moves the outer heaven is its own love for the unmoved mover whose perfection it tries to emulate by moving eternally in its perfect motion. By its own circular motion the outer sphere imparts the same uniform motion to the inner spheres. But as the motions of the inner spheres are also compounded from other varying movements there must be other subordinate agencies inspiring the inner subordinate spheres. Since the heavens through heat and light and seasonal cycles are the cause of the terrestial world, the deity (pure thought, without any physical action) is the final cause-- the *telos*-- of the universe. But we have seen that theoretical thought is also the essence and thus the *telos* of man. It is because of this divine quality of contemplative thought that Aristotle at times believed that this part of the human soul might be indestructible.

Aristotle's teleology, his concept of the *telos* as the inherent trend in every object to realize its perfect final form, governed his total approach to the acquisition of knowledge. It applies to the world as a whole in the *Metaphysics*, to man as an individual in the *Ethics*, and to human communities in the *Politics*. In Aristotle's psychology (*On the Soul*) as well as in his *Ethics*, contemplative thought, the search for knowledge for its own sake, appears as man's essence and *telos*. In zoology and botany the individual specimen, by growing to its mature form and reproducing itself, fulfils its purpose, the *telos* of its kind, the eternal perpetuation of its species. Thus in a sense the species is equivalent to the unchanging Platonic *Form* with which it shares its Greek name *eidos*, of which the Latin word *species* is the translation. But in Aristotle's view the permanent form, the species, exists in our world instead of the wild blue yonder of Plato's transcendental realm of Forms. Therefore the final form as *telos* remains accessible to sense perception, experience and human knowledge.

Every inquiry Aristotle undertakes is shaped by this conviction that every entity progresses towards its perfect form. Even his method of literary criticism, the first conscious analysis of literature in history, reflects his teleology. The *Poetics* start from the question: what is the purpose of each genre of literature, the specific enjoyment it tries to offer, its *telos*? Only when he has answered these questions can he proceed to determine the proper form and structure for each genre and to judge the merits of individual works of literature. For instance, in Aristotle's view the *Iliad* had reached its *telos*, perfection of the epic form beyond which further improvement was not possible.

Aristotle's teleological concepts had various effects. No matter what subject or science he embarked on he tried to trace the growth of knowledge in the respective field from as far back in the past as possible. He did so critically, rejecting some ideas, agreeing with others. Although his essential purpose was to show that his own theory on the subject was the last step, the *telos* of a development towards which his predecessors had been groping,[2] Aristotle's search for his antecedents produced several important consequences for the ever-growing role of literacy in the advance of civilization. His research into the past caused Aristotle to collect all available information and literature in his fields of interest-- and there seem to have been none that failed to interest him-- and thus to collect a comprehensive library which established the pattern for the foundation of the Library of Alexandria by the Ptolemies. The operation of a library requires the critical examination and, if possible, the restoration of original texts and their preservation for future generations. The library became a cornerstone of literate civilization; it inspired liberal education and systematic scholarship. Literary scholarship sparked the humanistic ideal of the perpetuation of all knowledge and ideas in literary form, with each generation adding to what it has received.

In spite of Plato's influence on Aristotle their philosophies were often diametrically opposed to each other. Plato's dualistic concept of a mortal body and an immortal soul, the concept of personal responsibility and of reward or punishment after death, became fundamental to most religious philosophies. Plato's outlook was essentially pessimistic. Any act or behavior that falls short of an absolute ideal is unacceptable. Since the knowledge of the higher ideas is not accessible to ordinary humans they are doomed to failure; therefore they must be coerced by the laws and rulers of the state to do what is right. Even Plato's philosopher-king can never attain full knowledge of the absolute good. Man is the frustrated victim of abstract inflexible generalities. This pessimism was adopted by the mediaeval hierocratic church. In Aristotle the individual takes precedence over generalizations. There are few universally applicable imperatives. The "good" is different in every kind of endeavor and situation. Ethical philosophy can set only certain limits, and within these limits the individual must judge and is capable of judging what is good under the particular circumstances. Universal truths can be learned from observation of individual phenomena; thus knowledge is attainable by all. Although science is the knowledge of universals, abstract speculation cannot overrule the facts of experience. Aristotle's greatest achievement was the creation of the language and methodology of science. He named and initiated almost all branches of science. That he was wrong in many of his findings because of faulty information or misinterpretations of observations does not change the fact that he made science self-correcting since every theory could be superseded if it was proven wrong by new observations and experience.

Aristotle's review of earlier theories had also some contradictory effects. His accounts became models to be followed by the later "writers of opinions" (doxographers) who set out to write chronological histories and summaries of philosophic doctrines as they understood them. As the doxographers relied heavily on Aristotle and Theophrastus, Aristotle's pupil and successor in the Lyceum, their accounts are of only limited value as independent sources.[3] Their writings, however, are of some importance to us, as they preserve some quotations from lost presocratic writings. On the other hand their excerpts and summaries tended in later antiquity to take the place of the original works in the preference of the readers. Thus the popularizing works of the doxographers and epitomizers probably contributed to the loss of original sources by lessening the demand for them. The trend towards reading and teaching from the popular handbooks instead of the original treatises led to misinterpretations, shallow repetitions of half-digested theories, and a superficial kind of literacy which turned out to be very detrimental to the understanding of Aristotle's own thoughts by late Roman and mediaeval teachers and students. But more important than these side effects were the positive consequences of Aristotle's retrospective accounts, since they emphasized the continuity of intellectual advance and the perfectibility of human knowledge. This consciousness became one of the driving forces in the humanistic western tradition because it presented the opportunity and challenge to the individual to make his own contribution. The very concept of progress, which was to play such an important part in later western thought, was in marked contrast to most other philosophies and religions, which saw the world either as static or as moving in ever-repeating cycles, from beginning to destruction to new beginning, in which the individual had no more importance than a grain of sand or a blade of grass.

Aristotle's treatises reinforced the trend towards written publication of scientific findings. From Aristotle on, the book and the library became the undisputed means for the preservation and accumulation of knowledge. He was the first to advocate public education in literacy administered by city governments, an idea that soon was to be put into practice by many of the Hellenistic *poleis* of the Near East. Plato's Academy and Aristotle's Lyceum were the first establishments of higher learning and models for the first institutions for scientific research and scholarship sponsored and supported by the rulers of states, such as the Museum attached to the Library of Alexandria.

In the span of 150 years from the beginning of the fifth century BC to the middle of the fourth the Greeks had transformed their conceptual outlook and their view of the universe as well as their view of themselves. Aristotle's work was a final step in that process (as he might have said, its *telos*). In the preceding pages, we have seen the part played by literacy in cognitive developments of which we are the heirs. But we are followers of the Greeks in our emotional as well as our intellectual lives. We are educated in a literary tradition that they originated which is permeated not only by their rationality, but also by their deep-seated motivations. Because of the near-universality of literacy in their society, as in ours, the literary conditioning affected the whole population rather than only a small literate elite. The dominant motivation of the Greeks, the main cause of their accomplishments as well as their failures and their eventual political downfall, was their ambitious competitiveness. In the oldest work of Greek literature, the *Iliad*, Achilles' father Peleus, sending his son off to war, gives him this admonition: "... always to be the best and outstanding above all others" (11.784). The *Iliad* remained the Bible and schoolbook of the young throughout antiquity. Peleus' words were not only the credo of the aristocrats. Hesiod, the farmer-poet, who rages against the oppressive lords, begins his *Works and Days* thus:[4]

> Strife is no only child. Upon the earth
> Two strifes exist; the one is praised by those
> Who come to know her, and the other blamed.
> Their natures differ: for the cruel one
> Makes battles thrive, and war; she wins no love
> But men are forced by the immortals' will
> To pay the grievous goddess due respect.
> The other, first-born child of blackest Night,
> Was set by Zeus, who lives in air, on high,
> Set in the roots of earth, an aid to men.
> She urges even lazy men to work:
> A man grows eager, seeing another rich
> From ploughing, planting, ordering his house;
> So neighbor vies with neighbor in the rush
> For wealth: this strife is good for mortal men -
> Potter hates potter, carpenters compete,
> And beggar strives with beggar, bard with bard.

Competition dominated every aspect of Greek life. Athletic contests appeared as early as the Homeric age. The Greeks reckoned time according to Olympic games. Pindar's extant poetry was devoted to the glorification of the winners in athletic games. Every public recital of poetry, every presentation of dramas was a contest for a prize to be awarded to a winner. Only the United States with its Oscars, Tonys, and Emmies has built the mystique of winning to a higher level. The competition for power in ancient Greece was even fiercer. The whole theme of the *Iliad* is the contest for prestige between Achilles and Agamemnon. When Achilles' pride was injured he did not hesitate to bring the whole Greek expeditionary force to the brink of destruction for the sake of his glory. Greek political leaders followed Achilles' example throughout the history of the city-states. When they lost their positions of power many sought help from the enemies against their own cities or joined the enemy. Hippias, Demaratus and Themistocles went over to the Persians. Alcibiades in the war between Athens and Sparta changed sides several times. The whole 150 years of the "Golden Age" were filled with wars for the hegemony over Greece and with internal conflicts for power between factions within the cities. The city governments, like the individual politicians, never hesitated to seek help from the enemies of Greece, such as the Persians, in their power struggles with other Greeks. Finally, the appeal for help by the cities, locked in war for the domination of Greece, gave Philip II of Macedonia the opening for his conquest of Greece. The self-destructive quarrels were the other side of the much-vaunted Greek striving for excellence, which brought the freedom of the *poleis* to an end.

Notes

1. Edward Rosen, "Dissolution of the Solid Celestial Spheres, *Journal of the History of Ideas* 46-1 (1985), 13-31

2. K. F. Cherniss, *Aristotle's Criticism of Presocratic Philosophy* (Baltimore 1935), 347-374

3. J. B. McDiarmid, "Theophrastus on the Presocratic Causes", *Harvard Studies in Classical Philosophy* 61 (1953), 85-155

4. Hesiod, *Theogony, Works and Days* and Theognis, *Elegies*, translated by Dorothea Wender, (London 1972), 59

7

The Hellenistic Period

Influences from the east had contributed much to the development of Greek classical civilization. The Greeks had transformed and advanced some of the knowledge they had gained, and spread it back to the east. Although there had always been commercial and cultural exchanges, they could not compare with the flood of Greek literate culture that swept eastward in the footsteps of Alexander's armies and made its imprint on the older civilizations. Out of this amalgam grew new modes of thought and eventually the religions "of the book", one of which would rebound to the west and determine the future of Europe, while another would dominate the Near and Middle East.

Although the political union did not survive Alexander's death in 323 the cultural unity of Hellenism remained all-pervasive and growing until the Romans in the second century BC restored political unification, and in the process became Hellenized themselves. Upon Alexander's death his lieutenants divided the empire among themselves, and each became the founder of a Hellenic dynasty. Their heirs, named after the founding generals, the Ptolemies, Seleucids, and Antigonids, kept ruling by the strength of their Macedonian and Greek mercenaries. Often they fought each other, sometimes they concluded alliances and dynastic marriages, or just observed an uneasy truce.

Greek civilization underwent changes as fundamental as those of the conquered people. The result was the culture we call Hellenistic, which shaped and unified the western world for almost a thousand years and in its revived form in the Renaissance gave birth to modern civilization. The term Hellenism is a modern creation, but aptly chosen to differentiate the new Greek culture from its classical parent. It was derived from the genuine Greek verb *hellenizein* which means to act like a Greek (in dress, manner, and especially language). The Greek suffix -*izein* has found its way as a verb-forming suffix into most European languages and appears in English as -ise, or -ize in the American spelling; it means to produce the quality denoted by the adjective to which the suffix is attached (such as fertilize, immunize, Anglicize, etc.). Thus, to Hellenize, besides its meaning "to act like a Greek." can also have the transitive sense of making someone a Greek. The means by which this process worked was Greek physical and literary education. Acting like Greeks and Hellenizing their children, an important segment of the conquered populations made Greek literate culture their own and established Hellenistic civilization in its dominant position within an amazingly short time. There were many reasons for this mostly willing acceptance by the conquered nations.

One reason was the acknowledgment of Greek military power. By conquering the known world the Greeks had proved their superiority. Throughout history it has been military strength that was admired most. The adjective "the Great" has always been reserved for conquering aggressors. It seems paradoxical that after the demise of the Greek cities as military powers their soldiers and tactics were not only able to maintain their warlike reputations, but also to provide Alexander with his aura of invincibility. It was primarily the Greeks military successes that gave them the image of superiority and raised the question as to what made them superior. The general answer of their subjects seems to have been the same as the Greeks' own-- Greek education.

Another, more obvious, reason for the willing acceptance of Greek ways was self-interest. For Alexander the fusion of the Greek and Persian civilizations may or may not have been a conscious purpose. In actuality the practical necessities of maintaining themselves in power dictated to Alexander and his successors a political course which fostered the syncretism of cultures as surely as if it had been sought by design. The Hellenistic kings and their instruments of power, the Greek-Macedonian professional armies of occupation, were such small minorities that they could govern only through the existing power-structures in their respective domains. The compliance of the local establishments was not too hard to obtain; after all, they were only exchanging one foreign ruler for another. To keep their positions of influence and wealth they needed the support of the Hellenistic monarch as much as they had needed that of the Persian king or the pharaoh. And the rulers needed the cooperation of the local elite to run the mechanics of administration, especially the collection of taxes. The language of the royal courts and their officials was, of course, Greek. The native political and administrative establishments which continued to operate at some level, varying from place to place, had to deal with the Greek authorities. Thus it was the people who counted most (the functionaries, the petty kings and client chiefs, and the wealthy elite) who were under the greatest pressure to "Hellenize," to adopt Greek ways, because they depended on the Greeks for their positions, their businesses and their social standing. Anyone to be successful in his ambitions among Greeks had to become one of them. The native elite in turn was the model for the lower strata.

In monolithic Egypt, with its rigid hierarchic and pyramidal structure where all power was concentrated at the court of the Pharaoh and his hieratic advisors, the Ptolemies had easily slipped into the Pharaoh's shoes and thus assumed centralized control of the scribal bureaucracy and a well oiled machinery of government. They ruled from newly founded Alexandria, where they had concentrated their Hellenic troops.

From the beginning Ptolemy I, Alexander's lieutenant, vigorously supported the promotion of Greek civilization in an alien environment. He had been a friend of Alexander from early youth and may have been under the influence of Alexander's tutor Aristotle. He later invited to his court Demetrius of Phaleron, who as governor of Athens had helped Aristotle to establish the Lyceum and had been one of his pupils there. The Ptolemies founded the Library of Alexandria with its attached Museum as a sanctuary of the Muses and of the arts and sciences they stand for. It was without a doubt inspired by Aristotle's Lyceum, and was the first government-sponsored institution of higher learning and research. The

Ptolemies invited to the Museum the outstanding Greek poets and scholars of their time and provided them with the means to pursue their studies. In return the guests at the Museum functioned as librarians and educators of the royal children. The library, which eventually contained all known Greek literature, became the heart and soul of classical scholarship, of Hellenistic poetry and science. The new Greek capital Alexandria grew to be not only the most prosperous commercial city but also the intellectual center of the Hellenistic world.

The Seleucids, who inherited most of the Asiatic part of the Persian empire, were confronted with a situation that was quite different from that of the Ptolemies in Egypt. They had to govern a sprawling land mass reaching for a time from the Red Sea to the Indus and one that was populated by many heterogeneous ethnic groups. Unlike Egypt, the Persian empire had relied on a decentralized administration by many satraps and client chiefs with various degrees of dependence, loyalty and autonomy. To control their vast domain the Seleucids had to station their troops in widely scattered garrison towns. Some of these were existing cities, but many were newly founded military colonies, (*katoikiai*), where Greek and Macedonian troops were settled. The soldiers were assigned plots of land for cultivation and, under the command of an officer, were responsible for the security of their assigned area. Such cities remained under the administration of the military commander. In order to broaden their power-base the Seleucids continued the policy of founding new *katoikiai* by encouraging enlistment of Hellenized native troops. Many of the later Greek cities had begun as such military colonies. When such a city had fulfilled certain requirements, it could petition for the status of independent *polis*. Since it was essential for the Seleucids to keep their Greek mercenaries and their families contented and to assure continued re-enlistment and recruitment in the isolation of a foreign land, they had to create for them an environment as similar as possible to their accustomed surroundings in which they could maintain their Greek lifestyle and educate their children as Greeks. Thus they faithfully patterned their planned garrison towns after the Greek *polis*, with its buildings for municipal administration, its gymnasium which also functioned as a school, an *agora*, theater, and the temples of the Olympian gods.

Many of these Hellenistic cities became prosperous centers of trade. Alexander, who had seized great hoards of gold and silver and control of the mines, coined enormous amounts of money, which he used for lavish compensation of his soldiers and for any services rendered to him. The flood of coinage issued by Alexander and his successors had introduced a money economy in many areas where none had existed before. Benefiting the most were, of course, the Greek *poleis*, but many older cities also profited from the new prosperity. Both kinds of cities offered many opportunities for commerce and attracted numerous Greek immigrants and local craftsmen and traders, but the Greek *poleis* were attractive for other reasons, too: they offered an appealing environment and a stimulating way of life. The citizens of the *polis*, through their elected council (*boule*), administered their own internal affairs. The *agora*, surrounded by colonnaded buildings formed a pleasant social center. Theater presentations, sports events, and religious festivals provided entertainment. The gymnasium offered not only physical recreation but often also public education for the children. Neither the Greek and Macedonian soldiers, nor the Greek immigrants who had come from the homeland to escape the widespread poverty there, had much education, but most of them commanded a basic level of functional literacy, and since there were usually sufficient books available, those who were interested could educate themselves further. The example of the *poleis* was attractive enough to stimulate the inhabitants of many of the older towns to imitate the model and to transform their own community into a Greek-style *polis*.

The Seleucids encouraged this process. Once a town had organized itself in conformance with Greek law, it could obtain recognition as a Greek *polis* from the king. This privilege emancipated the citizens from the status of subject population and gave them autonomy in municipal government as well as administrative control over the surrounding countryside. The free *polis* entered into direct alliance with the king and the other *poleis* and thus became part of the Greek ruling establishment. Many of the Greek cities referred to in the later literature were Hellenized native communities. As we observed in the discussion of self-government in the classical age, such municipal government depended on and could function only among a literate citizenship. From the *poleis* the Greek language and literacy trickled into the surrounding countryside. The way for the rapid penetration of Greek literacy had been facilitated by the advance of other alphabetic writing systems derived from the West-Semitic script. Through Phoenician, Aramaic, and Hebrew writing the literate classes of the population from Gaza to Sousa were already familiar not only with the principles of alphabetic writing but also with the names, the sequence and in many cases the shapes of the letters, as well as with a primitive teaching methodology in reading, writing and the explication of literature. Aramaic had become the *lingua franca* of commerce throughout the Levant, and the Aramaic alphabet had replaced cuneiform and other cumbersome syllabaries. Thus educated natives found it relatively easy to absorb Greek literacy. Greek became the *koine*, the common language of the Near East, and remained so even under the Roman Empire.

Political pressure and self-interest alone, however, could not have brought about a profound cultural transformation if it had not been for the vital force of Greek literature. Necessity and opportunism might have generated assimilation in speech and dress, but only Greek literacy and literary education could produce the Hellenization of thought-processes. None of the subject peoples had a literature that in scope and variety could compare with the Greek. This was especially true in expository writing, in historiography, in science, and in philosophy. The only body of literature comparable to the literary tradition of the Greeks was the Hebrew, but it too was mainly affective-mythological and lacking in the objective-logical element. Nevertheless it is noteworthy that the culture that would eventually emerge to dominate the Western world evolved from a fusion of these two richest literary traditions, both based on alphabetic literacy-- the Greek and the Hebrew. The more immediate result of Hellenistic empire-building, however, was that an elite of the subject populations, forced by circumstances to adopt the outward trappings of Greek civilization and education, succumbed to the exhilarating freedom of Greek rationality and literacy. Hellenized Syrians, Jews, Babylonians and Egyptians soon formed a new intelligentsia that, transcending all ethnic boundaries, would make its own contribution to Greek learning and literature.

The new surge of Greek intellectual activity with its origins in the Alexandrian Library was spurred by the realization that the classical age had come to a close with the demise of the sovereign city-states. Although, as we have seen, the *poleis* were still to play an important cultural role they were now mere municipalities conducting their internal affairs, while their ultimate fate depended on the supreme power of a monarchic government. To the Greek the very idea of freedom had always consisted in the fact that his city was a sovereign state in control of its relationships with the rest of the world. Aristotle was one of the last representatives of that era and seemingly unaware of the changes that had been set into motion in his own time; some of the trends were due to his own influence. The implications of Aristotle's teleological views in the *Poetics* were that the Homeric Epic and Attic Tragedy had reached their *telos*, their perfect form. This meant that nothing produced afterwards could ever surpass the classical works and would only be a let-down. Indeed, in "New Comedy" a genre of bourgeois Comedy of Manners and anti-heroic romances replaced classical drama and epic poetry respectively. In the early 3rd century BC, when the realization struck that the way of life which had produced the classics was irretrievably lost, this heritage seemed even more precious. But it was threatened from all sides.[1] Works existing in only a few fragile papyrus copies deteriorate, get lost, are corrupted in copying or are destroyed in war, or by fire, floods or other mishaps. Almost all the papyrus texts still in existence were preserved in the dry climate of Egypt and the neighboring desert areas; few could survive for long in the wet European weather. Texts of dramas and epics were continually changed by actors and reciters. The

Athenians even placed what was considered to be authentic copies in the archives and passed laws prohibiting any deviations from them in public performances. The survival of literature seemed especially threatened by the wars and upheavals after Alexander's death. As in later renaissance movements, the preservation of the classical literary treasures became an all-important goal.

Towards the beginning of the 3rd century BC, Ptolemy I invited the poet Philitas of Cos and the physicist Strato to Alexandria to help in the education of his son Ptolemy II -- Philitas as tutor in literary studies and Strato in science. Strato had been a student of Aristotle and Aristotle's successor Theophrastus, whom he followed as head of the Lyceum upon his return from Alexandria in 287 BC. Ptolemy II joined his father as co-regent in 285 and governed as King of Egypt from 283 to 247. The Museum with the Library took shape under their sponsorship. Ptolemy I in his later years wrote a history of Alexander's campaigns that seems to have been the most reliable source on this subject. His literary interests and affinity with the Aristotelians indicate that, in addition to any political purposes, Ptolemy was motivated by a genuine desire to secure the classical legacy. The activities at the Library took two directions. The Aristotelian circle surrounding Ptolemy I initiated a tradition of scientific research. The other current reflected the literary orientation of some of the heads of the Library. The librarians developed an efficient catalogue system. The collection, restoration and preservation of the texts became the main task of the librarians and gave rise to a new kind of learning, not only what we call classical scholarship, but also the study of language and a system of literate education that set a pattern for the Greek-Roman world and lasted almost into our own time.

In 338 BC Athens had instituted the *ephebeia* as the first publicly sponsored type of secondary education. It was mainly intended as a preparation for military service just at the time when the citizen soldier had become all but obsolete and was being replaced by the more effective professional mercenary. The *epheboi* were trained in a democratized version of the traditional aristocratic tutoring in gymnastics, equestrian sports, Homeric poetry, heroic music and choral dances.

Although the *ephebeia* had lost its meaning as military training, it became an important instrument of Hellenization in the conquered territories. Through the gymnasium and the ephebic training the Greeks in foreign lands were able to pass on their identity to their children. For the sons of ambitious natives acceptance into the *ephebeia* was the entrance to Greek *paideia*, education, assimilation and citizenship. A literary education was sometimes sponsored by the city or by wealthy citizens in connection with the gymnasium and the *ephebeia* in various arrangements, depending on local politics. And there were, of course, private teachers and private schools, offering the sought after Greek education. It has been said that the way to success in the Hellenistic city led through the gymnasium.[2]

Hellenistic education was to a large extent shaped by the scholars of the Alexandrian Library. It was originally intended as preparation for philosophy, and still carried in many respects the stamp of Aristotle. The very idea of state-sponsored education was first proposed in Aristotle's *Politics*. His admiration for the *Iliad*, which he had passed on to Alexander, assured its continued first place in Greek education. Among the thousands of Greek papyrus fragments found in Egypt, many used as mummy wrappings, a great number are students' exercises. Over a quarter of all existing literary papyri and fragments contain passages from Homer, with the *Iliad* leading the *Odyssey* about three to one.[3] The works of the fifth century, and especially those that had found Aristotle's favor in the *Poetics*, became canonized as classics. As H. I. Marrou has pointed out there was also a fascination with lists of "the greatest" in every field.[4] The preferred numbers, as in folklore, were 7 and 12: seven sages, seven wonders of the world, seven liberal arts; 12 labors of Heracles, 12 Olympian gods, 12 Apostles, division of the Homeric poems into 24 books each, even if it required padding the *Odyssey*. Aristotle's preferences and the selectivity of the grammarians were without doubt a reason for the survival of only the very small part of the ancient literature that has come down to us:

e.g. seven plays of Sophocles out of 123, seven of Aeschylus out of 70; none of the other tragedians survived except Euripides, whose audience appeal was so wide that over 30 plays were preserved. Of the quotations of ancient authors in the first sections of Stobaeus 314 are from extant works, 1,115 from works that have been lost.[5]

Furthermore, the rhetoricians and schoolmasters had little time for later literature. The short time span of one or two years devoted to secondary education imposed severe limitations not only on the choice of authors, but also on the selection of material from each author. Comprehensive education became even more difficult during the time of the Roman Empire, when the Latin authors of the late Republic and the Augustan era had become classics and were added to the curriculum, at least in the western part. Thus it is not surprising that anthologies, summaries and handbooks were in wide use and that literacy became more superficial the wider it spread.[6] The continual process of selection and narrowing of the variety of popular reading was responsible for the loss of most of ancient literature. The evidence of the papyrus fragments from the garbage dumps of even small Egyptian towns shows that a much wider range of literary works was still read in the first two centuries of our era than has come down to us.

When what we have called secondary education, *enkyklios paideia* (grammar, literature, rhetoric, and mathematics), filtered down into the municipal and private schools, it fell far short of living up to its name "encyclopedic." Highly eclectic from the start, it was further diluted by the varying abilities and preferences of poorly paid teachers. Mathematics probably seldom went beyond basic calculations. Despite the shortcomings of the program in practice, however, its principle set a standard that survived into our time. In antiquity it propagated an unprecedented level of literacy and unified the civilization of the Mediterranean world.

While Alexandria became the center of scientific and literary studies Athens retained its leadership in philosophic thought. The consciousness of a break in history that affected the approach to literature also redirected the evolution of philosophy. Classical philosophy had been focused on the *polis* as sovereign state. The city was expected to provide security and the fulfillment of most human needs-- economic, social, religious, and intellectual. For Hippodamus, Plato and Aristotle the quest for the happy life had meant an effort to make one's city the best possible community. Plato offered his totalitarian republic under a philosopher-king as the answer. Aristotle, following his empirical principles, collected and studied all constitutions he was able to obtain and the histories of the respective cities, and concluded that the democratic Athenian constitution of his time, although far from perfect, was the best attainable practical solution for the well-being of the citizens. But with the reduction of the cities to mere municipalities subject to the whims of an absolute ruler the citizens had lost control over their destinies. The answers of a socially oriented philosophy were not valid anymore. As a consequence philosophy turned both introspectively inward, and outward to a vastly expanded world. The question was no longer: "How can I improve my *polis* to satisfy my needs?" but rather: "How can I achieve a measure of happiness in an adverse environment over which I have no influence?" Thus, the philosophies of the Hellenistic age -- Cynicism, Epicureanism and Stoicism -- were directed towards the inner life of the individual and its defense against the world at large.

The Cynic philosphers, better known from the anecdotes centered on Diogenes (died 323 BC), and their outrageous behavior than from their teaching, claimed Socrates as their founding father by way of Antisthenes. The Cynics despised possessions and hypocrisy; they pioneered the concept of the unity of all mankind and considered themselves citizens of the world (*kosmopolitai*), an idea that had been given meaning by Alexander's conquest of the known civilized world-- the *oikoumene*. The mental break out from the confines of the city-state, in a somewhat different sense, had already been furthered by Isocrates, who had made literate education rather than ethnic descent the touchstone which differentiated Greeks from barbarians. The Cynics did not leave any significant literature.

Epicurus' (342-270) philosophy was based on the atomism of Democritus. The world consisted only of atoms and void. The random movements of atoms of different sizes and shapes, sometimes adhering to each other and sometimes separating, bring innumerable worlds into being and dissolve them again in a mechanical process without any divine intervention. Every phenomenon in the universe has a natural cause and can be understood on the basis of sense perception. Gods exist some place, but they lead their own blissful existence without any involvement in the world of humans. The way to human happiness is to enjoy the simple pleasures of life from day to day. The ideal state of the human mind is equanimity (*ataraxia*), attained by avoidance of all disturbing factors, such as mental or bodily pain, brought on by violent desires, fears, passions or ambitions. The greatest impediments to the serene state of *ataraxia* are fear of death, fear of the gods, and fear of punishment after death. These fears can be dispelled through the study of nature. Once it is understood that everything in the world happens through natural cause-effect relationships, there is no longer any need to believe in action by the gods. Death is just the dissolution of the atomic structures that constitute us and, since nothing of our individuality or consciousness survives after death, death is simply nothingness and not to be feared. All religion is superstition, and religious rituals and practices are immoral and to be avoided. So are desires for power, wealth or honors, as they disrupt the state of *ataraxia*. The best things in life are free: enjoyment of nature, the company of good friends, philosophic conversation, most bodily pleasures if enjoyed in moderation, and avoidance of intense emotions which might upset the inner tranquillity. Because Epicureanism advocated withdrawal from public life and opposed religion it never found favor with the Roman establishment, and still later became anathema to the Christian church. But it instilled an almost missionary enthusiasm in the Roman poet Lucretius, and inspired some of the most charming poetry of Horace and Ovid. The Epicurean philosophy, however, gained widespread acceptance in the Near East since it provided a rational basis for the spirit of "enjoy the day, for nobody knows what tomorrow will bring", which long before Horace's *carpe diem* had inspired the Gilgamesh Epic. Later, the age of reason would make Lucretius one of its own.

The Stoic school was founded by Zeno, a Phoenician from Cyprus (died 262 BC). He was succeeded by Cleanthes of Assos, Chrysippus of Cilicia and three more Asiatics, then by Panaetius of Rhodes, and Posidonius from Syria, the teacher of Cicero. Stoicism became the most important Hellenistic philosophy and practically the unofficial state religion of Rome. The last great works of Stoicism were the *Meditations* by the emperor Marcus Aurelius (AD 161-180). The Stoics carried the cosmopolitanism of the Cynics to its full conclusion: divine reason, the *logos*, permeates the whole universe, as the soul the individual. The *logos* gives form to the elements and shapes all physical phenomena. All the various national gods are just symbols for the different aspects and functions of the supreme deity. The religious myths, if read properly, are allegorical expressions of profound truths. The divine *logos* is also shared by man. It is what separates man from all the other animals and is a direct link between man and god. The traditional religious practices, such as oracles, divination and astrology, are a valid means of exploring the divine intent. It is the task of man to reinforce the *logos* within himself in order to subdue the animal part of his nature. Through communication with the *logos* humans can distinguish right from wrong, and thus judge their own morality. Each individual is put into the world for a divine purpose and through cultivation of his reasoning power can recognize this purpose; its fulfilment is the duty of the individual. In the plan of the *logos* each person has an assigned role to play out in his life. The emotions are part of our animal nature and prevent us from acting in accord with the *logos*. Thus suppression of all passions is the most important objective of the Stoic sage. Through concentration on his reasoning power, which is part of the divine *logos*, he can free himself from all affections and afflictions of his body, such as disease or pain, and from fear, anger, pity, and other emotions, and thus attain the ideal Stoic state of *apatheia*, complete mental detachment. When man acts in conviction of his moral duty he can bear any physical or mental torture.

There is a profound difference between Epicurean *ataraxia* and Stoic *apatheia*: Lucretius compared man to a spectator in the theater of life who might leave if annoyances outweighed the pleasures of the performance; the Stoic considered himself an actor on the world-stage who had the duty to play out his role while rising above all adversity. It was very convenient for the Romans to see as their duty the bringing of peace and justice to the world on their own terms. The Stoic concepts of the brotherhood of mankind and individual responsibility were instrumental in preparing the ground for Christianity, but Stoicism still had the tolerance for all other theologies which the later monotheistic religions so totally lacked.

From 300 BC on many prominent figures in Greek letters were Hellenized foreigners. Some tried to interpret their own cultural tradition to the Greeks. Writing in Greek, Berossus, a priest of Marduk, composed a history of his native Babylonia, and the priest Manetho did the same for Egypt. Both still had access to official records and were able to establish chronologies for the histories of their respective countries. Berossus' history was lost, but Manetho's reckoning by Pharaonic dynasties became the basis for Egyptian, Biblical, and early Aegaean chronology and is still in use with little contradiction by archaeology. Later Josephus wrote his history of the Jews and Philo Judaeus tried to interpret the Jewish tradition in terms of the Platonic philosophy. As mentioned above, Zeno the founder of Stoicism was a Phoenician, and many leaders of the school were Easterners, including Posidonius from Apamea, Cicero's teacher. The parodist Lucian of Samosata in Syria satirized all the Greek philosophic schools.

Two of the most important consequences of Hellenism for Western civilization were the encounters of the Romans and the Jews with Greek culture. Both peoples eagerly adopted Greek literacy and thought-processes and then reacted against them. The meeting of the two richest literary traditions, the Hellenic and the Hebrew, produced Christianity. Political domination and oppression by Greek and Hellenized Roman rulers eventually caused the Jews to withdraw into their own ethnic identity and tradition. The Roman acceptance of Christianity under conditions of military, economic and social stress, was part of a desperate attempt to save the crumbling empire.

Notes

1. Rudolf Pfeiffer, *History of Classical Scholarship* (Oxford 1968), 102

2. F. E. Peters, *The Harvest of Hellenism* (New York 1970), 198

3. H. L. Pinner, *The World of Books in Classical Antiquity* (Leiden 1948), 27

4. H. I. Marrou, *Histoire de l'education* (Paris 1948), 226

5. F. G. Kenyon, *Books and Readers in Ancient Greece and Rome* (2nd ed., Oxford 1971), 29

6. Peters, *Harvest*, 372-373

8

Hellenism and the Jews

In 586 BC the Babylonians under Nebuchadnezzar had destroyed the walls and the temple of Jerusalem and had ended the existence of Judea as an independent kingdom. A part of the population was led as captives to Babylon. When king Cyrus of Persia conquered northern Mesopotamia in 537 BC he allowed the Jews to return to Palestine. After the re-establishment of a fairly large Jewish community in Jerusalem the second temple was built to replace the one destroyed in 586 and the city became again the religious center of Judaism. A considerable number of Jews, however, had remained in Babylon, where they formed an increasingly prosperous community.

After Alexander's death the ensuing power-struggle among his successors was decided in the battle of Ipsus in 301 BC. *Koile Syria* -- essentially Palestine and Phoenicia-- passed into the possession of Ptolemaic Egypt. When Alexandria became the commercial center of the Hellenistic world it attracted a great number of Jewish immigrants, who formed there one of their largest communities. In addition to the types of cities discussed in the preceding chapter (the Greek *polis* and the military colony, the *katoikia*) a third type was sanctioned, named *politeuma*. This was a non-Greek city or ethnic community attached to a city, which had its own charter allowing the inhabitants "to live in accordance with their ancestral laws and customs." Sizable Jewish *politeumata* existed or eventually developed in Jerusalem, Alexandria, Babylon, Antioch, and other places. Hellenized Jewish mercenaries were settled by the Seleucids in *katoikiai* spread over Anatolia. Other Jews were scattered throughout the cities of Syria. Still, in their wide dispersion the Jews retained relations with each other and looked for religious guidance to the temple and its scribal bureaucracy in Jerusalem.

The interaction of Greek literacy with the Jewish literary heritage had profound consequences for the Jews and for the Western world. By the time the encounter took place the Jewish oral tradition had been committed to writing and edited by the scribal establishment to eliminate the earlier polytheism. Some themes of Sumerian origin, such as the creation and the flood, although purged, retain clearly discernible traces of polytheism, (e.g. *Genesis* 6. 2-4: the cohabitation of gods [*elohim*] with mortal women). But there were also later features common to the mythologies of all the people surrounding the Jews, especially the Canaanites. A tendency existed to identify Yahweh with Baal, the bull of heaven, who left his tracks as the Golden Calf. And a consort for the high god was apparently sorely missed. Since prehistoric times the earth mother, symbolizing fertility and death, had been central to most religions: Hathor, later Isis, in Egypt, Inanna in Sumer, among the Semitic tribes Ishtar and Astarte appeared in the Bible as "the abomination of Ashara." The pressures of these millennia old cults, practiced by all the people with whom the Jews were in contact, were hard to resist. The conflict between the polytheists and the monotheists, reflected in numerous passages (e.g. Elijah's victory over the Baalists in I *Kings* 17-19), lasted for centuries. The ultimately complete ascendancy of monotheism, as appearing in *Deuteronomy* 4 and *Isaiah* 44 - 48, did not occur until the final redaction of the scriptures in the post-exilic period. The expurgation of the polytheistic passages was the work of the literate elite, the temple scribes.

The Hebrew alphabet was still without vowels, and reading was a difficult process for anyone confronting the ambiguities of a written text for the first time. Reading and writing required special training, and continued to be the preserve of professionals. The scribes fulfilled the important functions of conserving the scriptures, interpreting the laws and supervising their practical day-to-day applications. These responsibilities gave them a privileged position which they had always jealously guarded. The protection of the

Mosaic law and of monotheism against foreign religions and influences was the foundation stone of the scribes' authority.

Therefore, when the leading strata of Jewish society enthusiastically embraced Hellenism, and Hebrew was threatened even as the language of religious services, the scribal temple establishment became the core of resistance against Hellenization and Greek literacy, although they were themselves influenced by it. Hellenization in the vast urban diaspora progressed much faster than in the largely agrarian society of Judea. By the middle of the 3d century BC the majority of the Jews, especially those in the diaspora, no longer spoke Hebrew and had Hellenized their names. The Israeli historian Victor Tchericover describes the situation at the end of the 3rd century BC as follows:[1]

> The Jews outside Palestine spoke, wrote and generally thought in Greek....the importance of these [inscribed Aramaic] potsherds is negligible compared with the abundant works of Jewish Hellenistic literature written entirely in Greek, although the overwhelming majority of its readers were Jews. To what degree Greek was the current language of the Jewish intelligentsia of Alexandria can be deduced, for instance, from the fact that Philo regards it as "our language" and has no qualms about attributing to the heroes of the Bible a knowledge of Greek etymology.

Another indication of the progress of Hellenization of the Jewish communities in the 3rd century BC was the translation of the Pentateuch, "The Five Books of Moses." It had become necessary to translate the Hebrew scriptures into Greek so that services could be conducted in the language understood by the members of the Jewish communities of Alexandria and the rest of the diaspora. This translation, the Septuagint, provided the text for Jerome's Latin version, the Vulgate, which became the canonized Old Testament of the Roman Church. The legend created about the translation is typical for that time. The source of the story is the Greek so-called *Letter of Aristeas* authored in the first century BC. The letter pretends to be written by one Aristeas, a Greek official at the court of king Ptolemy II, to his brother. It tells the following story:

Demetrius of Phaleron suggested to Ptolemy II to add the Jewish scriptures to the collection of the Library of Alexandria. Ptolemy dispatched Aristeas with a letter to Jerusalem requesting the high priest to send 72 Jewish scholars, six from each of the twelve tribes, to perform the translation (*ergo Septuagint.*)

The scholars went to the island of Pharos and spent 72 days, each of them individually translating the five books of Moses into Greek. After completion, when the 72 translations were compared, they miraculously turned out to be identical, indicating their divine inspiration.

The Septuagint became the Bible of the diaspora. It was also the beginning of a voluminous Jewish-Alexandrian literature in Greek. The Greek translation added a new dimension to Jewish thought and influenced the evolution of the religion. The abstract connotations and technical philosophic meanings of some of the Greek vocabulary transformed certain traditional biblical concepts. Assuming the role of sacred text the Septuagint itself became a powerful instrument of Hellenization.

Because of the scarcity of sources we know very little about the history of Jerusalem during the century of Ptolemaic rule (from 301-198). Perhaps this silence indicates that Egyptian rule was fairly benevolent without too much Egyptian interference in internal Jewish affairs. Aramaic remained the language of the common people and, due to the similarity of the two related languages, Hebrew continued to be understood and remained the language of the rituals and the temple establishment. But not even Jerusalem could escape the Hellenistic influences. There as elsewhere the wealthy and influential families who were in contact with the Greek administrators were attracted by the opportunities offered by a flourishing economy and the amenities of the Hellenic world.

We hear of some prominent Jews employed by the Ptolemies in positions of trust. From incidental information in papyri and accounts by Josephus we learn that in the beginning of the 3rd century, Tobiah was a cavalry commander of a military outpost in the Transjordan in charge of a typical Hellenistic force consisting of Greeks, Macedonians, Persians, and Jews.[2] He was married to the sister of the high priest Onias. Tobiah's son Joseph was later appointed by Ptolemy III to be tax collector for all of *Koile Syria*. Joseph's son Hyrcanus spent much of his time, and apparently much of his father's fortune, at the court of Alexandria. Thus one can see how one prominent family of the priestly establishment in Jerusalem became Hellenized within three generations.

In the second half of the 3rd century the contest between the Ptolemies and the Seleucids for possession of *Koile Syria* intensified. Although Judea was bypassed by the hostilities, the war had profound effects on Jewish internal politics. The leading families in their competition for power tried to use the conflict to their own respective advantage. In 240 BC the high priest Onias refused to send the annual tribute to Ptolemy III. When Ptolemy threatened to send troops as settlers to Jerusalem Joseph, son of Tobiah, had himself appointed as governing representative (*prostates*) of the king for the *politeuma* of Jerusalem, a position traditionally held by the high priest, and went to Alexandria to placate Ptolemy. He managed to establish such good relations that, as mentioned above, he was subsequently appointed tax collector for all the eastern Ptolemaic possessions.

From this time on we find the Oniad and Tobiad families in continual rivalry for power, vying alternately for the favor of the Ptolemies or the Seleucids according to the fortunes of war, with individual members of the two families frequently shifting sides and reversing roles. As the Hellenization of the aristocratic families and their involvement with Greek imperial politics progressed they became more and more alienated from the less privileged Jewish urban and rural populations. The war of the Greek dynasties came to a head in 198 BC, when the Seleucid Antiochus III defeated Ptolemy and annexed the Syrian provinces. In 175 the Tobiad Joshua, who had Hellenized his name to Jason, was able to convince Antiochus IV, probably by bribery, to appoint him to the high priesthood, an office belonging traditionally to the Oniad family. What is even more significant, he persuaded Antiochus to raise the status of Jerusalem from *politeuma* to that of a Greek *polis*. That the king agreed is striking evidence of how far the Hellenization of the city had proceeded. When Antiochus arrived in 172 to inspect and confirm Jerusalem as the newly chartered *polis* of "Antioch in Judea" he found all the institutions of a Greek *polis* in existence: The citizens' rolls had been drawn up, the council of elders had been reconstituted as a Council (*boule*), and a gymnmasium and *ephebeia* were dispensing Greek education. The elevation of Jerusalem to *polis* allowed the wealthy Hellenized families to participate in the commercial life of the far-flung Seleucid empire. They found new opportunities to increase their monetary wealth through trade and their landholdings through purchases, mortgages and foreclosures. The feelings of the traditionalists were outraged by the sight of Jews exercising nude in the gymnasium and by the usurpation of the high priesthood by someone not entitled to it. What had begun as a family feud had become a rift splitting the whole population. It would be too lengthy to follow all the intrigues, moves and counter-moves between the different factions. The next high priest, Menelaus, was able to maintain his position only through the help of Antiochus' mercenary troops. The price was high. Antiochus was in financial trouble and to satisfy his demands Menelaos had to continue to raise taxes and to keep reaching into the temple treasury while the agrarian population sank into deeper and deeper poverty. In 168 BC open rebellion broke out; Menelaos was imprisoned and the *polis* was abrogated. Antiochus' troops stormed the city and inflicted bloody reprisals. Menelaos was re-instated and a garrison of Hellenized Syrians was installed in the newly constructed citadel, the *akra*. The *polis* was restored.

Soon thereafter when Antiochus was forced to concentrate his forces at the eastern frontiers, where his empire was encountering increasing attacks, the revolt flared up again, this time led by the former high priest Jason, who had been displaced by the machinations of Menelaos. Antiochus sent a large army and in 167 BC occupied Jerusalem again. This time he intended to put an end for good to Jewish resistance. Antiochus outlawed the Jewish religion. He ordered the Torah rolls burned; the temple was rededicated to Olympian Zeus; all exercises of Jewish customs, such as circumcision and the keeping of the Sabbath, were forbidden. Jerusalem lost its status as *polis* and was reduced to a *katoikia*. This had dire consequences, as it meant confiscation of much of the arable land for assignment to the Syrian-Hellenic occupation troops. Antiochus' decree had the effect of unifying for the first time all the diverse elements in Judea against their Hellenistic rulers and their rich supporters. One group that felt most threatened was the temple scribes, the Hasidim. Antiochus' anti-Jewish decree doomed their existence and drove them into alliance with the oppressed peasants and the disenfranchised lower classes in the city.

According to *Maccabees* I the spark was provided by an incident in a small town. Mattathias of the Hasmonean family killed an official of the king who was trying to enforce Antiochus' decree and was subsequently killed in reprisal. His sons fled into the desert and gave the revolution the leadership it had lacked in previous uprisings, in which the forces of malcontents had been no match for the disciplined royal troops. Now the situation was different. The main body of Antiochus' army was engaged in a war with the Parthians in which Antiochus himself was eventually killed. The Hasmonean family, the three sons of Mattathias, known under the name of Maccabees, provided effective guerrilla warfare skills, first under the oldest son Judah and later under his brothers. Where they had acquired their expertise is not known. The war, supported by the rural population, pitted the Maccabees, the Hasidim, and their followers against the Hellenized Jewish and Syrian forces of Antiochus. Judah was able to defeat several contingents sent against him and eventually to occupy Jerusalem, with the exception of the Akra, the citadel, where the former Jewish leaders and the Syrian garrison were holding out.

In the meantime the stability of the Seleucid empire was threatened from every direction. The eastern provinces were under attack from India to Armenia and the Parthians continued their relentless westward pressure. Antiochus V was killed in Elam in 162 BC and a conflict broke out for the succession. The new king Demetrius had no choice but to compromise with the Jewish revolutionaries. He recognized the status quo in Jerusalem in exchange for the release of the beleaguered faction in the Akra and the acceptance of Alkimus, a Hellenized member of the Oniad family, as high priest. The Hasidim accepted the compromise, as it satisfied their objectives: the Mosaic law was reinstated, and thus they were restored to their former position and the high priesthood had been returned to the Oniad family. The Maccabees, however, were no longer content with a peaceful solution. Their struggle was taking on the aspects of a national war between Jews and Syrians for the possession of all of Palestine. The memories of king David's empire six hundred years before were still alive. In a movement foreshadowing modern history they set out to regain the land after centuries of absence. There apparently had been a population increase in Judaea and the landless farmers who had gained nothing in the compromise settlement kept flocking to the Hasmoneans. While their force continued to grow, the dissolution of the Seleucid empire accelerated. New pretenders to the throne kept popping up; one province after another fell to attackers or asserted its independence. Even the Ptolemies invaded Syria again. All this caused the Hasmoneans to raise their sights. As their military strength increased, their support was sought by the different pretenders to the Seleucid throne; and the Hasmoneans were willing to sell it to the highest bidder. The original war of liberation turned into a contest for the supreme power in all of *Koile Syria*.

When in 160 BC Judah Maccabeus was defeated in battle by a Seleucid force and subsequently killed, his brother Jonathan carried on and was appointed high priest and governor by one of the pretenders (Balas). Jonathan was now the highest official in Syria, representing both the central government and the Jewish state. He retained that position through two more changes of rulers, but the latest one (Tryphon) lured him into a trap and had him executed. Simon, the youngest and last of the three sons of Mattathias, continued the game of power politics until he obtained removal of all Syrian troops from Jerusalem and complete freedom from taxation, in other words virtual independence of the state of Judaea. Since the last descendant of the Oniads had emigrated to Egypt, Simon was legally able to assume the high priesthood. In 140 BC he convened the "Great Assembly (*knesset*) of the Priests and the People and the Elders of the Land" and had himself appointed commander (*strategos*) and governor (*epistates*). Combining thus the military, political and religious supreme power in his person, Simon the Hasmonean had become a sovereign ruler. He continued to expand the Jewish domination over the rest of Palestine. When the Seleucid king of the moment, Antiochus VII Sidetes, tried to rein him in, Simon defeated the army sent against him and continued his warfare against the "Greek" Syrian *poleis* in his gradual conquest of the rest of Palestine. Simon never assumed the title, but he nevertheless ruled as a Hellenistic king in absolutistic fashion, relying on his Greek-style army and bureaucracy, until he was assassinated in 135 BC.

After the death of Antiochus in 129 Simon's son Hyrcanus embarked on the conquest of the rest of Palestine. He campaigned against all of Judaea's neighbors: Samaria to the north, Transjordan to the east and Idumenaea to the south. In the conquered territories he "converted" the male inhabitants to Judaism by offering them the choice between being massacred or circumcised.

Our main sources for the history of the Jewish wars of liberation are *Maccabees I* and *II*. *Maccabees I* is written in Hebrew and probably more factual. Our preserved text of *Maccabees II* is in Greek and more propagandistic. Both were commissioned by the Hasmoneans and represent the wars as a conflict between the godless Seleucids and the Hasmoneans as the defenders of religious righteousness. The struggle, however, involved much more: it was a religious, ethnic and economic conflict. It had started as a reaction against the oppression by Hellenistic rulers and ended with the liberators converted into Hellenistic rulers by their own successes within the short span of a few decades. In all but name-- that came later-- the Hasmoneans were Hellenized monarchs. The language, literacy and education of the court, the bureaucracy and the upper classes were Greek. Their entourage had Hellenized their names. The names of all governmental institutions and offices were Greek. The original guerrilla force had become a professional army on the Hellenistic model, owing allegiance only to its paymaster.

John Hyrcanus went as far as importing a Greek mercenary force. Even the sponsorship of a self-serving history was a leaf taken from the book of Alexander the Great. They issued Greek style coinage with at least one face inscribed in Greek. The Hasmoneans, like the other rulers, went in for pomp and circumstance and expensive building programs, especially their own palaces. All this, in addition to their armies and bureaucracy, required great outlays of money. Like the Seleucids they not only exacted heavy taxes, but also despoiled the religious treasures, such as king David's tomb, to cover expenses. The situation in Jerusalem under Hasmonean rule had reverted essentially to the conditions that had given rise to the Hasmonean rebellion. The political power and the high priesthood were again in the hands of a Hellenized aristocracy. Under the burden of oppressive taxation imposed with the help of a mercenary army the gap between rich and poor was widening even more. None of these tensions are visible in the books of *Maccabees* and did not surface in the contemporary literature except by indirection until Josephus' histories in the first century after Christ. The conflicts seem to have been initially kept in check by the firm hand of the Hasmoneans, who were on the spot with their troops (unlike the Seleucids, who were far off in Antioch and distracted by other problems in their vast empire). Furthermore the Hasmoneans were Jews, and never tried to suppress that religion; their conquest of Syrian territory may have assuaged some of the land-hunger of the destitute farmers. Therefore the conflict did not break out into the open until the rule of Hyrcanus' son, Alexander Jannaeus.

When John Hyrcanus died in 104 BC he was followed by his son Aristoboulos. Aristoboulos began his regime by imprisoning his mother and his brothers. He called himself Philhellenos and was the first of the Hasmoneans to wear the royal diadem. When he died a year later his widow Salome Alexandra released his brothers from prison and married the older, Alexander Jannaeus, who was thirteen years younger than she. Jannaeus immediately set out to reconstitute the kingdom of David. He hired more Greek mercenaries and embarked on campaigns against Acco and Gaza in the west and Transjordan in the east. There he came into conflict with the Nabatean Arabs, was utterly defeated and lost his whole army in 94 BC. When he returned to Jerusalem, a new rebellion broke out. Apparently the opposition was centered again, as in the initial stages of the Hasmonean revolt, on the temple scribes, now known as Pharisees. They seem to have followed in the footsteps of the Hasidim, the earlier enemies of the Hellenized aristocracy. As absolute rulers the Hasmoneans wanted as few restrictions of their power as possible. Therefore they and their followers, known as Saducees, recognized only the books of the Torah as the source of Jewish law. This left them free to interpret the law in their own interest without restraint by the temple scribes who considered themselves the official interpreters of the written laws and the keepers of the oral tradition. The revolt led to a civil war lasting six years. Jannaeus finally gained the upper hand and took bloody vengeance on his opponents. According to Josephus, Jannaeus, sitting at a banquet with his concubines, watched as 800 of the rebels were crucified after their wives and children had been killed in front of their eyes.

Upon Jannaeus' death in 76, Salome Alexandra, the widow of two kings, ascended the throne herself. To re-establish some unity she reinstated the Pharisees in their former position and admitted them to the state council, the *sanhedrin* (from Greek *synhedrion*). When she died in 67 her two sons, Hyrcanus II and Aristoboulos II fought each other for the succession, drawing respectively the Idumenaeans and the Nabateans and eventually the Romans into the conflict.

Syria had become a Roman province in 64 BC. Pompey, who had campaigned on the Black Sea and in Armenia to secure the eastern provinces, arrived in Damascus in 63 BC. There he received emissaries of both Aristoboulos and Hyrcanus and also a delegation from the "people of Jerusalem," most likely the Pharisees. He is reported to have asked these delegates whom of the two pretenders they preferred. They answered that they did not want either one, but self-government under the high priest. Pompey did not make a decision just then, and sent his lieutenant Gabinius to Jerusalem. But Hyrcanus II, who was in control there, did not admit him and tried to defend Jerusalem. The city fell after three months of siege. Hyrcanus had to give up all the Greek cities outside Judaea and his royal title. All the conquests of the Hasmoneans and Jewish independence had been lost. For the next hundred years Palestine became a political football between the contestants for the supreme power in the Roman civil wars. Pompey, Caesar, Marc Antony and Octavian Augustus, all had an impact on the remnants of the Jewish state. Internally there were futile attempts at revolt by the last descendants of the Hasmoneans and conflicts between a variety of sects and ever more radical factions.

Not only the rich Sadducees had succumbed to Hellenization, but Greek literacy had also affected their traditional opponents. Even strict traditionalists like the Pharisees, in their exegesis of the scriptures, looked beyond the literal sense for symbolic interpretations in the Stoic manner. Concepts that previously had not existed in Judaism made their appearance, such as survival of a conscious soul and individual reward or punishment after death. The traditional belief had held only the tribe as a whole accountable to God for obedience to the law, and reward, or punishment for breach of the covenant, was expected to fall on the whole people. Even the polemics against Hellenism were written in Greek. Later the number of Greek loanwords in the Talmud shows the pervasive imprint of Greek literacy. Of all the ancient Jewish inscriptions found in Palestine in synagogues and on grave markers, about 80 percent are in Greek.

The general syncretism of cultures had absorbed the Iranian dualistic concept of the conflict between the forces of good and evil, the final battle of Armageddon and a last day of judgment. The Iranian idea of a final world conflagration had made its way also into Stoicism. With the disappointment in the rule of the Hasmoneans and their final defeat the hopes for victory of the Jewish people over all their enemies had more and more receded into the dim future of the Final Day (*to eschaton*). Prophecy and revelation, which had always been the stock in trade of Jewish and eastern holy men, became a popular literary genre. Apocalypse or revelation had been given a philosophic cloak by Plato in the myth of Er at the end of the *Republic*. One Jewish sect that was deeply involved in eschatology was the Essenes. Little was known about them until the discovery of the Dead Sea Scrolls in the late nineteen forties. Josephus had mentioned three main factions among the Jews (*Jewish Wars* Il. 8). To make the different schools of thought understandable to a Hellenized Roman audience he compared the Sadducees to the Epicureans, the Pharisees to the Stoics and the Essenes to the Pythagoreans (*Antiquities* 15.10.4).

After discovery of the scrolls in caves above the Dead Sea and excavation of the site of the Essene community at Q'mran much has been learned about the Essenes. They formed a bookish, monastic, communistic, perhaps celibate society. Admission was granted only after a long period of instruction, preparation and final initiation including a vow of secrecy. The life of the community was regulated by a strict discipline spelled out in a manual, which has been found. The Essenes lived according to an exact schedule of prayers, communal work, purifying ablutions, and communal meals for which they dressed in white garments as for most occasions. Although they spent most of their time in study some members went out into the cities and preached righteousness to the general population. The buildings of Q'mran contained a large scriptorium and library. The Essenes copied the scriptures, searched them for eschatological meanings, and created their own apocalyptic literature, which is dominated by the war between the forces of light and darkness and their final battle. This end they saw as close at hand and it was what they were preparing for. John the Baptist and Jesus seem to fit well into the Essene background and were at least familiar with it. Much of the New Testament language and imagery is strikingly similar to the Essene writings dating to the second and first centuries BC.

Josephus mentions still another group-- the Zealots, who would not submit to any authority but God and who were willing to die rather than lose their liberty (*Jewish Antiquities* 18.1.6). Thus we can discern in Josephus' accounts four different Jewish reactions to the Hellenistic and Roman domination. The Sadducees, mainly the aristocracies of birth and wealth, who are realists, do not believe in life after death, recognize only the Pentateuch and see their hope in an accommodation with the overwhelming power of the regime. The Pharisees, the literate temple bureaucracy, are also willing to compromise as long as the religious institutions and their own position as guardians remain respected. The Essenes have despaired of any viable political solution, have withdrawn from society and have put their hope on the final day when all wrongs will be righted. The Zealots will fight until victory or death.

Thus when the Romans finally appeared, they found a climate of bewildering cultural, political and religious cross-currents and conflicts which they could not understand and consequently aggravated to an eruptive intensity. Christianity grew out of these tensions. By the first century BC the governing families of Rome had been Hellenized themselves; they were literate in Latin and Greek. As the Romans gradually incorporated Greece and the Hellenistic east as Roman provinces they found it convenient to follow the patterns set by the Hellenistic rulers, and to establish their control of the occupied territories through the Greek *poleis*, whose language and customs they could understand. Where strong *poleis* were lacking the Romans tried to govern through some local Hellenized client-king or chief. This was the method which Pompey had successfully used around the Black Sea and the Aegaean and which he tried when he annexed Syria as a province in 64 BC.

But in Jerusalem the time for Hellenization had passed. The conflict between Hellenism and Judaism was beyond possible reconciliation. The Sadducees had no longer any support among the population. The Roman policies appeared a repetition of all that the Jews had fought against under the rule of the Seleucids and later the Hasmoneans. Riots and revolts increased in frequency. The Roman civil wars created conditions of great insecurity, and Syria and Palestine passed through the hands of all the contestants for power in Rome. Pompey was followed by Caesar, who, because he had been helped by Hyrcanus II when he was in trouble in Egypt, treated the Jews favorably. Then Caesar's murderers, Brutus and Cassius, took refuge in Syria. They levied troops and heavy taxes until they were defeated by Marc Antony and Octavian at

Philippi in 42 BC. In the meantime the Parthians had invaded Syria and deposed Hyrcanus. In order to regain control the Romans made Herod king of the Jews. Herod was an Idumenaean from the territory south of Judea, whose inhabitants the Hasmoneans had forcefully converted to Judaism. Herod and his father had been supporters of Hyrcanus and faithful allies of Rome through all the changes of power. Herod established himself with a firm grip. In 37 BC Marc Antony married Cleopatra of Egypt and gave her *Koile Syria* as a wedding gift. But before he could enact any changes he was defeated by Octavian in the battle of Actium in 31, and he and Cleopatra successively committed suicide in its aftermath.

Octavian Augustus, now sole ruler, consolidated his power and organized Egypt, Syria and Asia as imperial provinces under his direct control. He entrusted their administration to his best general and close friend, Agrippa. His policy was again the same as that of his predecessors: to unify the population through Hellenism. He supported the Greek *poleis*, founded new ones and tried to transform the older cities by adorning them with buildings in the Greek style. Herod had become a personal friend of Agrippa and vigorously helped him in the execution of Augustus' program. He surrounded himself with men well versed in Greek rhetoric and philosophy, among them Nicolas of Damascus, who wrote a world history in 144 books and chronicled Herod's actions; the works of Nicolas formed one of the sources of Josephus' books about Jewish history. Nicolas was probably responsible for attaching the label "the Great" to Herod's name. Herod launched his own lavish building program in support of Augustus' and Agrippa's policies. His outstanding accomplishment was the new harbor and city of Caesarea, which became the most important commercial and military port east of Alexandria. In 20 BC he began a monumental rebuilding of the temple in Jerusalem in order to gain favor with the Jews. In this respect he had little success. That is indicated by another phase of his building program: his elaborate palace fortresses, such as the Antonia in Jerusalem and his formidable refuge on the crag of Masada.

The Jews had from the beginning considered Herod a foreign tyrant. He was not even able to win the support of the Hellenized elite. To overcome their opposition against him he had 45 of the most influential aristocrats executed as he tried to enlist the help of the Pharisees. But it was getting too late for that, too. Many were withdrawing from political life and turning towards eschatological sects, such as the Essenes, later the Christians, or radical revolutionary factions. Herod died in 4 BC (actually a year or two after the birth of Christ since our chronology is based on erroneous calculations of the early church).

Immediately after Herod's death a rebellion broke out in Jerusalem against his son and designated heir Archilaos. Archilaos was able to crush the uprising and traveled to Rome to obtain Augustus' confirmation. In the meantime a Roman commander in Jerusalem plundered the temple and caused an uprising which, led by Messianic fanatics, spread to all of Judaea and the surrounding areas. Varus, the governor of Syria, with two legions put down the rebellion and had thousands of Jews executed or sold into slavery. After Augustus' death in AD 14, the infighting among pretenders to the Jewish throne and their intrigues in Rome continued under the emperors Tiberius, Caligula, Claudius, and Nero. Revolts and Roman repression followed each other with regularity and increasing hatred after Caligula tried to enforce the emperor cult in the temple of Jerusalem. Under Nero the conflict escalated again into open warfare. Roman garrisons were overpowered and massacred in the Antonia and in Masada, Herod's former palace fortresses, and in Jericho, while the Jews were slaughtered wherever they were in the minority: in Caesarea, Damascus, Alexandria and other cities. In AD 66 Gallus, the Roman commander of Syria, was put to flight by Jewish forces. For the first time the Sanhedrin officially sanctioned the war against Rome. In 67 Nero sent Vespasian with three legions to crush the revolt. But, as warfare between rival Jewish factions continued, and Jews continued killing Jews, Vespasian did not press the war. In 69, after Nero's death, Vespasian's troops declared him emperor. He left his son Titus in command in Judea and went to Rome. In April of 70 Titus laid siege to Jerusalem. After five months he entered the city, and the battle continued within the burning city until Jerusalem was utterly destroyed and most of its inhabitants killed. In 71 Titus celebrated his triumph in Rome. The sculptures on his triumphal arch in Rome show the triumphal procession carrying the seven-armed candelabra and the sacred vessels from the temple in Jerusalem. The band of Zealots occupying Masada held out for another three years and finally, when further resistance became impossible, committed mass suicide.

The Jewish state had come to an end, and so had the temple as the symbolic center of the religion. Twice more, Jewish rebellions flared up. In 115-116, when the Jewish communities of Alexandria and Cyrene were deprived of their civil rights they rose up in revolt and later also in Mesopotamia and Cyprus. Everywhere the revolts were suppressed with the loss of thousands of lives. The last attempt at the liberation of Palestine was the desperate uprising of Simon Bar Cochba under Hadrian. The war lasted from 132 to 135 and ended in total disaster. Jerusalem became a Roman colony under the name of Aelia Capitolina. A temple of Jupiter was erected on the temple site. No Jew was allowed to enter the new colony under penalty of death.

The clash of Judaism with the Hellenism of the Seleucids and Romans shaped the course of Western history. The accommodation policies of the aristocratic Sadducees and the revolutionary fervor of the uneducated classes led by the Zealots had both met catastrophic ends. The literate tradition of the Pharisees survived as the dominant force in Judaism. Although greatly influenced by Greek learning the scholars and rabbis sought the survival of Judaism in strict observation of the written and oral law and in a return to Hebrew as the exclusive religious language, especially since the Christians had made the Greek Septuagint their own. Henceforth the unifying center of Judaism was the literature, which could be carried to any place in the Diaspora, instead of a material building rooted to one site. As the ability to read the Torah became a requirement for every male Jew to be confirmed at his *bar-mitzvah*, the Jews were the only people conserving a universal (male) literacy through the dark ages after the fall of the Roman empire. Of the Messianic and eschatological cults only Christianity had survived by leaving the Jewish identity behind and fanning out over the Greek and Roman *oikoumene*-- becoming ecumenical. Its vehicle was the common Greek language, the *koine*. The "Good Message" (*Evangelion*) disseminated in writing could never have penetrated the whole Mediterranean world before the Greeks and Romans had made literacy near-universal.

Notes

1. Victor Tcherikover, *Hellenistic Civilization and the Jews* (New York 1970), 347

2. Tcherikover, 71, 130

9

Hellenism and Roman Literacy

The Romans unknowingly embarked on the road to power soon after they had freed themselves from Etruscan domination about 500 BC. In the next century they gradually absorbed the neighboring Italian tribes to the south and east. In the third century they were able to defeat a hostile alliance of the Samnites, the Etruscans, and the Gauls to the north. The conquest of most Greek cities in Southern Italy followed. Tarentum, the most powerful of the Greek cities in Italy, with some Italian allies held out against the pressure of Rome and appealed for help to king Pyrrhus of Epirus across the Adriatic. Pyrrhus landed an army in southern Italy in 280 BC. He defeated several Roman forces and later crossed over to Sicily to help Syracuse, the largest of the Greek cities, which were under attack by the Carthaginians. He was able to relieve the pressure on the Sicilian Greeks, but on his return from Sicily to Italy he suffered severe losses in renewed battles with the Romans and returned home to Epirus in 275 BC. By 270 all of the Italian peninsula, including the Greek cities, was in Roman hands.

There were now two major powers confronting each other in the western Mediterranean: the Romans with their land power and the Carthaginians with their sea power and colonies around the Mediterranean from the north coast of Africa to the west coast of Spain. War broke out between them in 264 over the possession of Sicily. The struggle between Rome and Carthage, the three Punic wars, continued with interruptions for over a century and finally ended with the destruction of the city of Carthage in 146 BC. During that same period the Romans occupied Sicily, Sardinia and Corsica, large parts of Spain, and finally the Carthaginian home territory in North Africa. These became the first Roman overseas provinces. In the intervals between the Punic wars, and sometimes concurrently with them, the Romans fought the Gauls to the north and the Illyrians across the Adriatic and expanded their empire in both directions.

As discussed above, the former empire of Alexander was divided among the three major Hellenistic successor dynasties: the Antigonids in Macedonia, the Seleucids in Syria (with the regions to the east), and the Ptolemies in Egypt. In addition there were some minor powers, among them the Attalid kingdom centered on Pergamum and the leagues of Greek mainland cities and islands. As the Romans kept expanding their power, they were more and more drawn into the continual rivalries and quarrels among the Greeks. The Roman policy was to make some allies among them and to support a balance of power so that none of them would become strong enough to pose a threat to Rome.

In 200 BC the Antigonid Philip of Macedonia and the Seleucid Antiochus III of Syria concluded an alliance to share the dominance of the Greek world at the expense of the Ptolemaic empire of Egypt, the Attalid kingdom and the Greek cities. The threatened parties promptly appealed to the Romans for help. This led to a series of Roman interventions over the next 50 years that resulted in the incorporation of Macedonia and Greece in the Roman empire and the increasing dependence of the Hellenistic East on Rome. The last resistance on the Greek mainland ended with the destruction of Corinth in 146 BC, the same year that Carthage fell.

The 250 years of almost continuous warfare and the conquest of the rimlands of the Mediterranean had caused profound economic, political and social changes in Rome and Italy. Because of their prolonged absences for military service many of the small farmers who constituted the backbone of the Roman army, had lost their farms to large landholders operating their estates with slaves who arrived as prisoners of war in an endless supply. The competition ruined more small farmers, who in turn went to Rome and joined a growing destitute proletariat. Power was held by a small coterie of senatorial families in Rome whose members monopolized most of the important offices. The provinces were administered as personal fiefs by ex-consuls or ex-praetors, who during their brief tenure as provincial governors tried to enrich themselves to the utmost possible. The large armies needed to hold and defend the far-flung territories could no longer be replenished by conscription, and the military leaders had to resort to enlistment of professional soldiers, who looked to them for compensation and rewards.

The next 150 years, from the fall of Carthage and Corinth in 146 BC to the establishment of Augustus' autocratic principate in 27 BC, saw continuous conflicts between rich and poor, country and city, the senatorial aristocracy of the *optimates* and the self-styled champions of the people-- the *populares*. Eventually ambitious military leaders would exploit these conflicts to reach for the supreme power in a series of civil wars that involved the whole country and the conquered territories. Usurpers like Marius and Sulla, Pompey and Caesar, Marc Antony and Octavian (later Augustus), decimated their opponents through proscriptions, fought new wars of conquest and against each other, and bled the provinces white for the maintenance of their private armies until republican government was overthrown and remained only as a facade of imperial rule.

The cultural effects of her conquests on Rome were just as profound as the political consequences. In the words of the much quoted verses of Horace: "Conquered Greece conquered the savage conqueror" (*Epistles* 2.1.156). Before the middle of the third century BC no significant, if any, Roman literature had existed. The extent of early Latin literacy is difficult to estimate. The earliest known Etruscan inscriptions are generally dated to the late 7th century BC although opinions among scholars vary widely. Perhaps the oldest known specimen is a model of a 26 letter alphabet inscribed on the margin of an ivory tablet from Marsiliane d'Albegna, now in the Archaeological Museum of Florence. The tablet, like several others of later date, may have served for writing instruction. It is variously dated to the 7th or 6th centuries. Etruscan literacy seems to have been quite widespread from the 5th century BC on. Inscriptions proliferated and more than 9,000 have been found.

The Etruscan alphabet was derived from the early West Greek, which it closely resembles, just as much of the Etruscans' mythology and their themes and styles in art had been borrowed from the Greeks. The Etruscans generally wrote from right to left and sometimes alternating lines "as the [plowing] ox turns:" *boustrophedon*. The Italian tribes adapted their scripts from the Etruscan. The Romans, who were apparently at times dominated by the Etruscans during the 7th and 6th centuries BC, derived many of their religious and political institutions and rituals as well as their alphabet from them. It is difficult to fathom the depth of Etruscan literacy; there is no evidence for any extensive works of literature. The inscriptions follow repetitive formulaic patterns with only slight variations. Their standardized form and content-- most of them are dedications or funerary inscriptions with many personal names-- make it possible to understand most of them in spite of the fact that their language is still unknown. The ability to read and write seems to have been common from the 5th century onward. Inscriptions on tombs and sarcophagi, on all kinds of pottery and metal artifacts, such as bronze mirrors, indicate that Etruscan craftsmen were able to write and that they expected their customers to be able to read. Thus one seems justified in inferring that the Romans, the Etruscans' pupils in so many respects, commanded a basic functional literacy. We know that they recorded laws, state treaties, religious calendars (*fasti*), and perhaps some important events. The mythical character of the Roman historical tradition concerning the early period, however, indicates that no systematic records existed.

The continuing expansion of the Roman territory and especially the acquisition of the overseas provinces certainly increased the need for a utilitarian literacy at least among persons in leadership positions. At the same time Greek civilization made its impact on the Romans. In 241 BC the annexation of Sicily brought many of the most prosperous *poleis* such as Syracuse under Roman rule. The occupation of the Greek peninsula and parts of the Hellenistic East followed in the second century. Greek historians, artists, philosophers and teachers flocked to Rome as ambassadors and visitors. Educated Greek slaves became members of Roman households. The Romans were overwhelmed with admiration for Greek achievements in the arts and literature. Greek became the second language of the noble Roman families.

Gilbert Highet observed that in the encounter of a civilization with a more advanced one assimilation usually proceeds in three steps: translation, imitation and transformation.[1] In the second half of the third century BC the first Latin translations of Greek literature made their appearance. Livius Andronicus, a former slave, translated the *Odyssey* and several Greek dramas. The second step followed when the first Roman poet, Ennius, treated Roman history in the Greek epic meter and style. In the second century Plautus and Terence wrote their plays in imitation of Greek New Comedy. Eventually in the first Pre-Christian century transformation of the Greek models resulted in mature original Roman literature.

When Octavian Augustus established his principate in 27 BC, the whole ecumene was united under Rome. After four centuries of foreign and civil wars raging throughout the Mediterranean area, peace had finally come. The effects of Augustus' victory were immediate. For the first time it was possible to travel in safety from the Black Sea to Gibraltar. Augustus' reorganization of the provinces alleviated the worst exploitation and would eventually lead to Roman citizenship for all free inhabitants. Thriving trade brought unprecedented prosperity. The general elation of the time and the admiration for Greek literature inspired poets like Ovid and historians like Livy. Encouraged by Augustus and supported by his unofficial propaganda minister Maecenas, Vergil and Horace poured out the praises of Rome and Augustus, and perhaps under the surface their misgivings about the rule of military might. Although the poets of the Augustan age used the Greek literary forms and mythological themes, they created a national Latin and at the same time almost timeless literature.

After Augustus' death in AD 14, the principate deteriorated under his successors into a more and more capricious tyranny. Opponents of the rulers were hauled into court on flimsy charges and their fortunes confiscated. At the death of an emperor the succession was fought for by intrigue, conspiracy, murder and warfare.

The oppression reached its peak under Domitian (69-94 AD). The voices of those writers and poets who had not lost their lives as had Seneca, Lucan and Petronius fell silent; the Greek philosophers and teachers were either murdered or exiled. But after Domitian's death the political climate improved. The emperor Nerva (95-98) tried to reconcile the opposition of the senators and intellectuals and the banished philosophers were readmitted. The emperors of the second century -- Trajan, Hadrian and Marcus Aurelius, steeped in Greek education and literature-- tried to provide enlightened government. Freed from suppression Latin literature flourished, and, fostered by the emperors, a conscious revival of Greek reached back to the classics in language and style. In Latin, Suetonius and Tacitus wrote their histories and Juvenal his satires; Pliny published his letters and Apuleius his novel, *The Golden Ass.* In Greek, Plutarch composed the parallel biographies of famous Greeks and Romans, and philosophic treatises. Epictetus and the emperor Marcus Aurelius wrote eloquent works in Greek pro-pounding their Stoic philosophy. It is typical of the fusion of Greek and Roman civilization that the Greek historians Dio Cassius and Appian wrote Roman histories in Greek while holding high office in the Roman administration.

Roman bilingual literacy probably reached its highest level in the 2nd century. Augustus had founded two large libraries, one for Latin works, the other for Greek. Tiberius, Vespasian and Trajan had followed in his footsteps. Trajan's library, the *Bibliotheca Ulpia*, consisted of two large basilicas, one on each side of Trajan's column on his Forum and each devoted to one of the two lan-guages. A basic utilitarian literacy had become nearly universal. Schooling in the Roman republic and the early empire, just as in classical Greece, was left to private citizens. While wealthy families had their children taught by educated slaves or hired tutors the less affluent committed their offspring to schoolmasters who had set up their businesses in various public places or in their own private es-tablishments. Most of them were notoriously ill-paid and we may assume that the quality of education they dispensed varied widely. The literary sources, however, and the omnipresent inscriptions and graffiti on surviving buildings, such as the many advertisements on the walls of Pompeii, make it clear that reading and writing were an integral part of daily life.

In the second century the municipalities began to take an interest in education, and with the help of wealthy citizens sponsored teachers and schools (Pliny *Epist.*, 4.13). Secondary education followed the pattern established by Hellenistic *enkyklios paideia*. The teaching of grammar, vocabulary, and the parts of speech became fairly standardized in the second century through the textbook by Dionysius Thrax (see Appendix). Certain Roman authors, mainly Vergil, Horace, Cicero, and Sallust, had been canonized as models and had been added to the sanctioned Greek classics. The Roman grammarian Quintilian advocated teaching Greek first, as it offered greater difficulty than the native Latin.

In practice the curriculum in most cases fell far short of a comprehensive education. As education had become near-universal it had been homogenized and had lost depth. Still, it offered a starting point for those who had sufficient interest and energy to pursue literacy in greater depth on their own. For those whose families could afford it higher education followed in the rhetorical and philosophic schools of Athens, Rhodes, Pergamum, and Antioch, or whatever other center of learning was flourishing at the time.

Although the knowledge of Latin outside of the Roman administration never became as common in the eastern part of the empire as Greek did in the west, bilingual literacy in the second century had become the driving force that converted a mass of heterogeneous conquered peoples into a culturally united commonwealth. It had established two common languages, a complex of common ideas, and a common identity which led to the extension of Roman citizenship to all free inhabitants of the empire in the beginning of the 3rd century.

Although scientific education and speculation in the Hellenistic-Roman period remained confined to a few centers and a small number of specialists, their accomplishments in a climate of widespread literacy had far-reaching consequences. Besides some significant advances in mathematics, astronomy and medicine perhaps their most important legacy was the systematization of existing knowledge and the creation of textbooks that would keep their validity for a thousand years. In addition to the all-pervasive influence of Aristotle's works these were the books that, once they had been put into print, provided the starting points for new inquiries during the Renaissance and thus for the beginnings of modern science. Because the Hellenistic textbooks were the most important product of ancient literacy that shaped European scientific thought when literacy returned after the Middle Ages their content, history, and transmission up to the first printed editions are reviewed in a separate Appendix. I believe this information is necessary for the understanding of the scientific revolution that followed the introduction of the printing press.

Here a short mention of a few must suffice:

Euclid's (330-275 BC) *stoicheia* (*Elements*) remained the standard mathematical text well into the 19th century.

Ptolemy's (ca. AD 150) astronomy and geography provided the basic knowledge and the techniques of cartography until the 15th century.

Galen's (ca. 130-200) medical writings remained authoritative well into the Renaissance.

These were some of the compendia of the Roman-Hellenistic era which 12 to 15 centuries later, when they became widely available in print, launched the Renaissance scholars and scientists onto their own inquiries. The selection is perhaps somewhat arbitrary. Theophrastus' botany, Strabo's geography, Archimedes' and Diophantus' mathematics, Vitruvius' books on architecture and civil engineering, the elder Pliny's encyclopedic hodge-podge, and others that had considerable long-lasting influence could be mentioned. All the works named were created before the end of the second century after Christ.

The last great flowering of bilingual literacy and literary creativity coincided almost exactly with the second century of our era. The emperors of that period from Trajan to Marcus Aurelius were on the whole intelligent, educated and well intentioned men, devoted to the classical tradition. They built libraries and fostered the anti-

quarian classicizing literary activities and speculations that sometimes have been labeled the second sophistic. For the first time the
emperors gave active support to secondary and higher education
and sponsored teaching chairs in rhetoric and philosophy in Rome
and Athens. Second century jurists formulated the legal philosophy
which later became the basis of Justinian's code.

Marcus Aurelius came as close to the Platonic ideal of the
philosopher-king as any monarch ever did. He devoted his life to
bringing justice, as he saw it, to the world. Although his view of
humanity was extremely pessimistic he considered it his duty to
work towards universal brotherhood. He lived his ideals without
much hope of realizing them. His *Meditations*, consisting of notes
to himself (*eis heauton*), are the most appealing statement of the
Stoic philosophy that has come down to us. It is also the last work
of ancient rationalistic philosophy, just as Galen's medical treaties
are the last notable scientific works of antiquity, both written in
Greek in the second century.

In the hindsight of history some of the symptoms of decay were
already visible. The traditional tolerance of a polytheistic society
had opened the doors to mystical cults of all descriptions. Most of
them, such as the cults of Isis or Mithra, and Christianity, came
from the East; others that had been long dormant among the country populations of Greece and Italy had a revival. Rome was over-
run by prophets, magicians and religious charlatans of every description. The reversion to irrationality in periods of economic and
social stress, personal insecurity and helplessness has been a repeated occurrence in history.

In a sense it was the revenge of the conquered East. The Greeks
had always been aware of the relative youth of their culture in
comparison with the ancient civilizations of the Near East. Plato
for instance had been overawed by the age of the Egyptian tradition. In his *Timaeus* he had an Egyptian priest tell Critias, Plato's
grandfather, "you Greeks are always like children which hold no
store of old belief based on long tradition, no knowledge hoary
with age" (*Tim.* 22b4, Cornford's transl.) When the eastern peoples
were conquered militarily and intellectually by the Greeks they

tried to compensate for their feelings of inferiority by playing on the Greeks' respect for antiquity. They downgraded Greek empirical science and reasoned logic by extolling the ancient wisdom of their own ancestors, a superior transcendental wisdom based not on mere sense-perception and human reason, but on direct communion with the supernatural. Their suggestions seemed supported by some of the more mystical facets of Greek philosophy, such as the Stoic concept of a direct communication between the human soul and the divine *logos*. The Eastern wise men claimed supernatural powers of prophecy, magic and miracle-working. Every self-respecting sage or holy man was expected to document his competency through miraculous "signs."

On a slightly more rational level Aristotle's cosmology combined with Hellenistic astronomy in an almost universal belief in astrology as the means to determine the influence of the heavens on human events. Later not even the opposition of the church could loosen the grip of astrology. It remained a preeminent influence throughout the Middle Ages and the Renaissance, and horoscopes still infest our newspapers today. In Rome astral cults and mystery religions flourished without official opposition. The only exceptions were the monotheistic religions, Judaism and Christianity, which at the beginning were not clearly distinguished by the gentiles. Their claim to a monopoly on the truth and their adherents' tendency to segregate themselves were considered offensive arrogance. The main resentment, however, was political. In Rome, as in the Greek *poleis*, public affairs were inextricably interwoven with religious rituals. For this reason Jews and Christians refused to participate in most city business. Their aloofness offended the population because they seemed to take advantage of citizens' right while shunning citizens' obligations. Denial of the city's gods was denial of loyalty to the city. Socrates had been executed for "denying the gods the city recognizes." In the Roman empire the Jews' and Christians' refusal to sacrifice at the altar of the emperor was equivalent to refusal of a pledge of allegiance. The demand of the city for involvement in its religious affairs offered no problems to other cults. The educated strata through Stoicism and Euhemerism

had learned to rationalize all religions as human wisdom symboli-
cally expressed; the common people could recognize sufficiently
familiar traits and functions in alien gods to identify them with their
own under different names. But Judaism and Christianity (and later
Islam), the first literate religions, professed to represent divine
revelation. One could not tamper with God's written words. The
book established a tyranny that flexible oral tradition had never
claimed. The written word tended to be taken literally rather than
as a symbolic paradigm.

The rule of the Antonines came to an end in 193 with the murder of Marcus Aurelius' son Commodus after a short and disastrous
reign. The next centuries saw a steady decline of intellectual creativity and rationality paralleled by the spread of Christianity.
Through the fusion of Greek and Roman literacy with the Hebrew-
Christian tradition the late Roman empire had a most important
formative influence on the subsequent course of European civilization.

The death of Commodus was followed by contests between
nominees of the Pretorian Guard and three frontier armies for the
succession. After an armed struggle and the death of several contenders, Septimius Severus emerged victorious in 197; the dynasty
of the Severi was to rule until 235. The finances of the empire had
long been under strain because of the need to garrison and defend
a border that stretched from Britain through all of Europe to the
Caucasus, from there south to the Persian Gulf, and from Syria
across North Africa to the Atlantic. This frontier was under continual attack or threat of attack by the Germanic tribes to the north
and the Persians to the east. The state finances were not helped by
the recurring wars of succession. The Severi held their throne by
the good graces of their armies, which were increasingly recruited
from border tribes within and without the fortified frontier. To retain their cooperation the Severi kept raising the army's pay and
adding to the financial burden. The resources of the empire had
mainly come from the wealthy citizens of Rome, the provincial
poleis and the Italian municipalities. Political persecutions over the
centuries had decimated the rich old families, and the self-govern-

ing cities had been gradually milked dry. To raise the needed funds the Severi resorted to increased central control over the affairs of the once autonomous cities. They also started the practice of debasing the coinage, giving impetus to progressive inflation. Caracalla, the successor of Septimius Severus, extended Roman citizenship to all free inhabitants of the Empire. This was certainly a unifying move increasing the identification of the individual with the commonwealth, but it also may have crossed Caracalla's mind that it would expand the estate tax basis.

The crisis reached its climax after the murder of Alexander Severus, the last of the line. During the 50 year period from 235 to 285, 26 contenders gained the *imperium*; only one of them died a natural death. The mutinous armies looted whole provinces. Of all the emperors from 235 to 284 only Gallienus managed to rule for 14 years until he was murdered by his own officers; none of the others lasted more than 6 years. At the same time the empire faced the attacks of the most powerful enemies in its history. The Goths stormed plundering through the Black Sea and Aegean areas. The Franks overran Gaul and invaded Spain. The Alamanni broke through Gaul into Italy itself. Yet Roman armies under their ephemeral leaders managed to ward off all the invaders; under Gallienus they turned the tide and kept the empire from disintegrating. The emperors kept recruiting Germans into the Roman army and enlisted and settled whole tribes on the frontier as defense forces. Service in the Roman legions and their auxiliaries was an important educational and assimilating force. No matter what their ethnic background, members of the Roman army learned Latin or Greek or both and learned to read and write. Their offspring were Romans.

When Diocletian ascended the throne in 284 he found the territory of the Roman empire essentially intact, but he had to confront again all the problems of his predecessors. Some of the worst had been the simultaneous wars on the western and eastern frontiers, requiring the emperor to be in two places at the same time or else to delegate command to a potential rival for the imperial power. Furthermore, internal lawlessness and inroads by foreign raiders jeopardized communications between the Latin West and the Greek East and impeded central control. To solve the administrative problems Diocletian named a co-regent, whom he thought he could trust and control. Both assumed the title "Augustus;" they divided the responsibility for the eastern and western provinces, thus sowing the seed for later division of the empire. To assure an orderly succession each Augustus was assigned a lieutenant with the title "Caesar," who would also take charge of some of the provinces for his Augustus. Diocletian, however, retained the supreme command and all the trappings of an absolute king. To strengthen the defenses he decided to restore and reinforce the fortifications all around the border and to increase the size of the army. To raise the means, he had first to rebuild the economy. For this purpose he devised the most totalitarian government ever seen in the Greco-Roman world.

Diocletian was the first to prepare a budget for the entire empire. He appointed regional prefects to take inventory of all the resources in their assigned areas. This included a census of inhabitants, a survey of all plots of land under cultivation and estimates of the crops and expected yields. This census was consolidated for the whole empire and matched with the annual budget. On this basis Diocletian and his officials assessed each community, institution and individual their taxes in money and kind. In addition Diocletian established complete price and wage controls; workers were prohibited from leaving their locality of work. Surviving fragments of an ordinance list ceiling prices for 900 commodities and 130 types of labor. Diocletian's program required an enormous bureaucracy of literate, well educated officials and civil servants, police and spies to enforce the edicts. Still, inflation persisted and a black market flourished.

Thus all freedom of the formerly self-governing cities and the rural population had been lost except by the owners of large estates who had the means to bribe or defy the agents of the central government. Conscription into the army, never ending exactions of taxes, depredations by marauders, and extortion by powerful bureaucrats reduced the population to such misery that it turned avidly to millennial cults and religions that promised an end to this world and the righting of wrongs in a future better world. As we have seen earlier, apocalyptic literature had been popular in the eastern provinces, where life had become unbearable under the predatory early Roman provincial administrations. The erosion of personal freedom and well-being fostered a desire for escape that manifested itself in the popularity of romantic novels in which the hero after a long string of ordeals finds salvation in the end. Eschatological religions spread everywhere.

The cult of the Great Mother in its various forms had been long established in the Mediterranean world. What goddesses of this type had in common was that they represented the fertility of the earth and that they had a consort or offspring who symbolized vegetation, and died every fall to be resurrected in spring. By ecstatic participation in the secret rites and mystical identification with the dying deity the initiates expected their purified souls to be resurrected to a happier life after death. In Ephesus the religion of Cybele was being converted into the cult of the Virgin Mary and attracted devotees from all over the ecumene. Because of the traditional orgiastic nature of these rites the church eventually was forced to suppress veneration of Mary and tried to substitute *Mater Iglesia*, but in the end had to throw in the towel and to tacitly sanction the Madonna cult. In imperial Rome the Isis religion for a time became the most popular cult of this nature.

An important offshoot of Iranian Zoroastrism was the cult of Mithra, who during the later empire became the most popular deity among Roman soldiers. Although an early Indo-European god who predated Zoroaster, he had become the fierce warrior champion of the Prince of Light, Ahuramazda, in the battle against the forces of darkness under Ariman. He slew the primeval bull, from whose blood the world was created. Mithra became identified with the rising sun and was elevated to heaven in the chariot of the sun. The initiates of Mithra had to bathe in the blood of a bull and to devote themselves to purity and duty. Mithraism apparently appealed to soldiers because they could identify their army with the forces of light. Later Mithra as a sungod blended in with the Invincible Sun (*sol invictus*). How widespread the cult was is evident from the great number of Mithra sanctuaries that have been found wherever Roman soldiers were stationed along the frontiers and in the larger cities. For instance, in Ostia alone 18 Mithra shrines were found and in Rome more than 50 sites have been identified.

Sun worship had a long history in Near Eastern religions. Sun and Moon were considered deities in almost all ancient religions. The increasing popularity of astrology accented the divine nature of the sun as the most important heavenly body and the source of life on earth. In representative art Sol or Helios was usually shown with the rays issuing from his crown, driving the fourhorse chariot and surrounded by the planets, all enclosed by the circle of the Zodiac with personifications of the four seasons in the corners. This tableau has been found in many sanctuaries, surprisingly including several Palestinian and Syrian synagogues dating from the third to the fifth centuries-- most recently on a well preserved mosaic floor in a third century synagogue in Hammath Tiberias in the Galilee.[2]

In the critical period of the third century, when the emperors were struggling to instill a sense of unity, the welter of different cults appeared to them as another cause of fragmentation. Therefore they tried to reinforce the emperor cult by combining it with the cult of *Sol Invictus* as official religion. A religion of the sun seemed to be the most universally acceptable. Elevating the sun to the top of the pantheon was only a minor step. Philosophy, too, had endowed the sun with divine powers. Plato had said that the sun not only enables us perceive the world, but also that it is the cause of its existence (*Republic* 6.507-508). For Aristotle the motion of the sun was the cause of life on earth. In the religion of *Sol Invictus* the emperor drew his divinity from the sun and ruled the empire as the sun rules the cosmos. From Septimius Severus to Constantine the emperors had themselves portrayed on their coins as *Sol Invictus* or next to him in the chariot of the Sun. The cult of *Sol Invictus* could accommodate the adherents of most religions except the Christians, who thus remained outside the pale as subversives.

Notes

1. Gilbert Highet, *The Classical Tradition* (Oxford 1949), 104

2. Hershel Shanks, "Synagogue Excavation Reveals Stunning Mosaic of Zodiak and Torah Ark", *Biblical Archaeology Review* 10 (1984), 32-44

10

Christianity and the Late Empire

Christianity had penetrated Rome by the second half of the first century. The correspondence between Pliny the Younger and the emperor Trajan (98-117) indicates that it was spreading rapidly in the eastern provinces. Christian literature of two types began to circulate. The first phase, from the mid-first to the mid-second century, consisted in translation of the oral tradition into written Greek histories of the life and sayings of Jesus. Eventually about 50 such good messages (*evangelia*) ascribed to various apostles were in circulation. Subsequently the church leaders undertook a sifting process and canonized as authentic only those four that we know now as the Gospels. The second type of Christian writings is patristic literature. The Christian apologists, like the Jewish before them, tried to show that their faith not only was consistent with the tenets of philosophy but perfected and refined them. Its literature was probably one of the reasons why the Christian church was able to win out against the competition of the other popular cults. In a literate age the persuasive power of an extensive, well organized body of literature was crucial, and none of the other religions offered anything similar. Furthermore only written documentation could support the Christians' assertion that they alone were in possession of the *ipsissima verba* of God. No religion depending on oral tradition could match this claim. Diocletian's attempt to stop Christianity by ordering the burning of its scriptures attests to the effectiveness he ascribed to them.

The wide dissemination of Christian literature, and thus possibly the rapid propagation of Christianity, was also aided by two innovations in the technology of book production: the replacement of papyrus by cheaper parchment and the introduction of the codex instead of the roll. The word parchment is derived from the name of the city of Pergamum, where it supposedly was invented because of a papyrus shortage. Herodotus, however, reports the use of treated skins as writing material in Asia Minor as early as the 7th century B.C., and some of the Dead Sea Scrolls are written on leather. The manufacture of parchment or vellum was apparently the refinement of a long established usage. The Latin term *membrana* appears in Martial for the first time at the end of the first century after Christ. The codex seems to have gained popularity about the same time or a little later, but not necessarily in connection with parchment. In the third century, papyrus bookrolls, parchment rolls, papyrus codices, and parchment codices existed side by side; it took several centuries until the parchment codex emerged as the standard form of the book. Both parchment and the codex were favored by the Christians because of the cheapness of the material and the advantage of the compact book format, which allowed easy access to any passage without unraveling yards of scroll. A codex could accommodate the whole New Testament in one volume instead of at least five scrolls. F. G. Kenyon has shown that the use of papyrus rolls diminished parallel to the decline of traditional literature, while the use of the parchment codex increased with the proliferation of Christian writings.[1]

The last flurry of creativity in Greek philosophy occurred during the upheavals of the third century. Plotinus, a product of the philosophical school of Alexandria, was active in Rome from 243 to 270. Although he disdained the East's obsession with magic, miracles and prophesy he still was imbued with its mysticism. He tried to blend Platonic and Aristotelian transcendentalism; his supreme being, "the One," the source of all being, was both Plato's *Idea of the Supreme Good* and Aristotle's detached *Theoretical Thought*. He added several more levels of being to Plato's hierarchy, of which the material world of experience is the last and lowest. Plotinus' student and editor, Porphyry, led the last effective intellectual resistance against Christianity. The debates conducted in writing by both sides created a sizeable body of literature. Plotinian Platonism, however, was too esoteric to be widely understood or to appeal to the mass of the people.

There had been sporadic persecutions of Christians ever since the time of Nero. The Christians had inherited, along with their Jewish background, the resentment of the populace and of the rulers, a resentment that increased with the successive Jewish revolts in Palestine, Alexandria and Cyrenaica. Charges of disloyalty against Christians and Jews had been engendered by their refusal to participate in religious rituals, especially the emperor cult. At the beginning the Christians were considered an extremist Jewish sect, but as they gained adherents of other ethnic groups the difference was recognized. But while the Jews, although disliked, had been granted the right under the usual tolerant Roman policy "to worship their ancestral gods," the Christian converts of different nationalities could claim no such privilege to justify their aloofness. Some of the earlier persecutions, e. g., in Gaul and Syria, had been outbreaks of mob violence or attempts by authorities to divert or blunt the grievances of the population; but in the second century toleration was still the general policy of the emperors, and the early Christian apologists directed their writings to them. When local riots beset the Christians they appealed to the imperial authorities for protection and usually obtained relief.

To the emperors of the third century, facing wars on two or three fronts and challenges from rival pretenders within, the foreign body of the Church, spreading its branches throughout the provinces, took on the appearance of a grave menace to the unity of the empire. This impression was heightened by some of the apocalyptic literature, such as the *Revelation of St. John*, in which the prophesies of doom for the wicked were transparently aimed at the Roman Empire. The recruitment of the destitute and even slaves, for whom the promise of salvation and resurrection in a better world held the greatest attraction, increased the suspicion of subversive intentions. The willingness of the Christians to die rather than perform the common ritual sacrifices to the Roman gods and the emperor seemed a fanaticism that made the Christians even more dangerous. Septimius Severus was the first to issue empire-wide edicts against them. He enjoined them from proselytizing and set heavy penalties for converts. Tertullian, the Christian apologist, retaliated by declaring that "the only permissible military service was in the army of Christ. A Christian must refrain from sacrificing not only to the emperor, but also for the emperor." This intensification of the conflict, however, soon abated and gave way to a period of toleration. But when the Gothic invasion put the empire in mortal danger in 250 Decius issued an edict requiring all citizens to appear before commissions and to demonstrate their allegiance by sacrificing to the Roman gods. In return they received certificates attesting their loyalty. Those refusing were to be executed. Decius, fully absorbed in the war against the Goths, was killed within a year, and after his death enforcement of his edicts petered out. This became the general pattern: when the military situation deteriorated, the persecutions intensified; in periods of relative stability, enforcement of the measures abated. During the second half of the third century the Christians were able to expand their foothold throughout the empire, especially in the cities and the upper strata of society.

The most comprehensive attack against Christianity was launched by Diocletian. His reorganization of the empire into a totalitarian structure required also religious conformity. Diocletian was thorough in his attempt to eliminate Christianity. In 303 he prohibited all assemblies of Christians and ordered all churches and scriptures destroyed. The fact that Diocletian thought he could stem the tide of Christianity by destroying its written expressions shows the power he ascribed to literacy and literature. In the eastern provinces, under his own direct, and his Caesar's (Galerius') control he had the clergy arrested and forced to sacrifice to the official gods. After his abdication in 305, his successor Galerius applied the edict to all residents, man, woman and child. The persecutions in the east lasted for ten years. In the west Caesar Constantius I Chlorus never implemented Diocletian's edicts, other than the banishment of some bishops from Rome. Eventually, shortly before his death, even Galerius relented and issued a letter proclaiming toleration of Christians. The last empire-wide persecution of Christians had ended. From now on it would be the Christians who persecuted all dissenters, including other Christians.

In 312 Constantine, Constantius Chlorus' son, managed to make himself sole ruler in the western part of the empire. He had long been a devotee of the sun cult which had been vigorously promoted by some of the emperors of the third century. He had struck coins inscribed to "the Invincible Sun, my Comrade (*Soli invicto comiti*)." Gradually, probably under the influence of his mother, he veered towards Christianity. He allied himself with Licinius, one of the eastern rulers. Together they issued in 313 the decree of Milan which declared religious tolerance throughout the empire. Licinius became sole ruler of the East when Galerius died in the same year. Constantine and Licinius shared the power for 11 years until 324, when Constantine was able to eliminate Licinius and to obtain the throne for himself alone. Constantine's conversion to Christianity is said to have occurred in 312, but the symbols of *sol invictus* still appear on the Arch of Constantine in Rome, constructed in 318. In Constantinople, his new capital, founded after he secured the sole reign, his monumental statue showed him as Helios wearing the radiating crown of the sun. He granted the church financial and legal privileges and placed many Christians in high positions. He was, however, conscious of the sensitivities of the non-Christian majority and refused to take any actions against other religions. He built churches in many cities and generally made conversion to Christianity attractive. There is every indication that in his own mind he considered himself a Christian. Amidst the confused muddle of religions in his time his blend of Christianity and sun cult was probably not unusual. He postponed his baptism until shortly before his death. This was common practice among converts, in order to face the final judgment with a freshly laundered soul.

Constantine's Christian beliefs did not restrain him from murdering his wife, his eldest son, a nephew and the nephew's wife. He had Licinius, his fellow ruler, and Licinius' son killed in spite of an earlier promise to spare their lives. Constantine saw in Christianity a force that could bring the long sought unity to an empire more divided than ever as the linguistic and economic gap between the eastern and western part of the empire, the contrast between the rich and the poor, and the tensions between urban and rural continued to widen. Constantine tried by all means at his command to strengthen the bureaucratic regime inherited from Diocletian and he took it for granted that he would exercise the same control over the church. In the initial exuberance of being not only tolerated, but receiving active support from the emperor, the Christians did not object to his assumption of command over the church. While Constantine hoped to achieve religious unity through the church he did not neglect the traditional and still strongest ideological bond: the classical heritage. Civilization was identified with Greek and Roman literacy, literature, rhetoric and, increasingly, Roman law. As Marrou observes, no one doubted Isocrates' dictum that "the art of rhetoric teaches to think correctly and to act correctly while teaching to write."[2]

Government and church considered a literate education an essential qualification for the service in their hierarchies. Constantine, like his predecessors, continued the policy of regulating and supporting primary and secondary schools in the municipalities, where private initiative had faltered in the general social decline. He sponsored chairs of rhetoric and philosophy in the larger cities. He had his sons brought up as Christians, but he gave special recognition to Libanius, their teacher in classical literature and philosophy and outspoken critic of the Christians.

Although classicism and philosophy were the rallying point of the traditionalist and rationalist opposition to Christianity the Christians, too, fostered traditional learning. While the families, helped by the clergy, imparted religious training to their children they sent them to the same schools as the nonbelievers. The church under Constantine assimilated its structure and administrative methods to those of the empire. Although voices had been raised within the church for a long time condemning an erudition filled with the exploits of the Olympian pantheon they had no effect. In order to penetrate the educated urban class the church needed educated men. The running debates with its opponents from the various philosophic schools required men who could meet them on equal ground. As the church changed from a loose organization to a centralized hierarchy, demand for educated leaders increased. When Constantine opened to the Christians access to the imperial officialdom, many were eager to give their sons the only education available in the traditional schools. Some of the schools were run by Christians; in others, Christians and non-Christians taught the same curriculum side by side. It still was the view of the church that literacy was a prerequisite to true Christianity. After all it was a religion based on the "scriptures" and a growing body of written interpretations. Incidentally it never occurred to the Christians raised in the mythological environment to question the existence of the Olympian gods. Instead they resorted to downgrading them to manifestations of the forces of evil; thus the Greek *daimones* became demons. Yet Constantine officiated as Pontifex Maximus at the same time as he championed the church. His ambivalence was not unusual. Eusebius, a church historian and his religious adviser, celebrating 30 years of Constantine's reign orated thus: "The divine Logos, which is above, throughout and within everything, visible and invisible at once, is the lord of the universe. It is from and through the Logos that the emperor, the beloved of God, receives and wears the image of supreme kingship,... and like the light of the sun illuminates these farthest from him with his rays... As there is only one God,... so there is only one emperor."[3]

In his search for unity through Christianity, however, Constantine was disappointed. All the conflicts within the Church which during the persecutions had been smoldering under the surface broke into the open when toleration lifted the lid. Dissensions were inevitable because of the inherent logical contradictions in the Christian doctrines. Most of the controversies revolved about the human and divine natures of Jesus, his relationship to God the Father, and how to reconcile their duality with monotheism. The addition of a third entity, the Holy Ghost, making it a trinity, did not help much. Because these problems were not susceptible of a rational resolution they surfaced again and again over the centuries. The debate raged throughout the empire, with bishops on both sides throwing anathemas at each other and at times resorting to violence. Constantine finally lost patience seeing his policies jeopardized by a controversy over what he considered an insignificant theoretical question.

In 325 he summoned a council of bishops from all parts of the empire to Nicaea to settle the problem. He forced them to reach a decision. Constantine enforced the ruling, which affirmed the divinity of Jesus, by excommunicating and banishing the dissenters led by Arius and thought the matter settled, but after his death Arianism remained a powerful movement for another two centuries, until the Arians were finally suppressed by force of arms. Constantine's policy was still toleration of all religions. He did not resort to persecutions of any sect except the Donatists, whom he considered political rebels.

Before his death Constantine had carefully prepared the succession. His three surviving sons and his nephew Julian were to share the rule under the tetrarchic system that Diocletian had established. But the arrangement did not last. After Constantine died in 337 Constantius, who in the family tradition had managed gradually to kill off most of his relatives, emerged as sole ruler in 350. The council of Nicaea had set several precedents that determined the direction of developments for the rest of the fourth century. It had established an orthodoxy to which all Christians were expected to conform. It had tacitly sanctioned the emperor's authority over the church. Constantine had set another precedent by persecuting the Donatists in violation of his own declaration of toleration of all religions. Nicaea and Constantine thus had prepared the way for the practice of the official church of suppression of all dissenters within its own ranks. Subsequently the persecutions of heretics and pagans would make the numbers of earlier Christian victims insignificant in comparison. After almost a thousand years of varying and relative freedom of thought total intolerance descended over the western world for an equal period of time. The church fathers of the fourth century, including St. Augustine, were unanimous in their demands for the eradication of all heretics and pagans. The emperors, aiming for a monolithic state, gladly obliged. Constantius ordered the closure of the temples and for pagans and heretics he decreed the death penalty.

The term pagan (*paganus*-- originally villager) assumed its new meaning at that time: with the progressive degradation of the rural population into serfdom their resentment against the central government, which became more and more identified with Christianity, strengthened the peasants' natural religious conservatism. Later the term was also applied to the the urban upper classes, who resisted Christianity on intellectual grounds. Philosophical schools were still operating with imperial sanction in Athens, Alexandria and Antioch. Many Christians studied under pagan teachers. Such church luminaries as John Chrysostomos, Basil of Caesarea, and Gregory of Nazianzus attended the lectures of Libanius, their most articulate opponent. Constantine's nephew and Constantius' successor, Julian "the Apostate," was a product of the Hellenistic Neo-Platonist urban society.

Julian had been raised as Christian and instructed by Eusebius, the Arianic bishop of Nicomedia. From age 14 to 20 he studied classical literature. He avidly read the works of Libanius while practically held in exile by his cousin Constantius, whose co-ruler he was destined to become. In 351 Constantius allowed him to resume his studies at Pergamum; in 355 he appointed him Caesar and entrusted him with the defense of Gaul while he himself was involved in the war with Persia. Julian was successful in freeing Gaul from its Germanic invaders. Constantius, shortly before his death, appointed him his successor. Being now on his own, Julian gave free rein to his Hellenism, renounced his Christianity, and reinstated toleration of all religions. He rescinded the privileges of the clergy and reopened the temples that had been closed or taken over by the church. He also tried to restore the confiscated properties to their pagan owners. His goal was to revive the ideals of Hellenic thought. Since he realized that Christianity owed much of its success to the strength of its organization and the emotional appeal of its rituals, he tried to reform the Olympian religion under the dominant power of Helios in a quasi-monotheistic blend with

Neo-Platonic and Stoic philosophy and to organize it as a national institution like the church.

Julian did not persecute the Christians, but his declaration of tolerance was followed by violent confrontations between pagans and newly aggressive Christians, resulting in victims on both sides. The only direct action Julian took against the Christians was the removal of Christian teachers from the state supported schools, since he felt that the Christians could not in good conscience do justice to his Hellenic ideals. Julian's efforts came to nought; he died in June 363 after only 18 months in office-- most of them spent in the war against the Persians, in which he was killed at the age of 32. Even his Christian opponents acknowledged his stature, while castigating his actions against their religion. Prudentius said in a poem: "Yet of all the emperors one there was in my boyhood, I remember, a brave leader in arms, a lawgiver famous for speech and action, one who cared for his country's weal, but not for maintaining true religion, for he loved myriad gods."[4] St. Augustine commented: "He had unusual talents, which were led astray through his ambition for power by a sacrilegious and detestable inquisitiveness (*City of God* 5.21)." Julian was the last who tried to stem the tide of Christian domination.

After Julian's death the period from 363 to 378 was marked by continuous inroads by the Germanic tribes, who themselves were being pushed by Asiatic peoples arriving from the East. The eastern and western parts of the empire were rapidly drifting apart and the knowledge of Greek was disappearing from the West.

The crisis came to a head under Theodosius I (378-395). He managed to bring the Goths under control by mobilizing 40,000 foreign settlers who previously had been admitted to the empire. He thus contributed to the further Germanization of the Roman army. Under the influence of the Nicaean faction of the church, which now claimed the title all-encompassing (catholic), he undertook the enforcement of its tenets by a series of laws. The so-called code of Theodosius contains 13 edicts against pagans and 61 against non-conforming Christians, depriving them eventually of all civil and legal rights. Raids against pagans in the countryside became frequent, temples were destroyed or converted into churches, statuary was smashed. In 390 a Christian mob in Alexandria set fire to the Serapeion and burned the last remnants of the great Alexandrian library.

The death of Theodosius was followed by the de facto division of the empire into an eastern and a western half. During the 5th century the power in the Western Empire was wielded by a succession of Germanic army commanders in whose hands the emperors were powerless puppets. Finally they were no longer able to stem the tide of ever new invaders. Gaul, Spain, North Africa and, lastly, Italy were lost. Rome was sacked three times, and the last West Roman emperor was deposed in 476 by Odovacar, the leader of Germanic mercenary troops of various tribes.

During the same time the Eastern Empire, beset by the inroads of the Huns, the Persians, and the rebelling Gothic confederates, barely held together. Slavic peoples occupied much of the Balkans. The struggles within the church continued unabated, fueled by the contest for power between the patriarchs of Constantinople, Alexandria, and Antioch as well as by dogmatic disputes which still hinged on the nature of Jesus. The patriarch of Alexandria, Cyril, proclaimed the theory of one single divine nature of Jesus Christ which became known as monophysitic. The same Cyril in 415 in Alexandria had led a mob on a rampage against the Jews and the pagans. Among their victims was a woman of great genius, Hypatia, head of the philosophic school of Alexandria and an outstanding mathematician. She, together with many others who had sought refuge in a church, was literally torn to pieces by the rioters.

Pressed by external attack and internal conflict the last emperor of the fifth century, Anastasius (491-518), was finally able to ward off a take-over by his obstreperous Gothic allies by commissioning their leader Theodoric to reconquer Italy and thus to get him out of his own empire. Theodoric was successful and established himself in Ravenna, the new capital of the West.

Justinian came to power first as co-ruler with his uncle Justin and as sole emperor after Justin's death in 527, by which time the western provinces had become Germanic kingdoms. Most of Gaul was ruled by the Franks, Spain by the Visigoths, North Africa by the Vandals, and Italy by Theodoric's Ostrogoths. With the exception of the Franks, who still held fast to their tribal polytheistic religion, the occupiers were Arianic Christians. The Ostrogoths were to a considerable degree Romanized and did not interfere with the cultural institutions of the Roman population.

Justinian was the last Latin speaking emperor of the Eastern Empire. He was governed by one overriding purpose: the restoration of the Roman Empire. To tighten his autocratic grip over church and state, Justinian aimed for the total eradication of paganism. In 529 he closed the last philosophic schools in Athens.

In the years from 535 to 554 Justinian's mercenary armies were able to conquer North Africa, Sicily and the other Mediterranean islands, Italy and finally the western coastal strip of Spain. The wars had stretched the resources of the empire to the limit. Italy was devastated, the eastern defenses were weakened, Bulgarian and Slavic tribes kept streaming into the Balkans. The Persians overran Syria and captured Antioch, and were finally bought off by the payment of a yearly tribute.

Justinian died in 565. Three years later the Lombards invaded Italy and occupied all but Rome, Ravenna and the southern part of the peninsula. The settlement of the Balkans by the Slavs had severed the overland connection between East and West and had made the separation permanent. With the death of Justinian Latin faded as official language in the East. The Roman papacy lost all influence in the East, but had built up its strength and prestige in the chaos and power vacuum of the West. The Spanish possessions were lost early in the 7th century and by the middle of the century the Moslem Arabs had conquered Syria and Egypt and were sweeping into the rest of North Africa. Greek-Roman civilization in western Europe had come to an end.

The classical achievements in empirical science and rationalistic philosophy had been essentially completed before the third century and the same holds true for the masterworks of literature. Scientific and literary creativity atrophied with the end of relative individual freedom after the death of Marcus Aurelius. The battles for survival of the empire from the third century on had been fought and won only at the cost of enormous physical hardships and regimentation which culminated in the totalitarianism of Diocletian, Constantius, and Justinian.

The backbone of Roman civilization had been a trust in human rationality based on a system of literate education. But with oppressive rule and the individual's loss of control over his fate came a loss of confidence in human capabilities, an escape into mysticism, and a return to irrationality. It was perhaps Tertullian who most strikingly expressed the abdication of reason in commenting on the Trinity: "It is certain because it is impossible; therefore I believe it (*certum est, quia impossibile est. Ergo credo*)." Mysticism was as manifest in philosophy as in religion. Plotinian Neo-Platonism had completely divorced itself from the empirical base of earlier philosophies. Introspective meditation had taken the place of deductions from the observed physical world. Plotinus described the intuitive process as the "flight of the alone to the Alone." Julian the Apostate, who wanted to re-establish the reign of Hellenic thought, was involved in theurgy and magic. The church fathers, beginning with St. Paul, had expressed their disdain for scientific inquiry. Tertullian said "we have no need for curiosity after possessing Jesus Christ, nor for research after the benefit of the gospels (*On prescriptions against heretics*, 7)." Lactantius expressed himself similarly. St. Ambrose (337-397) dismissed scientific inquiry with the words: "For wherein does this assist our salvation?" St. Augustine himself, who had come to Christianity via Neo-Platonism, thus expressed his contempt for inquiries into nature : "God and the soul, that is what I desire to know. Nothing more? Nothing whatever!" (*City of God* 11.3) For the next millennium under church rule "idle curiosity" about the physical world and its workings was unnecessary, even sinful, since earthly existence was only a short stage of preparation for eternal life after death.

Justinian left a deep imprint on European history. The Byzantine Empire, unified and consolidated within its shortened and more defensible borders, was to survive for almost another thousand years, longer than the Roman Empire before it. While the

Byzantine fleet and army held off the onrush of successive waves of Persians, Arabs, Mongols, and Turks, the Byzantine church sent its missionaries into southern Russia, to bring to the Slavic world not only Christianity, but also the (modified Greek) Cyrilian alphabet and a modicum of literacy. The Byzantine monks and scholars continued Greek classical literary scholarship and education side by side with Christian indoctrination. In the monasteries librarians and lexicographers preserved the Hellenic heritage until western Europe, after its long eclipse, was ready to receive it again just before Constantinople fell to the Turks in 1453. With Justinian's brief reconquest of Italy monasticism had spread to the western world. There the monasteries became the centers of clerical education and islands of Latin literacy and of some learning when the remnants of civilization were submerged by the barbarian tide.

During the late empire uniform written laws had been expected to keep the empire together. Comprehensive law-codes were commissioned by Theodosius and Justinian (see Appendix 334). It became a medieval *topos* that the law is the soul which rules the body of the state. Law schools had been founded in Rome, Beirut and Constantinople. Justinian's code was one of the most important legacies of the late empire to the West and was to play a considerable part in the revival of classical learning. The Italian secular universities of the Renaissance had their beginnings in the study of Roman Law.

When the western empire finally collapsed the general disbelief and consternation throughout the ecumene made it clear that the Rome had become an idea and an ideal. Rome represented security, justice, culture and comfort long after most of these amenities were gone. The power of Roman civilization as an ideal was demonstrated by all the claims to the successorship of "eternal Rome." In the West the Germans called their dominion the "Holy Roman Empire of the German Nation," and their emperor took the title of the Caesars as Kaiser. In the East, Constantinople called itself the second Rome and wore the mantle of the Caesars until 1453. When Constantinople fell to the Turks, Moscow claimed the name of the third Rome and her rulers assumed the name of Caesar as Tsars. The mystique of Moscow's destiny as the third Rome still lingers in the Russian subconscious. All these attempts to assume the role of the Roman empire indicate the realization of the great void left by its demise.

During the next centuries literacy in western Europe survived only within the clerical establishment and to a lesser extent at some courts of royalty and the reigning aristocracy. Both western Europe and the Byzantine East reverted to conditions of severely restricted literacy under theocratic governments and caste systems reminiscent of the ancient empires of Mesopotamia and Egypt.

In the religious context there is a reverse side to literacy. When an oral religious tradition is written down its symbolism tends to succumb to the authority of the written text. The "holy writ" will be taken literally. This is especially apt to happen when "The Book" claims direct divine revelation. When the Roman church gained secular powers its official exegesis of the Latin Bible acquired the force of law. In contrast to its attitude in the late Roman empire favoring literacy among Christians the medieval church discouraged the lay population from reading the scriptures, lest someone might stray from the sanctioned interpretations. Any deviation was branded as heresy. Throughout the European Middle Ages the "tyranny of the book" was complete, while at the same time popular literacy disappeared.

The developments were similar in Islam. In the early stages an intellectual elite among the conquering Arabs eagerly embraced Greek learning and science. Many philosophic and scientific works were translated into Arabic from the Greek or from Syriac versions. Advances were made in mathematics, astronomy and medicine. In the 12th century many of the Arabic texts found their way through Spain, where even in the Christian part learning had never been completely interrupted, to the rest of Europe and prepared the way for the renascence of scientific inquiry. It is a fortunate coincidence that the recovery of Greek learning through Arabic texts had begun in Europe just when Islamic fundamentalism - the tyranny of the book (this time the Koran)-- stifled independent scientific speculations in the Moslem world. Today, four hundred years after the beginning of modern rationalism and scientific thought, "The Book," in one form or another, is again on the offensive from Teheran to Jerusalem, to Rome, to Washington.

Notes

1. F. G. Kenyon, *Books and Readers in Ancient Greece and Rome* (Oxford 1951, Folcroft Library edition 1971), 113, 117-118

2. H. I. Marrou, *Histoire*, 414

3. Eusebius, *Speech on Constantine's 30th Anniversary* 3.4-5, 5.1-4, as translated by Robert Browning, The Emperor Julian (Berkeley 1976), 221

4. *Ibid.*

Notes

11

The Renaissance: Humanism

The 150 years from 1450 to 1600 in western Europe show many parallels with developments in the Greek world from 450 to 300 BC. Both eras were characterized by a spectacular growth in popular literacy sparked by innovations in the technology of writing. In Greece the simplicity of the alphabet had opened wide access to the skills of writing and reading. In Renaissance Europe the introduction of printed books brought for the first time wide dissemination of literary material and was most effective in the creation of a literate lay public. In both periods the spread of literacy generated a new confidence in human capabilities. The growing self-awareness was expressed in new styles in art and architecture and in the search for the vanishing intellectual treasures of an idealized classical age.

The Greeks had elevated to an ideal the cultivation of the mind through a comprehensive education (*paideia*). Its goal was freedom from ignorance (*eleutheria*). Aristotle's goal of education was *philanthropia*, love for humanity. The Romans, too, had believed in the liberating power of a literate education; their term for the objective was *liberalitas*. Cicero used the word *humanitas* for the quality of a personality whose potential was developed through literary education and philosophic inquiry.

Just at the time when the ideal of literate education spread through the Hellenic world there arose the realization of the fragility of the literary heritage, which was preserved only in a few perishable papyrus copies. The Library of Alexandria was then founded to rescue and protect the endangered literary legacy.

In the 14th century, when the growing secular Italian city states assumed many of the governmental and judiciary functions that for centuries had been preserves of the clergy, interest re-awakened in the laws and institutions of the ancient self-governing communities. The search for model constitutions in Roman law and history rekindled interest in all facets of Roman literature, which, although never quite forgotten, had become confined to a few oases of classical learning. Like Alexandrian scholarship, Renaissance Humanism began with a frantic effort to find and save the ancient texts. The modern term humanism originated with the early humanists themselves. In 1401 Bruni (of whom more later) used the Ciceronian term, stating that Petrarch had revived the "*studia humanitatis.*"[1] The term renaissance, too, in its Italian form *rinascita*, originated in the 15th century when it was addressed to Poggio by a fellow scholar.[2] As in the 4th century BC the awareness that a whole cultural heritage was in danger of slipping away inspired not only the search for ancient manuscripts but also the efforts to restore the original texts, which had been corrupted in repeated copying, often by scribes who were no longer familiar with the original form of the language and the technical aspects of some of the subject matter. Just as the study of grammar and semantics was one of the foremost concerns of Alexandrian scholarship the philological study of the classical languages became the most important part of humanistic learning. With the study of the ancient literary genres came the desire to revive and emulate them as well as other aspects of classical culture. The ancient works of literature, sculpture and architecture became subjects for imitation and new creativity which transformed the classical models into the new style which we now call Renaissance.

One of the most important moving spirits who gave impetus to the revival was the poet Petrarch (Francesco Petrarca, 1304-74). An avid collector, discoverer, copier, and editor of classical manuscripts, he spread his enthusiasm through personal visits, correspondence, and most of all through his own poetry inspired by the classical models. The movement found a warm reception with the ruling elites and institutions of learning in northern Italy. Florence under the Medicis became an important center of the revival. Beginning with Collucio Salutati in 1375 and throughout the 15th century, outstanding humanists appointed by the Medicis held the chancellorship in Florence. Salutati through his emissaries was able to collect a library of 800 Latin manuscripts and was instrumental in the revival of the study of Greek by bringing to Florence as teacher the Greek scholar Chrysolaras.

Salutati was followed by Leonardo Bruni, one of his own and Chrysolaras' pupils. Bruni was one of the first to devote himself fully to the translation of Greek works into Latin and thus to make Greek literature accessible to his contemporaries. Among his translations were Plutarch's *Lives*, some dialogues of Plato, and Aristotle's *Politics* and *Ethics*. He was succeeded by Poggio Bracciolini, one of the most successful manuscript hunters.

Some scattered influences of the classical revival extended beyond the Alps and to the west, but essentially the Renaissance remained confined to Italy and southern France until the advent of printing. Only after the first presses had been established in Rome in 1464 and in Venice shortly thereafter did the flood of the first printed editions carry the Renaissance to the rest of Europe and again make the establishment of comprehensive libraries possible, thus setting the stage for the intellectual ferment of the 16th century.

There had been precursors of the revival at various times. Throughout the Middle Ages isolated islands of learning had existed and some scholars had tried to preserve the classical heritage. Manuscripts were protected in monasteries and later in university libraries and scriptoria. But as long as the works of the ancient authors existed only in a limited number of copies, they were always subject to deterioration from neglect, dampness and mildew, destruction by mice, fire or war-- and most of all -- errors in copying. It is nearly impossible to copy a lengthy manuscript without mistakes and this was especially the case with manuscripts full of scribal idiosyncrasies and abbreviations.

Knowledge of Greek had all but disappeared from western Europe, and what Greek literature survived owed its existence to Byzantine, Arab, and Jewish scholars whose efforts enabled it to find its way back later into western Europe from Constantinople,

Baghdad and Spain. The Byzantine Greek and translated Arabic texts had obviously been exposed to the same vicissitudes as the Latin texts in western Europe. Awareness of the danger to the literary legacy had manifested itself before; the Carolingian renascence of the 9th century had been a partially successful effort to rescue civilization from total oblivion. The 12th century renewal of learning had been spurred by the influence of the reviving scholarship and of Greek learning radiating back from centers in Spain. But both revival movements, restrained by the scarcity of books and the limited extent of literacy,remained restricted to small groups of scholars and soon lost their momentum. The 12th century revival, which had spread a somewhat wider circle, was eventually stifled by the church authorities.

Thus it is quite possible that the Italian Renaissance would have suffered the same short-lived fate as the earlier movements if the printing press, providing hundreds or even thousands of copies of texts that previously could have been counted on the fingers of one or two hands, had not made the rescue of the ancient works permanent. For the first time the survival of the remnants of classical literature was secured forever. At the same time the abundance of relatively cheap books on all kinds of subjects propagated literacy to numbers of people unequalled since the end of the Roman empire. Only after the proliferation of printing presses in Italy did the revival of learning expand into every part of the continent and to the British isles.

Gutenberg had perfected his press sometime between 1440 and 1450. The first full-sized printed book known to have come from any European press was a Latin Bible, printed by Fust and Schoeffer, usually called the Mazarin Bible because a copy dated 1456 was owned by the cardinal of this name. Printing spread rapidly throughout Germany, and by 1500 at least 63 cities in German-speaking countries had presses in operation. From there, German printers spread their art throughout Europe.

The first printing press in Italy was established in 1464 by Arnold Pannarz and Conrad von Schweinheim, two German priests, in the monastery of Subiaco near Rome. From 1469 on, when Johannes

Speyer published in Venice two editions of Cicero's letters *ad familiares* and Pliny's *Natural History*, that city became an important center of humanistic publication. In the first fifty years of print, from 1450 to 1500, about 40,000 editions were published in all of Europe; of these, between 15,000 and 17,000 in Italy, 38 percent of these in Venice.[3] These figures are extremely significant in several respects: (1) They illustrate the enormous flood of books. If we assume only 300 copies per edition, this represents 12 million books, but a figure of 20 million is more likely, as editions of a thousand or more copies soon became common. It is certainly a much larger number than all the books ever produced in the world before the age of print. (2) The numbers show the importance of Venice as the initial fountainhead of the new literacy and learning propagated by the printed book.

Venice was at the height of its power and prosperity as a center of capitalistic commerce and wide-ranging maritime trade. This was, of course, the reason why it attracted many of the early German printers. At the same time the mercantilism of Venice determined the direction of the new print-culture. Printing was from the beginning a secular enterprise governed by the profit motive, and in the beginning relatively free from church or government interference. Venice's flourishing export trade offered a market comprising all of Europe in addition to a prosperous and sophisticated local population of approximately 100,000, one of the largest in European cities. As 77 percent of the editions were in Latin, language barriers did not restrict distribution. Printing reached Italy at a most favorable time, when humanistic activity was at a peak and demand for classical texts was widespread throughout the centers of the Italian Renaissance. Printshops were also established in Bologna, Rome, Florence, Naples, and other cities, but the predominance of Venice had become firmly established.

In 1468 Cardinal Bessarion donated his manuscript library of 800 manuscripts, including 500 in Greek, to the city of Venice. Bessarion was a Byzantine scholar who had come to Italy as a delegate to the council of Florence, one of the attempts to reconcile the Eastern and the Western churches. After the failure of the council he stayed in Italy, joined the Roman church and became a priest and eventually a cardinal. He was also an eminent humanist, who was responsible for one of the first expansions of humanist learning into Germany by bringing the German astronomer Regiomontanus to Venice and giving him access to his library on Greek mathematics and astronomy, which he gave to the city before his death. During the years 1471 and 1472 Venetian presses produced 134 first editions of classical authors. It is characteristic of the intellectual climate in Venice that, while of all the books printed outside of Venice during the 15th century 48 percent were religious and 52 percent secular, and in Italy 60 percent were secular, the percentage of secular books in Venice was more than 73 percent, most of them classical. In 1489 Aldo Manuzio, known as Aldus Manutius, established his famous printing enterprise, the Aldine Press, which was to influence the art of printing and classical scholarship throughout Europe for the next fifty years.

Aldo Manuzio was not only a learned humanist in his own right; he surrounded himself with the outstanding scholars of his time. His printshop became the focal point of a learned society, the *sodalitas philhellenon*. Erasmus of Rotterdam, John Colet and his friend Thomas More, the great French classicist Guillaume Budé, as well as many others, visited Aldo and his establishment. Most important was the help Aldo received from native Greek scholars and teachers such as Marcus Misurus and Janus Lascaris in his pioneering publication of the Greek classics. He developed a Greek type based on the handwriting of Misurus and published a Greek grammar by Lascaris. Lascaris contributed much to the teaching of the Greek language in Italy and later in France. In 1496 Aldo Manuzio published the first printed edition of Theocritus and in 1498 that of Aristophanes. Between 1495 and 1498 he produced the first edition in Greek of Aristotle's works, in five volumes. In the single year of 1502 Aldo published five first editions, and a total of 27 in 21 years. Under Aldo and later under his son Paolo the Aldine Press set the standard for scholarly publication. While the German printers essentially had tried to imitate the manuscript letter forms, Aldo initiated a much more readable type (based on the ancient Roman inscriptions) which set the pattern for publications in Latin. In 1501 he introduced a new octavo format and a smaller cursive type, which in Anglo-Saxon countries became known as italics, to produce cheaper classical texts than the expensive unwieldy folios in larger quantities.The modern book had been born. Soon the Aldine classical texts filled the libraries of Europe and became popular with students and teachers alike. It was the Aldine texts that carried the Renaissance across the Alps and the English Channel. The ground, of course, had been prepared for some time. The Italian universities had always attracted students from many parts of western Europe. Small humanistic circles had formed in Spain, the Netherlands, France, and Britain. Hans Baron states that it was "...the period from 1490 to 1520 when the Renaissance, issued forth as a movement of European scope..."[4] This is no coincidence, because it was the exact period when the first editions flowed from the Aldine Press. As Elisabeth Eisenstein remarked, there was no longer any need to travel to the books; the books were coming to the readers.

The growth of trade and the prosperity of the cities, combined with the availability of relatively cheap books on all kinds of subjects, had stimulated an increasing interest in literacy and education. Printing presses were operating in more than 60 German cities. Centers of humanism sprang up, often around print shops. Regiomontanus, the protégé of Cardinal Bessarion, one of the earliest German humanistic scholar-printers, was to play an important part in the revival of Greek science and the beginnings of modern astronomy.

As mentioned above, most of the material printed north of the Alps was of a religious nature. It was inevitable that the traditional Christian literature should become an important subject of humanistic scholarship. The towering figure in this field was Erasmus of Rotterdam. Born in 1466 or 1469, he went to school in Deventer and was ordained a priest in 1492. Deventer was the seat of a religious lay movement that called itself *devotio moderna*. The objective of this school was Christian piety based on the most accurate reading possible of the scriptures and the pursuit of classical linguistic studies with this end in mind. The movement spread through northern Germany, founding schools in many places. Because of their insistence on "pure texts" the schools had their own print-shops, which contributed to the propagation of the movement. The restoration of the biblical texts remained the main purpose in Erasmus' life. In the year after his ordination he went to Paris to continue his classical studies, and in 1499 he was invited to Oxford by one of his pupils. There Erasmus became a friend of John Colet, an English humanist who had studied in Florence and Venice. Colet and Erasmus agreed on the need to combine the spirit of ancient *humanitas* with Christian piety. They shared the Socratic belief that ignorance is the source of all evil. Both realized the insufficiency of their own knowledge of Greek. Colet made the statement: "without Greek we are nothing." Therefore, Erasmus went back to Paris to continue his studies in that language. When Erasmus returned to London in 1505, Colet was dean of St. Paul's. Through him Erasmus became acquainted with Thomas More. In 1508 he traveled to Venice, where he divided his time between Aldo's print-shop, the library, and the *sodalitas philhellenon*. From 1509 to 1514 he paid another visit to England. He spent two years at Cambridge, teaching Greek and working on his edition of the Greek New Testament and Jerome's Latin text of the Bible, which, as the *Vulgata*, is still the authoritative version of the scriptures of the Catholic Church. Later he divided his time between Basel and Louvain. He stayed in Basel from 1521 to 1528 to work with his printer, Johann Froben, on the publication of his Greek New Testament. Froben was another of the prominent scholar-printers, and his shop was the nucleus of a spontaneous association of humanists that included, besides Erasmus, Beatus Rhenanus, Simon Grynaeus (the editor of Euclid's *elementa*), and others. The Reformation caused Erasmus to leave Basel in favor of Catholic Freiburg, but he returned to Basel in 1536, one year before his death. In the same year John Calvin's *Christianae religionis institutio* was printed in Basel, the first publication of Calvin's fundamental doctrine that we know as Calvinism.

Erasmus' lifespan coincided with the highwater mark of the European Renaissance, which he had helped to propagate, and with the Reformation, which he opposed-- although he had unwittingly contributed to it. His residence in many countries and his studies gave him a fervent feeling for European unity, of which the Latin language and Christianity were the two common bonds. Printing made the Reformation possible. It is estimated that Luther's publications sold well over 300,000 copies in the first three years following their publication in 1517 (Eisenstein 303). Luther himself acknowledged: "...it is a mystery to me how my theses, more so than any other writings, indeed those of other professors, were spread to so many places." He considered printing: "God's highest and extremest act of grace, whereby the business of the gospel is driven forward." (Eisenstein 304) Earlier "heretics" did not have the advantage of the printed medium; their ideas died with them at the stake. Ideas printed in hundreds of thousands of copies cannot be easily suppressed. Most of the intellectual warfare of the Reformation was conducted in print by both sides. The writings of the reformers divided Christianity forever. Their objective, to put the Bible into the hands of every believer, was possible only by means of printed translations. It was the vernacular Bibles that spread popular literacy but broke the bond of the common Latin language.

When Erasmus began his career the unity was still intact. He expressed his vivid concern for it in the famous words: "I want to be a citizen of the world, a fellow citizen of all or rather a visitor, for I wish it may be granted to me to be inscribed in the rolls of the City of Heaven." His friends in many countries constituted the "Republic of Letters:" Aldo Manuzio in Venice, Guillaume Budé in Paris, John Colet in Oxford, Thomas More in London, Robert Étienne in Geneva, and Johannes Reuchlin, the first to introduce the study of Greek and Hebrew in Germany, to mention just a few.

Erasmus believed that the decline that followed antiquity was manifest in the deterioration of the language, and therefore that all revival of learning must begin with the rebirth of the ancient languages and the restoration of the ancient texts and scriptures, which had been corrupted through centuries of scribal transmission. Being himself a product of the era of print he considered it his fundamental task to disseminate the wisdom and knowledge of the past by means of purified printed editions. As mentioned before, Erasmus was convinced of the Socratic thesis that knowledge is the basis of virtue and ignorance the cause of all evil. True religion, *Philosophia Christi*, depended on knowledge and he repeatedly asserted that knowledge can never be dangerous to religion. Man's supreme duty was to "find out, to understand, to know (*recognoscere, intellegere, scire*)." Since he thought that true religion depended on the correct understanding of correct texts he devoted himself to the preparation of revised editions of the scriptures, the classics, and the church fathers. In addition he was much concerned with education and pedagogy and consequently with interpretation, translation and commentaries. His emphasis on education was a major influence on the renewal of the ancient ideal of *humanitas*, the development of the human potential through education.

Erasmus produced an enormous amount of work. His New Testament was published in Basel in 1516. In the same year, his edition of Jerome's *Vulgata* went to press; later, revised editions followed in 1519, 1522, 1527, and 1535. The 1535 version printed by Robert Stephanus became the official *textus receptus*. Pope Leo X, a Medici, considered Erasmus' Bible an outstanding service to the Church. Luther used it as a main source of his German translation. Since Erasmus considered Luther's doctrinaire approach lacking in *humanitas* he opposed him strongly. It was Erasmus' tragedy that he was eventually attacked by both sides: by the Roman Church because his work had furthered Protestantism, and by the Protestants because he opposed them as the destroyers of Christian unity. The split between humanists and hidebound traditionalists on both sides went even deeper. Erasmus responded to the opponents of learning with some satirical works of which his *Praise of Folly* is the best known. To the very end he worked for tolerance and reconciliation. It was to a large extent Erasmus' merit that the "community of learning" still held together despite the widening divisions. An outstanding example was the Pfefferkorn affair.

Johannes Pfefferkorn, with the support of the Dominicans who dominated the University of Cologne, waged a campaign against Jewish books and proposed that all Hebrew writings should be confiscated and destroyed. In 1511 the Dominicans requested a decision to this effect from the imperial court. Johannes Reuchlin (1455-1522), after studying Greek in Paris and Hebrew in Rome, had almost singlehandedly introduced the study of Greek into Germany and had also lectured on Hebrew. He vigorously opposed the move of Pfefferkorn and the Dominicans. A bitter campaign in print ensued between the humanists and the obscurantists. When the matter came before the court Reuchlin submitted a written opinion in which he exposed the ignorance and fanaticism of the bookburners. They countered in 1513 by accusing Reuchlin of heresy. Reuchlin presented testimony to the Pope in which the Emperor, the King of France, and many bishops and clergymen attested Reuchlin's orthodoxy. The following year, Erasmus and the outstanding scholars of many countries published a collection of letters in defense of Reuchlin entitled *illustrorum virorum epistolae ad Ioannem Reuchlinum*. This was followed by an anonymous collection of fictitious letters addressed to the accusers satirizing their ignorance and parodying their views. In Rome all the cardinals took sides against Reuchlin. He probably escaped serious harm only because the pope was a humanist Medici. The Hebrew books had been saved.

Erasmus dedicated his last work, in 1535, to Cardinal Fisher, head of the theological school at Cambridge. The same year, Fisher and Thomas More were executed because they opposed Henry the Eighth's divorce and the split from Rome. It was Erasmus who had coined the epithet "a man for all seasons" for Thomas More.

Johannes Reuchlin had published a Hebrew grammar and dictionary and had lectured at the universities of Ingolstadt and Tübingen. He stated that he could never have done so without his books from the Aldine Press. On his death in 1522 he left his library, which included almost all Greek texts printed in Italy, to his hometown of Pforzheim. It was his grandnephew Melanchthon (Philipp Schwarzerd, 1497-1560) who formalized humanistic education, including Greek, in Germany. After publishing a Greek grammar in 1518 he was appointed professor of Greek at the University of Wittenberg on Reuchlin's recommendation. There he met Martin Luther and embraced Protestantism. His approach, which tried to combine humanism with Lutheranism, became the model for Protestant education in Germany for the next two centuries and earned him the title *praeceptor Germaniae*. Two of his pupils headed Protestant schools. One of them, Joachim Camerarius in Nuremberg, published an edition of Ptolemy's astrology, the *tetrabiblion*, with a Latin translation by Melanchthon, and in 1538, together with Grynaeus, the first Greek edition of Ptolemy's *megiste syntaxis*, the *Almagest*. This edition was used by Copernicus.

Thus at the beginning of the 16th century the wide availability of classical texts from the Italian presses spurred considerable humanistic activity in Germany. Soon however the increasing religious tensions seemed to absorb most energies. Erasmus complained at one time that in Germany nothing seemed to be published except against or for Luther. Eventually the thirty year religious war (1618-1648) paralyzed most literary activity in the German lands and restricted their participation in the discoveries and intellectual advances of the 17th century. The true classical literary renaissance of Germany had to wait for the 18th century.

The south of France had been open to Italian influences quite early, but it was not until the end of the 15th century that humanism really conquered Paris. Guillaume Budè, a friend of Erasmus and Reuchlin, went on several missions to the Medicis in the Vatican and visited the Aldine Press. In a sense he was already a product of the print-age, as his knowledge of Greek was essentially self-taught from books-- although he later learned more from Lascaris, whom the French court invited for several visits to Paris. Budé was the driving force for humanism in France. He persuaded Francis I to found the Collège Royal, which was later renamed Collège de France. Budé conceived the Collège as a new "Museum" patterned after the *mouseion* of Alexandria, a sanctuary for the cultivation of all arts and sciences, where scholars and poets would revive the Greek literature and inspire each other to emulate the classical achievements. From the time of its opening in 1530 the Collège became the center of French humanism.

The first lecturers appointed were pupils of Lascaris and Budé, among them Toussain, a friend of Erasmus and teacher of Jean Dorat, who together with Adrianus Turnebus (Turnèbe) was to assume the lectureship in 1547. Most of the luminaries of the French Renaissance attended the Collège Royal, such as Muretus (Marc Antoine Muret) the teacher of Montaigne, Francois Rabelais the great essayist, John Calvin the reformer and Jacques Amyot, who translated Plutarch's *Lives of the Great Greeks and Romans* into the French version which was later translated into English by Thomas North and became a rich source of material for Shakespeare. A famous group at the Collège was the Pleiade. The name shows its inspiration by Budé since it was borrowed from a similar seven member group at the Museum of Alexandria; they had adopted the name from a constellation of seven stars. The founding member of the French Pleiade was Dorat (1508-1588), one of two *lecteurs royaux* in Greek; he wrote poetry in Greek, Latin and French. Dorat was a popular lecturer, who communicated his enthusiasm for Greek literature to his students and tried to stimulate them to compete creatively with the ancient models. Other members of the Pleiade were Jean du Bellay, the theoretician of the group, who stated its objective to marry the French language with the Greek poetic forms, and Pierre Ronsard, the most creative and successful member, who wrote four books of odes in the manner of Pindar. The group had considerable influence on the three great French dramatists-- Corneille, Racine and Molière.

With the royal patronage for the revival of learning came an increasing demand for the classics and an immediate response by the printshops. Here, as in Italy, scholarly printers contributed much to the advance of humanism, especially in the field of Greek classics, which had so far been known mainly through the Aldine editions. The outstanding French private publishing house was the establishment of the Étiennes, known by their humanistic name as the Stephani. It was founded in 1502 by Henri Étienne. He was one of the first to use a new Greek type commissioned by the king

(Francis I), who had founded not only the Collège Royal but also the Presse Royale.

Robert Étienne, Henri's son and a scholar in his own right, published a comprehensive Latin dictionary, the *Latinae Linguae Thesaurus*, which was not superseded as the authoritative Latin Thesaurus until 1771. In 1550 he published an edition of Erasmus' text of the Greek New Testament. The following year he moved to Geneva and converted to Protestantism. In Geneva in the same year he printed another edition of the Testament - the first edition that divided the text into verses. In 1556 he applied the same system to his edition of the Old Testament in Latin. This innovation was adopted by all Protestant printers, and later his verse numbers were also accepted by the Catholic Church. The Stephanus Bible became the standard text and was never altered until the complete critical revision by the German humanist Lachmann in 1831. When Robert Étienne went to Geneva and changed his faith he left his son, Henri II, in charge of the Paris operation. The Geneva branch was taken over after Robert's death by his other son, Robert II. The Catholic branch in Paris and the Protestant business in Geneva continued to maintain the best relations throughout the religious wars which filled the second half of the 16th century.

Henri Étienne II (Enricus Stephanus), a pupil of Dorat at the Collège Royal, was an outstanding Greek linguist and indefatigable editor, printer and publisher. He published 74 Greek texts, 18 of them first editions, and 58 in Latin. The most important were his Plato of 1572 and his Greek Thesaurus, commonly referred to as "the Stephanus." The Thesaurus, twice re-edited in the 19th century, has remained the standard reference work until finally in 1987 an international project at the University of California at Irvine completed a new computerized Thesaurus which includes in its data base all Greek literature up to the year AD 600. It is ironic that the Thesaurus, his main work, bankrupted Henri Étienne, and he died in poverty.

During the upheavals of the Reformation and the Counter-Reformation Geneva had become the refuge and publishing center of the Calvinists, just as Basel had become the Lutheran center for southern Germany. Later, the cities of the Netherlands became the sanctuary for the publication of all the banished views; the Dutch and Belgian printers served all sides with equal eagerness. The religious controversies nourished an enormous flood of printer's ink. From the Netherlands all the proscribed opinions found their way back into France, Germany, Italy, Spain and England. Perhaps the best example is furnished by one of the most successful printers, Christopher Plantin, who had moved to Antwerp from Paris. He put printing on an industrial basis, for at the height of his career in 1576 he had 22 presses in operation, despite numerous competitors. This compares with two to four presses of such prominent publishing houses as the Aldine Press or the enterprises of the Étiennes. During all the religious controversies (conducted mostly in print) and the physical persecutions by the diverse pro- or anti-Rome establishments, the scholarly publishing firms provided a meeting ground for humanists of all persuasions. They remained focal points in the correspondence network of the international community of learning. Catholic and Protestant scholars cooperated in the editions of polyglot Bibles as well as in vernacular Bible translations. By supporting the Protestants Plantin managed to survive the Calvinist revolt of 1566, when hundreds of churches were destroyed. When Spain brutally crushed the uprising, and Plantin's life was in danger, he produced an elegant edition of a polyglot Bible for the king of Spain and obtained his patronage. From 1571 to 1576 orders from Philip II of Spain kept 12 of Plantin's presses busy. During the same time, he published a botanical encyclopedia, a German thesaurus, a Latin dictionary, atlases for the cartographer Abraham Ortelius, and several compact editions of classical works. In 1576 he moved to the site which is today the Plantin Museum. In the same year Spanish troops sacked Antwerp and massacred 7,000 inhabitants. Plantin bought himself free through payment of an enormous ransom. Soon the Dutch regained the city, and Plantin became the official printer to the new authorities and dedicated a new edition of his herbal to William of Orange, the founder of the Dutch Republic. When the Spaniards advanced again he entrusted his shop to his son-in-law and moved to Leyden, where he set up a new shop and became printer to the newly founded University. He eventually returned to Antwerp, where he died in 1583. His life illustrates the force that the independent commercial printers exerted as defenders of intellectual freedom by their legitimate pursuit of profit, while the official institutions such as the universities were under strict partisan control. After the Netherlands gained their final autonomy from Spain the cities of Belgium and Holland more than ever became the refuge for religious exiles and centers of independent learning and printing. Throughout all the conflicts the printed word alone assured the survival of ideas against all attempts at repression. By the middle of the 16th century the North surpassed Italy in classical scholarship. The classics, however, were only a small part of the output of the printing presses. In order to operate profitably within the ever increasing competition the publishers needed markets far beyond the Latin-speaking educated elite. The production of translations and books in the vernacular languages increased continuously. The printers had to cater to every taste in order to survive. Generally the preponderant share of the printed material was of a religious nature, with the only exception being in Venice, where editions of secular books outnumbered those on religious subjects by three to one. The line between religious and secular, blurred as it is, is an after-the-fact distinction of our time. It would not have occurred to the humanists, who, contrary to popular belief, generally were profoundly religious. They made no distinction between the works of pagan antiquity and Christian writers, especially since the concepts of chronology were still extremely vague.

In the second half of the 16th century the controversies of the Reformation released an even greater mass of religious writings. The Reformation movement itself could never have gained momentum without the vehicle of print. The spread of Protestantism in turn, with its emphasis on Bible reading, encouraged not only a proliferation of Bible translations, prayer-books and psalters in the various vernacular languages, but also systematic education in reading and writing. Besides and beyond humanistic and classical subjects a veritable deluge of popular printed matter poured from the presses: Abecedaria, primers, almanacs and how-to-books on every conceivable craft, skill, or art from magic to medicine, from arithmetic to astrology, as well as old and new belletristic literature. All of this increased popular interest in literacy and education.

To promote sales the publishers advertised their books widely by sending out flyers and catalogues. Printers staged book fairs, sent their agents to the major cities of Europe and carried on a far-reaching correspondence with their potential clientele. Thus the literate public was kept aware of new editions and the latest literature on every subject. Notwithstanding an over-supply of superstition and just plain trash that issued from the presses, knowledge and ideas were disseminated faster than ever before. Literacy rates multiplied. It is estimated that literacy rates in the more advanced cities by the end of the 16th century were better than 50 percent.[5]

By the turn of the 16th century the classical revival had gathered enough momentum to inspire the literary creativity of such dramatists as Shakespeare (1564-1616), Christopher Marlowe (1564-1593) and Ben Jonson (1573-1637) in England; Lope da Vega (1562-1635) and Calderon (1600-1681) in Spain; and Corneille (1606-1684), Racine (1639-1699) and Molière (1622-1673) in France. Since it was known that music played an important part in Greek drama, music was combined with drama in Italy and generated the creation of opera. Drama was the most spectacular product of the literary Renaissance, but all other genres were equally revived and transformed by the ancient paradigms.

Notes

1. Rudolf Pfeiffer, *The History of Classical Scholarship 1300-1850*, 14-15

2. Elisabeth Eisenstein, *The Printing Press as an Agent of Change* (Cambridge 1979), 137n.

3. L.V. Garulaitis, *Printing and Publishing in 15th Century Venice* (Chicago and London 1976), 60

4. Hans Baron, *New Cambridge Modern History* I (1957), 75.

5. Carlo Cipolla, *Literacy and Development in the West* (London 1969), 60

12

The Renaissance: Science

The revolution in communications wrought by print, and the resulting revival of ancient learning, prepared the way for a new beginning of scientific inquiry. Some recent historians of science have expressed the opinion that the intellectual direction of humanism was all backward-looking, antiquarian, concerned more with form than content, and lacking interest or understanding of science. The humanists, it is alleged, were still prisoners of scholasticism and philosophic dogma, and thus rather a retarding influence. Both charges are without merit. That the humanists were uninterested in science is an unjustified generalization. Even if it may have applied to some, it is certainly proven wrong by the scientific achievements of others. Regiomontanus, Copernicus, Johannes Kepler, and Galileo were all products of humanistic learning. They were motivated in their scientific inquiries by the philosophic Aristotelian quest for perfection and simplicity in nature, the same ideal of order and beauty (*cosmos*) that gave rise to classical and Renaissance art. The denial of the humanists' contribution to science is often based on an artificial dichotomy between a supposedly Aristotelian speculative deductive approach and a scientific empirical method. It was precisely the humanistic resurrection of the original Greek Aristotle, who stressed experience and induction over dialectics, that laid the scholastic dogmatic distortions of Aristotelian thought to rest. Furthermore, as Albert Einstein observed, "there is no empirical method without speculative concepts and systems; and there is no speculative thinking whose concepts do not reveal, on closer investigation, the empirical material from which they stem."[1] The critics fail to recognize that scientific inquiry had to start from some base. That base was knowledge that already existed in books, especially the Hellenistic textbooks.

As Elisabeth Eisenstein in her penetrating study has pointed out, problems had to be recognized before they could be solved, questions had to be asked before they could be answered.[2] The accumulated knowledge of the past had lain hidden in often corrupt manuscripts in an unknown language, or buried in misunderstood secondhand summaries and translations, distorted by the religious bias of commentaries. The humanists performed the indispensable task of reviving the Greek language and restoring the corrupt texts and making them accessible in print, in the original as well as in accurate translations. In the process the humanists formed a bridge between the past and the future; some of them, as we shall see, also became pioneers of the new scientific beginnings. Only when, through the work of the humanists, printed editions had made it possible to examine the findings of the ancient authorities side by side did errors, contradictions and inconsistencies manifest the problems, raise the questions, and point the way to new investigations.

Before true empirical science could evolve, many preconditions had to be met. Printing was an essential contributing factor to the realization of most of them. Ancient science had reached a certain level, but had not advanced much after the Hellenistic surge. Observation had been limited by the power of the naked eye. In the absence of the requisite technology it had been impossible to verify competing theories by controlled experiments. By the 16th century, technology had made considerable progress. Improved techniques of metal working and gear cutting facilitated the construction of sophisticated mechanical apparatus. In this field, too, printing made its contribution. During the Middle Ages skilled artisans had jealously guarded their trade secrets, passing them on from father to son and keeping innovations secret within their families, or at least their guilds. But when printing offered an advertising medium that held out promise of a worldwide market, instead of the local monopoly assured by secrecy, workshops became eager to publicize their inventions and the improvements of their products. In this way the knowledge of technical innovations was disseminated rapidly through printed flyers containing descriptions and sometimes drawings. Craftsmen and instrument makers learned from each other, and the pace of technological advancement accelerated. By the end of the 16th century mechanical clocks had made their appearance. The art of the lens-maker reached the point where not only spectacles became common, but finely ground lenses led to the development of telescopes and microscopes and thus a tremendous expansion of human observational powers. The renewed appreciation of classical representative art and architecture revived understanding of the mathematical canons and of the laws of optics and perspective on which these arts were based. The new art of copper engraving, married to the craft of the printer, brought realistic pictures of plants, animals and the human anatomy, and thus a knowledge of nature, to a wider public than ever before. Even mathematics, which as a purely theoretical science had been least hampered by the lack of mechanical apparatus, had become more manageable through the adoption of the Arabic numerals. Printed books illustrated with engraved accurate drawings made geometric and mechanical principles understandable.

Charles Singer observed: "The 16th century marks a frontier for another reason. Until about 1500 the East was culturally as active as the West. Many devices came west from both Near East and Far East. By 1500 the process had been reversed and the history of science can be told without reference to the East."[3] The turning point noted by Singer marks exactly the transition from manuscript to printed communications, when the publication of the ancient texts hit its stride. There can be little doubt that of all the many and various developments which turned the Middle Ages into modern times, the printing press has provided the most important catalyst. The question arises why the invention of printing with moveable type in China and Korea about three centuries earlier had not produced the same effect there. The answer lies in the immense complexity of the Chinese writing system, which kept reading and writing the esoteric arts of an exceedingly small privileged minority, while the simplicity of the alphabet made European books accessible to all those sufficiently interested and motivated. The following examples will show the part played by printing in the birth of modern science.

Renaissance Medicine

Hand in hand with the revival of ancient literature had gone the rediscovery of ancient art. Just as writers and poets tried to emulate the classical masterworks painters and sculptors strove to live up to the ancient canons and models. Lifelike representation of the human body demanded a knowledge of its structure. The artist and the physician shared a common interest in anatomy, and both were helped by the printing press in two ways. Many more of Galen's works had appeared in print than had been known in the Middle Ages (see Appendix, 328-332). In 1490 Galen's complete works in Latin (with a few exceptions, only recently recovered from the Arabic) had come off the press of Philippus Pincius in Venice, followed by the first Greek edition from the Aldine Press in 1525. Galen's treatise on dissection (*De anatomicis administrationibus*) was to become a favored textbook for artists and physicians alike. The other benefit of the printing press was its ability to produce multiple exact copies of drawings through woodcuts and later from copper engravings. Thus the imaginative art of Albrecht Dürer (1471-1528) and the scientific illustrations of the human anatomy by Andreas Vesalius (1514-1564) in print could within a short time reach a vast public.

Vesalius united the artist and the scientist in his own person and took full advantage of the age of print. He was born in Brussels and studied medicine in Louvain and Paris. In Paris he became thoroughly familiar with Galen's works and assisted his professor Gunther of Andernach in preparing the first Latin edition of Galen's newly discovered *De anatomicis* for publication. It was printed by Simon des Colines, a relative of the famous scholar-printer Charles Étienne, who also helped with the project. Thus Vesalius was drawn at an early stage of his career into the field of learned publishing. His knowledge of Galen inspired him to work for the restoration of anatomy "as it was of old in Alexandria."[4] Vesalius was attracted to Padua, like Copernicus before him and Harvey after him. This was not surprising, since Padua not only had a renowned medical school where dissection was practiced since the 15th century[5] but also was a center of secular humanistic re-evaluation of the classics within the orbit of Venice's feverish publishing activity.

While continuing his education in Padua, Vesalius edited parts of a new edition of Galen. In 1542, at the age of 28, he was appointed professor at the University of Padua. He conducted extensive anatomical research and presented his findings in his exquisite drawings of the skeletal and muscular structures. He was an extremely popular professor and attracted as many as 500 students at a time.

In 1543 he published his pioneering work in anatomy *De fabrica corporis humani*, the first comprehensive work on this subject since Galen. Vesalius tried to verify every aspect of Galen's views by firsthand observation and experiment and documented the results in exact detail in his drawings. In the ancient view the veins carried the blood while the arteries were filled with air. The blood was thought to be continuously manufactured by the liver from food and air and distributed through the veins to the right ventricle of the heart and all the various parts of the body. There it was consumed as nourishment. Galen, however, realized that blood flowed also in the arteries and he anticipated the discovery of the lesser circulatory system (through the lungs); he thought that some of the blood seeped through invisible pores in the dividing wall of the septum from the right ventricle into the left ventricle and that there also was a secondary flow from the right to the left through the pulmonary artery (he called it the "artery-like vein") through the lungs into the small branches of the pulmonary vein (Galen's "vein-like artery"). This was how Harvey later interpreted Galen's passage in *De usu partium* (6.10) when he acknowledged his debt to him. The concept of the continuous production of blood from the intake of food and air, and its use as nourishment by the body, implied a rather small volume of bloodflow-- not much more than a trickle.

Vesalius doubted many of Galen's theories but in the end wound up accepting them, as he had no viable alternative. He was especially skeptical of the idea that blood entered the left ventricle of the heart through pores in the septum, of which he could find no evidence. He never mentioned Galen's hypothesis of a flow through the lungs, which later became known as "the lesser circulation," and seems not to have been aware of it. Yet some of his contemporaries were familiar with it. Servetus quoted Galen's statement on this subject almost verbatim, although without attribution (which is not unusual for that period) in his book *Restitution of Christianity*, written in 1546 and published in 1553-- the year he was burned as heretic by the Calvinists, condemned to death by Protestants and Catholics alike. Galen's statement is also quoted without attribution by Columbus, Vesalius' student and successor at the University of Padua.

That Vesalius' work was an immediate success is attested by numerous plagiarized works and pirated editions. Because his research was squarely based on Galen's methods rather than his dogmas it marked the revival of empirical scientific medicine. When Vesalius retired a year after the publication of the *Fabrica* to become personal physician to the emperor Charles V at the age of 29 he had strengthened the university's medical tradition, basing it firmly on observation and experiment which, through his successors, would lead to Harvey's discovery of the true workings of the circulatory system and to modern medicine. Vesalius' *Fabrica*, with its accurate description of the human anatomy in word and picture, was a turning point in medicine and its popularity clearly demonstrated the power of the print medium. A comparison with Leonardo da Vinci a generation earlier will illustrate this point.

Leonardo, with his insatiable intellectual curiosity, for the sake of his art made his own anatomical studies in order to gain a deeper understanding of the structure and the mechanics of the living body in motion. In a recently discovered manuscript he describes in moving words the ordeals he underwent for this purpose. The only cadavers he could obtain were those of old and sick people from prison or poorhouse. Without refrigeration or preservatives in the Mediterranean heat he continually had to overcome his nausea while dissecting the putrid corpses and delving into their inner organs. His art reflects his thorough knowledge of the workings of the skeletal and muscular systems, but his studies went much further. By painstaking dissection and experiments he made discoveries surpassing many facets of existing knowledge. For instance, he discovered two additional chambers of the heart, the left and right auricles, and the exact workings of the valves, which showed that some of the then current theories concerning the bloodflow had to be wrong-- as the valves would allow only flow in the opposite direction. He documented his findings in precise drawings, but because Leonardo did not commit anything to print his findings remained hidden in his scattered notebooks and did not affect the state of knowledge in his time. Some of his pioneering discoveries had to be re-discovered generations later.

Realdus Columbus (Realdo Colombo), Vesalius' pupil, was appointed his successor at Padua in 1542. His book, *De re anatomica*, was published after his death in 1559. He was the first who actually observed that the pulmonary vein contains blood which flows to the heart, and thus confirmed Galen's theory of the lesser circulation through the lungs which Vesalius had ignored. After his death he was followed by Gabriel Fallopius, another pupil of Vesalius who among other things studied the bloodflow to and around the brain. He and his outstanding student Fabricius carried on the Galenic-Vesalian tradition of thorough study of the ancient sources combined with continuous verification and testing through personal observation and experimentation.

Fabricius of Aquapendente held the chair of anatomy at Padua from 1555 until 1619, when he died at the age of 89. He was steeped in the theories of Aristotle and Galen, but he was also an excellent observer. He was the author of the first illustrated book on embryology and the first to publish accurate pictures of the structure of the eye. In 1574 he published *On the Valves of the Veins* and showed on the basis of his own experiments that the flow in the veins was towards the heart. He was an excellent teacher and had a far-reaching reputation. It was under his tenure that Harvey came to Padua.

William Harvey (1578-1657), attended Caius College in Cambridge. The college had been named after John Caius who had studied at Padua under Vesalius. Caius had been also an avid student of Greek and had edited some of Galen's treatises. Thus the Galenic Vesalian-Paduan connection was strong at Cambridge. This tradition and the contemporary fame of Fabricius probably combined to lure Harvey to Padua, where he arrived in 1597 after receiving his degree from Cambridge and became a student of Fabricius. Harvey later acknowledged his debt to Fabricius, who had always stressed firsthand observation. In 1602 he received his medical doctorate from Padua and also from Cambridge after his return the same year. He established his medical practice and in 1615 was appointed lecturer at the College of Physicians in London. He continued the dissection of animals to gain insight into human physiology and urged his students to do the same. In his lecture notes, which still exist, he quoted most often Aristotle and Galen and showed thorough knowledge of the works of Vesalius, Fallopius, Colombo and especially of his teacher Fabricius. His reputation must have grown rapidly, for in 1618 he was appointed court physician to King James I. In 1628 he published his revolutionary book *Anatomical Dissertation on the Motion of the Heart and Blood in Animals* (*Exercitatio anatomica de motu cordis et sanguinis in animalibus*), which, with the first correct understanding of the circulatory system, gave medicine a new beginning.

Harvey had at an early stage accepted the view of Galen, whom he repeatedly quotes, that the blood flows from the right ventricle of the heart through the pulmonary vein to the lungs and from the lungs through the pulmonary artery to the left side of the heart (the lesser circulation). Through his own animal studies he had recognized that the contraction of the left ventricle (*systole*) impels the blood into the aorta, from where it is distributed through the arteries to all parts of the body. He and Fabricius had also rediscovered the functions of the valves which Leonardo da Vinci had described more than a century earlier, namely that the blood can only flow *out* from the right ventricle into the pulmonary artery but is prevented by the valves from returning, and similarly that the blood can only flow *out* of the left ventricle into the aorta. But the crucial observations and the reasoning that led Harvey to the discovery of the "greater circulation" were the following:

Harvey had recognized that the rhythmical systolic contractions which emptied the left ventricle into the arteries caused the beating of the pulse 72 times per minute. Assuming a capacity of two ounces of blood in the left ventricle, this means that each hour 72 times 60 times 2 ounces, that is 9640 ounces of blood, would enter the arteries. This equals approximately three times the weight of the human body. Thus the ancient theory of a continuous production and consumption of blood is manifestly impossible, since neither could the food intake generate nor the body hold such a quantity.[6] Harvey saw only one possibility: the blood moves in a continuous circle; as it is pumped out through the arteries it returns through the veins to the right auricle of the heart. This was the way it had to be, because in the arteries the flow was from the larger into the smaller ones that branch into ever smaller vessels always away from the heart. In the veins he had observed the opposite; the blood ran from the smallest ones, which combined into ever larger ones toward the *vena cava* and the heart.

There remained, however, unsolved problems: How did the blood get from the arteries to the veins, or in the lungs from the pulmonary artery into the pulmonary vein? Galen and Harvey had both by inference concluded that a connection must exist but had never been able to observe any; Harvey could only quote the unproven hypothesis of Galen. Galen had theorized that a process occurred which he called *anastomosis*: the smallest vessels, both arteries and veins, terminate in minute openings (*stomata*, literally "mouths") through which the blood empties into pores within the tissues. When the *anastomoses* are close enough together, communications take place (*synanastomoses*), but are hidden to sense perception.[7] Although Harvey was unable to discover *how* the transfer took place he obtained circumstantial evidence through experiments on animals and himself that a passage of blood *does occur*. These experiments consisted essentially in restricting the bloodflow by pinching arteries or veins and observing the resulting swelling or shrinking of the vessels above or below the obstruction. It remained for Marcello Malpighi more than 30 years later to describe *how* the transfer of blood between arteries and veins occurs, when through a microscope he could actually see the capillary network in the lungs of a frog forming the connecting link.

When Harvey propounded his thesis before the College of Physicians and when he published the *de motu* in Frankfurt in 1628 he found little resistance, and he gained acceptance of his discovery within his lifetime. Harvey died in 1657 at the age of 80.

In 1661 Malpighi at the University of Bologna had confirmed the existence of the lesser circulation through the lungs. In the following year the Royal Society was formed in London as a forum for discussion and for support of scientists in other countries. In 1667 the Italian learned society, the *Academia del Cimento*, founded by followers of Galileo ten years earlier, was suppressed by the Church authorities. Henceforth Malpighi published his works on embryology in London. The center of gravity for free inquiry shifted to England and to France, where the *Académie des sciences* was founded in 1667. With the issue of regularly published scientific journals by both of these societies the print medium made another enormous contribution to the advance of knowledge at the very time when the Church drove scientific publication in Italy underground.

The advances in anatomical and biological knowledge exemplify the evolution of scientific thought during the Renaissance under the influence of the new literacy fostered by printed publications. When printed editions made the ancient medical writings widely available Galen's works, especially his textbook on anatomical procedure (which had been little, if at all, known during the Middle Ages), became the guide to new research. Vesalius started in the 16th century where Galen had left off in the second and from Vesalius a direct line of progression led to Harvey and the Royal Society. During the hundred years between them, as we have seen, the University of Padua played an important part. As Charles Singer has observed,[8] most of the early advances in medicine came from Padua.

The University of Padua as Venice's institution of higher learning reflected Venice's intellectual ferment. Unlike Oxford, Paris or the German universities, which had developed from theological schools, the Italian universities had originated from schools of law and medicine, and generally had no permanent theological faculties or official theological curricula.[9] Therefore, they offered less resistance to free inquiry. Of all the Italian universities Padua was the most prosperous and had the oldest medical school. It required its students to prepare themselves by the study of philosophy, which essentially meant Aristotle. But under the humanistic influence some professors moved from rigid scholastic Aristotelianism to a more objective re-evaluation of Aristotle's works, shifting emphasis from his doctrines to his methods and reviving interest in his biological works. Anatomical demonstrations became part of the curriculum, and many of the professors published their findings in print. With a revitalized Latin there were no language boundaries and Padua attracted inquisitive minds from all over Europe. Vesalius was Flemish, Copernicus Polish or German, and Harvey English. Multilingual literacy seems to have a stimulating intellectual effect, since we find it associated with almost all the historical watersheds that widened the horizon of human thought and knowledge.

Some writers have asserted that the humanistic revival was a hindrance rather than a help to Renaissance scientists. A statement by Harvey is quoted from his introductory letter which accompanied the *de motu* to the College of physicians. In it he says: "... I do not profess to learn and to teach anatomy from books or maxims of philosophers, but from dissections and from the fabric of Nature herself (*De motu*, 8)." The context is a polemic against those conservative scholastics ..."who suffer themselves to be so addicted to the slavery of any man's reports and precepts and so lose their liberty that they no longer give credence to their own eyes..." In fact, Harvey was a convinced Aristotelian. In his *De generatione ani-*

malium, he said "I follow Aristotle like a leader (*tamquam ducem*)."
He was totally imbued with Aristotle's teleology and quoted repeatedly his statement that "nature does nothing without a purpose." Harvey looks always for Aristotle's "final cause" when he is
trying to determine the function of an organ or part of the
anatomy. He clearly overstated his case when he said that he did
not learn or teach from books. He knew and continually quoted all
the pertinent literature, ancient and contemporary-- especially
Aristotle, Galen, Columbus, and Fabricius. Without the books he
would not have known what and where to look for in "the fabric of
nature" or to recognize what he found there. This had been the
fate of Leonardo da Vinci, who was poorly educated and was
forced late in life to study Latin and to seek help in reading Galen
to be able to pursue his anatomical investigations. Harvey acknowledged his debt to Galen: "that divine man (*viro divino*)." He
followed the methods and procedures of Aristotle and Galen, and
both of them "would have approved of Harvey," as Galileo said,
that "Aristotle would have accepted me among his followers."

   The wide and fast distribution of literature through print had
been largely responsible for the recovery and restoration of the ancient texts which provided the starting point for the new inquiries.
It now provided the same efficient dissemination of new findings to
all these interested in the field. Soon the exchange of scientific information became more systematized through the regular publication of transactions and journals by the newly chartered learned societies and their proliferating offspring.

Astronomy and Copernicus

In the late Middle Ages there existed essentially two views of the
world-- the Aristotelian and the Ptolemaic. The Aristotelian tradition, much distorted in Latin translations and handbooks, had
never been fully interrupted, but after the fall of the Roman Empire knowledge of the Ptolemaic system had fallen into oblivion in
western Europe together with the knowledge of the Greek language and mathematics. When it reappeared in the West during

the 12th century it was in the form of translations into Latin of the *Almagest*, the Arabic translation of Ptolemy's work (see Appendix, 322-324). Its mathematical intricacies, with epicycles and eccentricities, could not compete with the simplicity of the Aristotelian model of concentric circular orbits around the earth.

The first printed book on astronomy, by Georg Peurbach (1423-1461), was titled *New Theories about the Planets* (*theoricae novae planetarum*). Peurbach was a humanistic professor of rhetoric at the University of Vienna who had traveled in Germany and Italy. He studied astronomy from a mediaeval Arab manuscript of the *Almagest*. In his book he gave a lucid explanation of Ptolemy's system of epicycles and tried to reconcile it with the Aristotelian cosmology; he was convinced that by going back to uncorrupted Greek texts the problem could be solved. He improved on the *Almagest* by calculating with sines instead of chords, and he prepared a table of sines with 10 minute intervals. Working with Peurbach, first as his student and later as partner, was Johann Muller (1436-76), known as Regiomontanus after his native city of Königsberg. During their association Peurbach and Regiomontanus made observations of eclipses and measurements of solar altitudes. In the process they discovered errors of several degrees in the Alphonsine Tables. These tables were named after King Alphonse X of Castille, who after the re-conquest of Andalusia had gathered a group of Arab and Jewish astronomers to document their findings for him. The Alphonsine Tables, which were essentially based on the *Almagest*, had remained in continuous use since their original compilation in 1232. Regiomontanus had also prepared a first edition of an astronomic poem by Manilius. In 1461 the Greek humanist, Cardinal Bessarion of Venice, visited Vienna, where he took an interest in Peurbach's and Regiomontanus' work. He invited them to accompany him to Venice so that they could use his library of Greek scientific works which he later willed to the city of Venice. Peurbach, however, died before their departure and Regiomontanus went alone with Bessarion. In Italy Regiomontanus studied Greek, and collected and copied Greek manuscripts. When he returned from Italy he took a position with Matthias Corvinus, King of Hungary, who had acquired a large library of Greek manuscripts. During his stays in Italy and Hungary Regiomontanus became acquainted with most of the works of the ancient Greek mathematicians and astronomers. In 1471 he returned to Germany and settled in Nuremberg. (Corvinus' library was destroyed in 1527 when Hungary was conquered by the Turks.)

In Nuremberg Regiomontanus found backing by some wealthy humanists and was able to set up his own observatory and print shop. The first works he published, in 1472, were Peurbach's *New Theories*, the first printed scientific book mentioned above, and his own edition of the poem of Manilius. He gained fame by publishing his *ephemerides*, tables in which the positions of the planets (including sun and moon) had been calculated for the 32 years from 1475 to 1506, and he also printed advertisements for astronomical instruments. An important document he published in 1474 was an advance list, of which copies are still in existence, of some 45 items he planned to publish. It contained most of the extant ancient works on astronomy and mathematics followed by his own intended works. Unfortunately his premature death in 1476 prevented the realization of his plans but his list of ancient scientific books became a valuable guide for his successors. Several works he had completed before his death were published posthumously--among them a treatise on the comet of 1472, which he had observed (printed in 1532) and his *de triangulis*, the first systematic book on trigonometry, published by Erhard Radolt in Nuremberg in 1533, 57 years after Regiomontanus' death.

Radolt was another pioneer humanist-scientist-printer who had set up shop in Venice. There in 1476 he printed a *calendarium* by Regiomontanus. This was the first book with a separate title page and dated in Arabic numerals. Radolt also printed the Alphonsine Tables in 1483 and the first complete Latin edition of Euclid, translated from Arabic (see Appendix, 321-322). In 1490 he moved to Augsburg and printed Regiomontanus' *tabulae directionum*, orientations with respect to the seeming daily rotation of the sky. Peurbach's and Regiomontanus' most important work, *Epitoma in Almagestum Ptolemai*, was printed in Venice in 1496 by Johannes

Hamman. Regiomontanus' life and work illustrate the revolutionary transition from the age of manuscripts to the age of print. As a student he had to travel from place to place to get access to manuscripts. He was extremely fortunate to find in Bessarion and Corvinus two sponsors with extensive manuscript libraries. Still, Regiomontanus had to work from a corrupt secondhand Arabic copy of the *Almagest*. He had to spend untold hours copying and excerpting to prepare for his own research. In their work he and Peurbach pointed out many errors in the data and inconsistencies in the accepted tradition. By going into print he gave mathematical astronomy an unprecedented impetus. All successive astronomers had the advantage of printed books and astronomic as well as trigonometric tables which Regiomontanus had pioneered.

Copernicus' library contained all of Regiomontanus' works. As a student Copernicus used and annotated a printed set of the *ephemerides* and later Radolt's 1490 edition of Regiomontanus' *Tables of Directions*, as well as Hamman's 1496 edition of his epitome of the *Almagest*. When Copernicus was 65 years old he received Petreius' 1535 edition of Regiomontanus' trigonometry (*de triangulis*) and used it to correct his own data in his *de revolutionibus planetarum*, which was to be published eight years later by the same printer. Later Tycho Brahe and Johannes Kepler were as familiar with Regiomontanus' works as Copernicus'. All these scholars were connected through the printed communications whose focal points were the northern Italian and southern German universities and printshops. Rheticus, who directed the publication of Copernicus' book, brought to him the first edition of the complete Greek text of the *Almagest*, published by Grynaeus and Camerarius in Basel in 1538. It was based on the same manuscript which Regiomontanus had studied in Cardinal Bessarion's library. While Regiomontanus had to travel to the manuscripts in Venice and Buda, and had to copy or excerpt them, all the books Copernicus needed came to him in his remote little town in Poland in edited and easily readable printed form.

Copernicus' sometime associate and valuable helper, Joachim Rheticus, who provided many of the books to him, was a student at

Tübingen, Nuremberg, and Wittenberg (where he received his degree, and eventually was appointed professor of mathematics). In Tübingen Johann Stoeffler taught mathematics and continued the publication of the *ephemerides* which Regiomontanus had begun; Melanchthon and Johannes Schoener were some of his pupils. Schoener wrote a preface to Regiomontanus' treatise on the comet of 1472, which was being printed posthumously in Nuremberg. He was Rheticus' teacher at Nuremberg, and it was he who eventually encouraged Rheticus to visit Copernicus in Poland and to find out about his theories, as Copernicus was not publishing anything. Rheticus addressed the first report on the Copernican theory to Schoener. All these contacts bridged the religious gulf between Copernicus, who was a Catholic canon, and the German Protestant universities-- especially Wittenberg, where Melanchthon and Luther held sway.

The relationships briefly sketched in the foregoing illustrate several points. The renewal of science was an integral part of the humanistic revival. The Greek classics were still the starting point of scientific inquiry, but through the new medium of print each piece of recovered knowledge, each correction of data, each new discovery immediately became common knowledge of the community of learning. The converse also can be seen. The untimely death of Regiomontanus, before his *de triangulis* could go to press, delayed his trigonometry from becoming known for 50 years. And as Eisenstein observes, if Rheticus had failed to overcome Copernicus' reluctance to commit the *de revolutionibus* to print, the heliocentric theory could have remained hidden in Copernicus' study in Frombork for decades to come.

Nicolaus Copernicus was born in 1473 in Thorn (Polish Torun) on the Vistula. His father died early and he was brought up by an uncle. After his uncle became bishop of Varmia he appointed Copernicus canon at the cathedral at Frauenburg (Frombork). Copernicus first studied at the University of Cracow, then went to Italy, where he stayed (with interruptions) until 1506, studying the classics, medicine and law. After his return he published a Latin translation of an obscure Greek epistolographer, Theophylactos

Simocattes, which he dedicated to his uncle. As Edward Rosen put it, "But it was not only in this concern with classical antiquity, that Copernicus showed himself a man of the Renaissance. He also strove to achieve the many-sided accomplishments of that humanistic ideal, the universal man. He was competent in canon law; he practiced medicine; he wrote a tract on coinage; he served his cathedral chapter as an administrator and diplomatic representative; he painted his own picture; he made many of his own astronomical instruments; and he established the heliocentric system on a firm basis."[10]

Copernicus' interest in astronomy apparently began during his student days in Cracow. He was pursuing this subject in Bologna in 1496, the same year Radolt's edition of the epitome of the *Almagest* appeared in nearby Venice. In it Regiomontanus raised great doubts about Ptolemy's account of the motions of the moon. Copernicus later raised the same objections. In Bologna Copernicus studied astronomy under Domenico Novara, living in his professor's house and assisting him in his observations. In 1500 he made his own observations of a conjunction of the moon with Saturn and noted the results in a copy of Regiomontanus' Tables of Directions; the same year he observed a partial eclipse of the moon in Rome. In 1501 he went to Padua to study medicine and stayed there for two years, before obtaining a doctorate in canon law in 1503 at Ferrara. After his return to Poland he assumed his various administrative and political duties, at first with his uncle, the bishop of Varmia, whom he also served as personal physician. After his uncle's death he established his residence at Frombork in 1510 and performed his offices as canon and later chancellor of the cathedral-chapter.

He observed eclipses of the moon in 1509 and 1513, and when he was installed in Frombork he had his observatory built and constructed his own instruments. He devoted himself especially to the study of the motions of the planets and, as he said later in the *de revolutionibus*, became more and more disillusioned with the Ptolemaic system. It is not clear exactly when Copernicus formulated his heliocentric theory. The first written version of it was a handwritten treatise which he circulated unsigned among his friends. It was entitled *commentariolus*, the "little commentary." In it he presented his theory in general terms, but did not work it out mathematically; he promised to do so later in a "larger work." Following the example of Euclid's *elementa* he began the treatise with a series of axiomatic statements. That this first conceptual formulation of his heliocentric theory was directly inspired by Archimedes' paraphrase of Aristarchos' hypothesis (appendix, 324-325) emerges clearly if one puts Copernicus' statements side by side with the quotations from Aristarchus' lost book:

Aristarchus	Copernicus
The fixed stars and the sun remain motionless, the earth revolves in the circumference of a circle about the sun, which lies motionless in the middle of the orbit, and	All the orbs revolve around the sun as the midpoint and therefore the sun is the center of the universe while the firmament and the outermost heaven remain motionless. The ratio of
the sphere of the fixed stars, situated about the same center as the sun, is so great that the circle... in which the earth revolves, has such a proportion to the fixed stars as the center of the sphere bears to its surface.	the earth's distance from the sun to the height of the firmament is so much smaller than the ratio of the earth' radius to its distance from the sun that the distance of the earth to the sun is imperceptible in comparison with the height of the firmament.

The similarities between the statement ascribed to Aristarchus and the formulation by Copernicus, not only in content but also in the wording, are too striking to be coincidental. Both use the same, more figurative than mathematically correct, ratio between the radius of the earth orbit and the distance to the fixed stars to drive home the almost infinite nature of that dimension which accounts for the absence of any measurable parallactic displacement. (It was not until 1838 that a stellar parallax was actually measured.)

Copernicus spent the next twenty years fulfilling his promise made in the *commentariolus* to work out the mathematics of his hypothesis. In the meantime his reputation had reached Johann Schoener at the University of Nuremberg and, as mentioned earlier, on Schoener's suggestion Rheticus (an eminent mathematician in his own right) went to visit Copernicus in Frombork in 1539 with a gift of many of the recently printed mathematical and astronomical books. Rheticus was well received by Copernicus and stayed with him for almost two years. Copernicus was still not willing to have his work printed, but he gave Rheticus permission to publish a summary, the *narratio prima*, which Rheticus had printed in Nuremberg in 1540 in the form of a letter to Schoener. The reaction to it was so favorable that a second editon was issued in 1541 in Basel. The success of the *narratio prima* together with the urging of Rheticus and his other friends persuaded Copernicus to allow Rheticus to publish the *de revolutionibus planetarum*. The first edition appeared in 1543 from the press of Petreius in Nuremberg, and Copernicus received a copy shortly before his death the same year.

Copernicus' reasons for rejecting the Ptolemaic system were twofold. First there was the realization that the data did not accurately reflect or predict the motions of the planets. When Peurbach and Regiomontanus had reached that conclusion they had ascribed the errors to the inadequacies of the Arab translations and to the deterioration inherent in the scribal transmission of manuscripts. They had believed that a return to the Greek originals would solve the problems. They were right up to a point, but besides the errors introduced by translation and copying there were also errors in the original observations which had been multiplied by the passage of 1500 years, as well as incorrect estimates of the precession and other inaccuracies. Thus the data of the *Almagest* and the Alphonsine Tables based on it simply no longer reflected the actual positions of the planets.

Copernicus' main cause of dissatisfaction with the Ptolemaic astronomy, however, was the nature of the system itself. As a true
product of the classical heritage he was imbued with the Hellenic
conviction that *cosmos*, order and beauty, demanded a unified system of divine simplicity and perfection. It was the same quest for
unity that had led to the Presocratic philosphers' search for the one
common element that constituted all matter, Parmenides' concept
of one indivisible unmovable Being, Plato's idea of the supreme
good as the cause of all, and Aristotle's eternal universe of concentric spheres. The Hellenic quest for unity always was and still is at
the root of most Western science and philosophy. Einstein was
looking for the all-encompassing unified field theory to his dying
day and his successors still are. Copernicus rejected the Ptolemaic
system because it did not satisfy this need for unity and perfection.
In his own words in his prefatory letter to the pope:[11]

> ... They [the authors of the Ptolemaic system] have not been able to deter-
> mine even the most fundamental thing - that is: the shape of the universe - or
> to derive the certain symmetry of its parts from these things. What happens
> to them is as if someone were to put together from different places hands,
> feet, head and other limbs, all parts excellently painted, but unrelated to a
> single body and in no way fitting each other; the result would be a monster
> rather than a man.

Copernicus thought he had found the unifying principle of the
planetary system in the relationship between the distance of a
planet from the center of its orbit (the sun), and the time it takes
the planet to complete one orbit. The outermost-- Saturn--
requires 30 years, the next-- Jupiter-- 12, and Mars two. He
calculated the time of the inner planets, Venus and Mercury, as
respectively seven months and 80 days. The earth, having a one
year orbit and lying between Mars and Venus, fits this pattern of
the heliocentric system of Aristarchus and Copernicus' search for
inner harmony. Therefore it is surprising that he never mentioned
the name of Aristarchus in his book. Copernicus' strange silence
concerning the prime source of his idea has puzzled many
historians. We know that he was well aware of Aristarchus' author-

ship of the heliocentric theory. This is quite clear, not only from the comparison between Archimedes' quotation of Aristarchus and Copernicus' own words cited above but also from a passage in Copernicus' manuscript in which he referred to Aristarchus by name. But later he crossed out the three pages which contained this reference so that it never appeared in the printed version of the *de revolutionibus*. It seems unlikely that he suppressed Aristarchus' name out of vanity to present himself as the originator of the idea. On the contrary, he quotes most extant classical sources that testify to theories of a moving earth, from the Pythagoreans to Heraclides of Pontus, to Plutarch, in order to lend greater justification and authority to his own thesis. Much has been made of Copernicus' expression of agreement with Neo-Platonic and Neo-Pythagorean mysticism, which forbade initiates to reveal the esoteric secrets to the common crowd that would be unable to deal with the divine truths. These beliefs are also adduced as reason for his reluctance to commit his work to print. As Eisenstein notes, however, Copernicus had much more valid misgivings about the publication of his theory and the mention of Aristarchus' name. There is a passage in Plutarch which reads as follows:

> Only do not, my good fellow, enter an action against me in the style of Cleanthes, who thought it was the duty of the Greeks to indict Aristarchos of Samos on the charge of impiety for putting in motion the Hearth of the Universe, this being the effect of his attempt to save the phaenomena by supposing the heaven to remain at rest and the earth to revolve in an oblique circle, while it rotates , at the same time, about its own axis. (*Moralia* vii, *de facie lunae* 923A, trnsl. Harold Cherniss and Wm. C. Helmbold [Harvard 1957])

Since Aristarchus' theory appears to have been considered heretical by some, even in pagan antiquity, Copernicus might not have wanted to put ideas into the heads of his enemies at a time when the religious tensions were heating up, especially as he was vulnerable for several reasons. Copernicus had been admonished several times for an alleged affair with his housekeeper. He was suspected of being soft on Protestantism because of his sympathy with tolerant Erasmian views and for sheltering Rheticus, a heretic from Wittenberg, in his house for two years. And contrary to the opinion of some modern scholars, Copernicus seems to have been fully aware of the revolutionary consequences of his theory. This is indicated by the care with which he separated the technical data and charts from the underlying theory when he sent an almanac to Vienna in 1535, by his refusal to comply with a request for a copy of his findings which Cardinal Schoenberg requested from him in 1536, and of course most of all by his long hesitation before publication of the *de revolutionibus*. But the clearest indication is his apologetic dedication to the pope when he finally did consent to have it printed:

> I doubt not that intelligent and learned mathematicians will support me if they, as this science demands, are willing to reach a thorough rather than a superficial understanding and appreciation of the proofs of these matters that I am offering in this work. But that learned and unlearned alike may see that I am not trying to evade anyone's judgment, I preferred to dedicate these studies to your Holiness, rather than to anybody else, since even in this remotest corner of the earth in which I live, you are regarded as the most eminent because of the dignity of your office as well as your love of letters and science, so that by your authority and judgment you can easily restrain the slanderers from biting , although the proverb says that there is no remedy against a sycophant's tooth. It may happen, too, that foolish blabbermouths, even though they are ignorant of mathematics may claim the right to pronounce judgment on my work by reason of some passage of scripture basely twisted to suit their purpose. (*Kopernikus*, prefatory dedication, p.6,)

In the light of this dedication, it would appear that Copernicus' "Pythagorean" or "Neo-Platonist" qualms about divulging the secrets of philosophy to the uninitiated are simply a veiled anticipation of the expected attack by his enemies. He had also blunted the impact of his work by limiting himself to the traditional technical language of mathematicians and astronomers, a forbidding presentation to lay-persons, and by playing down any philosophical or religious implications. He followed the structure of the *Almagest* chapter by chapter recomputing the tables according to the heliocentric theory. In the process he followed Regiomontanus' improved technique of using sines instead of chords. He had corrected some mistakes, he had substituted some of his own observational values, but generally the work still relied on the ancient data and so it was not much more accurate than the *Almagest* in describing and predicting the positions of the planets. But his computational procedures presented a vast advance beyond the old methods and led to greatly increased accuracy once better observational data were obtained. Although the book was immediately condemned by Luther and Melanchthon in Protestant Wittenberg, it made little impact on the world at large, perhaps because of its restrictive technical nature. One of the reasons the book did not evoke any opposition by the Roman Church at the time was the fact that one of the editors, Osiander, against the wishes of Copernicus and Rheticus, had included a preamble in the printed edition calling the heliocentric theory a mathematical hypothesis to describe the motion of the planets, rather than a statement of fact. Thus for a period of time after its appearance the *de revolutionibus* was apparently read mostly by astronomers who, even if they disagreed with Copernicus' theory, appreciated and used his computational procedures. The real storm broke 70 years later when the full impact of the Copernican system on traditional beliefs was finally recognized.

In the Judeo-Christian-Aristotelian amalgam that had emerged from Thomas Aquinas and scholasticism, God had created the world and the earth at its center for man. The world was finite, enclosed by the rotating firmament-- the sphere of the fixed-star heaven. Between the immobile earth in the center and the crystalline outer sphere with its attached stars, and suspended from it, were the concentric spheres of the planets, including sun and moon, all rotating at different angles and speeds. The heavenly spheres were pure, eternal, motionless, divine. Below the innermost sphere, in the sublunar terrestrial world, matter was mixed, perishable and flawed. Man, although the ultimate object of creation, was sinful by nature, leading a transitory existence on earth with the sole purpose of being redeemed by faith and the grace of God, so that after death he might enter the divine world of the heavens. The Copernican theory overthrew this concept in its totality: heliocentricism had removed the earth and man from the center of creation; the sun had become one of the stars and the earth just another planet. This implied that planets and stars were no more divine than the earth. Another consequence of a moving earth was the fact, already noted by Aristarchus and now pointed out by Copernicus, that if there were no noticeable changes in the angles at which fixed stars were observed from different orbital positions of a moving earth, the distance to the fixed stars must be infinitely greater than ever imagined. The absence of parallaxes indicated a vastly expanded, possibly infinite universe. Furthermore the assumption of a crystalline heavenly sphere had been based on the observation that all the stars seemed to rotate in unison without ever changing their relative positions to each other; therefore something had to be holding them in place. But if the stars stood still and their rotation was an illusion caused by the earth's rotation, there was no longer any need to believe in a solid firmament. If the universe was unlimited, with stars stretching to infinity-- possibly with their own planets, like the sun -- innumerable worlds might exist, and the concept of a center of an infinite universe became nonsensical, as Cardinal Nicolas of Cusa had noted almost a hundred years earlier. So did the idea of a universe created solely for the benefit of man. This is what gave the Copernican theory an explosive potential far exceeding that of a mere astronomic hypothesis. It contained the seeds of a total revolution in the scientific, philosophical and religious view of the world.

The question has been posed repeatedly why the Copernican revolution came just when it did. Many causes have been named, and without a doubt most of them contributed something, but as Elisabeth Eisenstein and Edward Rosen showed so convincingly, many of the factors that have been cited had existed for a long time without producing similar results, while the one innovation -- the transition to print-- which can be exactly pinpointed in time, though usually mentioned, is not given the full weight it deserves. Rosen noted that Copernicus could not have accomplished his work 50 years earlier. Almost all the books which provided Copernicus with his conceptual tools came off the presses during his lifetime, most of them precisely during Copernicus' formative study years. In contrast to Peurbach and Regiomontanus, who had had to work from a single medieval translation of the *Almagest* and to travel from one manuscript source to another, Copernicus working alone in his study in Frombork, "in the remotest corner of the earth," as he described it, had a whole library of recent scholarly editions of ancient and contemporary sources right at his fingertips. His literary resources were immeasurably greater than those of any astronomer before him. They included, besides the aforementioned books, trigonometric tables, a Greek-Latin dictionary, and astronomic *calendaria*. If it has been said that Copernicus ushered in modern science, it might also be said that the age of print ushered in Copernicus and his work.

Notes

1. Introduction to Galilei's *Dialogue Concerning the Two Chief World Systems*, ed. & transl. by Stillman Drake, (Berkeley 1967), XVII

2. Elisabeth Eisenstein, *The Printing Press as an Agent of Change*, 470-477 and *passim*

3. Charles Singer, *A Short History of Scientific Ideas* (Oxford 1959), 187

4. Eisenstein II, 571; Walter Pagel and P. M. Rattansi, "Vesalius and Paracelsus", *Medical History* 8 (1964), 324

5. C.B. Schmitt, *Studies in Renaissance Philosophy and Science* (Cambridge, Mass. 1983), 504

6. William Harvey, *Exercitatio anatomica de motu cordis and sanguinis in animalibus* (Frankfurt 1628), chpt. 9, 44; Gweneth Whitteridge translation, 80

7. *De motu*, chpt. 7, 38-39; Whitteridge transl., 68

8. Charles Singer *The Discovery of the Circulation of the Blood* (London 1956), 42

9. P. O. Kristeller, *The Mediaeval Aspects of Renaissance Thought* (New York 1961), 43

10. Edward Rosen, *Three Copernican Treatises* (3d ed., New York 1971), 3

11. F.& C. Zeller (edd), *Nikolaus Kopernicus* (Munich 1949), 9

13

From Copernicus to Newton

Copernicus' years as student fell into the last decade of the 15th century, when the Renaissance was essentially still confined to Italy and when the first printed editions of the classical authors were rolling off the printing presses. His mature years spanned the first half of the 16th century, when the humanistic revival swept over the rest of western Europe, fed by the scholarly presses of the Manuzios, the Étiennes and others in Italy, France and the southern German provinces. Copernicus' *De revolutionibus* appeared in 1543, the same year as Vesalius' *De fabrica corporis humani*. By that time, for all practical purposes, most of the extant classical works had been published in print. The Reformation had gained its momentum. Martin Luther had broken with the Catholic Church in 1517, the Church of England had seceded from Rome in 1534, and in 1536 Calvin had published his Protestant manifesto. During Copernicus' lifespan printing had transformed the Western world. Humanistic scholars had completed the revival and absorption of ancient learning and were well on their way, striking out on their own in many fields. Copernicus, who died in 1543, appears to personify the transformation of intellectual life in the early 16th century.

Although the next generation of astronomers was reluctant to adopt Copernicus' heliocentric system it recognized the superiority of his mathematical procedures and calculations. Thus Copernicus' book became an indispensible tool for astronomers whether they accepted his theory or not. During the second half of the 16th century a most disparate cast of characters, scattered from Copenhagen to Florence, contributed willingly or unwillingly to the full development and confirmation of the Copernican theory. What they had in common was their humanistic upbringing and convictions and their unfaltering devotion to astronomy and observation.

In 1551 Erasmus Reinhold, sponsored by the Duke of Prussia, developed the "Prutenic (Prussian) Tables", based on Copernicus' methods of calculation and data but without acknowledgement of his theory. These were the first complete astronomic tables since the "Alphonsine Tables" of the thirteenth century and considerably more accurate. But since these tables, like the Alphonsine tables and Copernicus' calculations, were essentially still based on the ancient Ptolemaic data, they still rested on some flawed observations and errors magnified by the passage of time. Rheticus, Copernicus' devoted assistant, spent the rest of his life computing the most comprehensive trigonometric tables so far devised, calculating sines, tangents and secants to 15 digits at 10 second intervals. But one of the most important pioneers of empirical astronomy was Tycho Brahe, whose life appropriately spanned the second half of the 16th century as Copernicus' had spanned the first. He provided what was needed most: new and more accurate data.[1]

Tycho Brahe

Tycho Brahe was born in 1546 in the Danish province of Scania, the son of a privy councilor of the Danish King, Frederick II, and governor of the castle of Helsingborg opposite Elsinor, which guarded the entrance to the Baltic. Denmark was at the height of its power and prosperity. The Danish King ruled also over Norway and the later German provinces of Schleswig, Holstein, and the free city of Hamburg, as well as some provinces now part of Sweden-- among them Scania. Much of the wealth of the crown came from the recent confiscation of the lands and other possessions of the Catholic Church after Denmark had turned Protestant. Most of the power rested with the aristocratic clans, such as the Brahe, the Gyldenstierne and Rosenkrantz families of Shakespearean notoriety, and others who constituted the privy Council (Rigsraad).

Like Copernicus, Tycho was brought up by a politically influential uncle and educated in the humanistic fashion. In his time there was no longer any need to travel to Italy in order to study the classics. Tycho entered the University of Copenhagen at the age of 13, not an unusual age at that time. Students were allowed to speak only Latin or Greek during class and meal times. Later, all through his life he would compose Latin poems to express his feelings about important events. Again like Copernicus, he was destined to study law, but soon became interested in astronomy. His professors were unable to help him in this field and suggested that he read the *Almagest* and the *Ephemerides* of Stadius, which were based on the Prutenic Tables. Strictly supervised by his tutor he was continually short of money and time, but managed to buy the books and to study them at night. He remained in Copenhagen from 1559 to 1562 and then went on to Leipzig.

There he continued his studies of law and philosophy under Camerarius, the prominent humanist and editor of Ptolemy's *Tetrabiblios* and the *Almagest*. He began his studies of mathematics, learned the use of astronomic tables, and gradually acquired more books and instruments for observation. Soon Tycho discovered that neither the Alphonsine nor the Prutenic Tables agreed with his own observations. In 1565 his uncle died and left him his fortune. Tycho was now financially independent and able to devote himself fully to his studies of mathematics and astronomy. In 1569 he went to Augsburg, where he became acquainted with Hieronymus Wolf, a friend of Camerarius and an outstanding humanist and mathematician. As mentioned earlier, Wolf and Camerarius had been pupils of Melanchthon at Wittenberg. Both had also been students of the French humanistic school of Turnebus and had an encyclopedic knowledge of ancient literature and science. Both headed Protestant schools and were thus still under the towering influence of Melanchthon.

Tycho was a great admirer of Copernicus and collected Copernicana all his life. He greatly valued an instrument once owned by Copernicus that he had received as a gift. He treasured Copernicus' writings and annotated his own copies. He acquired Copernicus' self-portait and published it with his own in his main work.[2] In his observations he used all of Copernicus' methods, but he never could bring himself to accept his theory. It may have been the condemnation of the heliocentric system by Luther and Melanchthon and the influence of Melanchthon's protegés, Camerarius and Wolf, that prevented him.

Wolf helped Tycho to have his own instruments made in Augsburg. During his stay there from 1569 to 1571 Tycho designed and commissioned instruments of unprecedented size and accuracy: a 5 foot globe, a quadrant of 19 foot radius, and an equally large sextant. These instruments were constructed by the foremost craftsmen in the arts of jewelry and instrument-making, and were graduated so finely that angles could be read to an accuracy of 10 seconds. Tycho used them for his planetary observations and established his reputation through his correspondence with most of the prominent astronomers of Europe. In 1571 he was called home because of the death of his father and inherited the lordship of his home territory. His family persuaded him to stay and helped him to establish a chemical laboratory, a glass-making plant, a papermill and a small observatory where he installed his Augsburg instruments.

On the night of November 11, 1572 he suddenly discovered an extremely bright star in the constellation of Cassiopeia that had never been there before. The phenomenon was noticed throughout Europe and excited astronomers and laymen alike. Some thought it a comet although it had no tail. Beza, the friend of Calvin, declared it to be the Star of Bethlehem announcing the second coming. Tycho immediately concentrated on exact observation. Since the new object had no parallax and always occupied the same position to the fixed stars, he came to the conclusion that it must be a star. He published his findings in his first printed publication *De nova stella* in 1573. The nova gradually became dimmer and after 18 months disappeared altogether. This phenomenon dealt a severe blow to the traditional Aristotelian belief in the divine unchangeable nature of the fixed-star heaven. It also stimulated the general interest in astronomy and enhanced Tycho Brahe's fame. The king of Denmark offered Tycho the small island of Hveen as a personal fief and as location for an observatory for which the crown would bear most of the cost. Later a canonship and additional fiefs were added.

On Hveen Tycho Brahe built an elaborate castle in Renaissance style, which, as a true humanist, he called Uraniborg after the Muse of Astronomy. An inscription over the entrance read: "Neither power nor riches, the rule of the arts alone is lasting (*Nec fasces nec opes, solum artis sceptra perennant*) ." But more importantly, adjoining his castle he established the most elaborate and efficient observatory yet conceived, with steel-constructed rotating instruments of accuracy not to be surpassed until the advent of telescopic observation. Tycho was the first to plot the positions of the planets at regular intervals. The accumulation of exact data was the greatest service Tycho performed for astronomy. His catalogue of 800 stars was the first such catalogue since Ptolemy's and remained the standard reference work for a hundred years. The mean error in comparison with modern works was about one minute of arc.

After consulting with Plantin, the Belgian publisher, he established his own printshop at Hveen. The first things he published were his Latin poems and woodcuts of all his instruments. Then followed his own astronomic works. He had planned to publish the results of his lifework in several volumes. The first part he never finished because he kept revising it and it was finally edited and published by Kepler after Tycho's death in Prague in 1602. The second part, *De mundi aetherii recentioribus phaenomenis*, Tycho printed in 1588. It contained his observations of the nova of 1572 and the comet of 1577, his findings on refraction of the light by the atmosphere, and his own cosmology.

In 1588 Tycho's patron and friend, King Frederick, died. This was a catastrophe for Tycho, for his arrogant and violent temper, which among other things had caused him the loss of his nose in a duel, had made him many enemies. He had antagonized the nobles by his marriage to a peasant woman and he had violated the rights of his peasant tenants. He had greatly neglected his duties as lord of his fief and was remiss in the collection of taxes and the maintenance of public assets for which he was responsible. One of his duties for which he received a stipend was the maintenance of a lighthouse to guide ships through the straits between Elsinor and Helsingborg, but there were continual complaints by sailors and fishermen that the light was out. After the death of Tycho's royal protector all these complaints came to a head. He was successively deprived of all his fiefs and revenues except Hveen, which he had been given for life, but without the income of the lost estates he was no longer able to maintain his complex. In 1597 he felt forced to leave and to seek a new sponsor.

In 1598 he printed a volume entitled *Astronomiae instauratae mechanica* (The Instruments of Awakened Astronomy), graced with his and Copernicus' portraits as mentioned above. He dedicated it to the German Emperor Rudolph II. In it he described all his instruments and their use, with exact illustrations, a brief outline of his findings and a summary of his accomplishments. Tycho sent copies to many provincial rulers, but his greatest hope was the Emperor Rudolph. And indeed his book, his reputation, and the recommendations of his friends were successful in gaining him an invitation to the imperial court in Prague in 1599.

Rudolph II had always been interested in learning and scholars. He was trying to make the University of Prague, the oldest German university, the intellectual center of Europe and thus was glad to enlist the services of the greatest living astronomer. Rudolph offered Tycho a generous salary, the choice of any of three castles near Prague and all the support he might require. Tycho, of course, gladly accepted. He chose the castle of Benatzky, situated on a hill and offering a wide unobstructed horizon. He immediately sent for his family and his instruments in Hveen and began to remodel the castle from top to bottom. He also felt the need for a truly competent collaborator in addition to his previous assistants, whom he had also summoned to Prague. He had been greatly impressed with the work of Johannes Kepler, whose book, modestly entitled *Forerunner of Cosmological Inquiries containing the Mystery of the Universe (Prodromus dissertationum cosmographicarum continens mysterium cosmographicum)*, had appeared in 1596, when Kepler was only 25 years old. For Kepler Tycho's invitation came just in time.

Johannes Kepler

Kepler was born in 1571 in a small town south of Stuttgart. In school he acquired an extraordinary knowledge of Latin, and he entered the University of Tübingen in 1589. He studied mainly theology and philosophy, but probably through the influence of the astronomer, Michael Maestlin, he became not only interested in mathematics and astronomy, but also a convinced Copernican. Because of this flaw in his orthodoxy he was unable upon his graduation to obtain a position with the Lutheran Church in his home state of Swabia and had to accept an appointment as professor of ethics and mathematics at the Gymnasium in Graz, the capital of the Austrian province of Styria. As official *mathematicus* he was expected to make astrological forecasts and he complied by composing a *Calendarium et Prognosticum* for 1595, in which he prophesied unrest among the peasants and flight of the Austrians before the attacking Turks. When both predictions were fulfilled he gained a considerable reputation and in 1597 he married a young noblewoman in Graz. The same year he published the *Mysterium Cosmographicum* which came to the attention of Tycho Brahe. The book is totally inspired, if not possessed by the spirit of humanism, classical philosophy and Christian piety. To defend his belief in a purposeful Copernican world order of ideal mathematical perfection, Kepler refers to all the Greek sages from Thales and Pythagoras on. He quotes Plato and Aristotle, King David and St. Paul. He chases the Platonic phantasy that the relationship of the celestial spheres is determined by the ratios of the spheres circumscribed around the five "perfect" polygons. Still, the work showed so much original mathematical genius that it impressed not only Galileo, who at that time was a closet Copernican, but also Tycho, who was emphatically opposed to the heliocentric theory.

For Kepler Tycho's invitation was a god-send, as he was about to be expelled from Austria and to lose all of his possessions because of his Protestant views. Kepler arrived in Prague in January of 1600. The ensuing short and stormy cooperation of Tycho and Kepler was one of the most fortunate events in the history of astronomy. In spite of the violent clashes of their diametrically opposed personalities each learned the greatest respect for the other's talents and achievements. Tycho's years of painstaking observations and collection of exact data had provided a totally new basis for astronomy. Kepler completed Tycho's work and used the data to open up unprecedented new perspectives. While still a student Tycho had determined that the Alphonsine Tables based on Ptolemy's *Almagest* were about a month out of phase and that the Prutenic Tables based on Copernicus' *De revolutionibus*, which still depended on ancient data, were several days in error. It was of the utmost importance to present to the world Tycho's own data, gathered at regular intervals with vastly improved instruments, in the form of a new set of astronomic tables. This was the project Tycho undertook with Kepler. The tables were to be called the Rudolphine Tables in honor of their patron.

Tycho died in the following year, 1601, and Kepler was appointed in his place as "Her Holy Majesty's Mathematicus." It remained for Kepler to complete the Rudolphine Tables. He published them in 1627, and eventually completed, edited and published the other incomplete or unpublished works of Tycho Brahe.

As mentioned earlier, Tycho had held Copernicus in great admiration; he had adopted his methods, but he had been unable to reconcile himself to a moving earth. He cited the timeworn argument, already proposed by Aristotle, that falling bodies would not be able to hit a point vertically below them if the earth were in rapid motion. He also failed to find any parallax to the fixed stars, despite the sensitivity of his new instruments. This seemed explainable by the large distance of the stars from a motionless earth, but with the earth shifting its location in a large orbit around the sun, a yet infinitely longer distance would be required to make the parallax disappear, much larger than anyone brought up in the tradition of a finite bounded universe could accept. But perhaps even more important to Tycho may have been the religious argument of the Lutherans of Melanchthon's Wittenberg school with whom he had had such a close relationship during his study years. Therefore, although he recognized the apparent validity of Copernicus' arguments against the Ptolemaic system and even some adverse evidence in his own observations, he tried to overcome the contradictions by creating his own planetary model. In the "Tychonic system", which was a compromise between the Ptolemaic and the Copernican systems, the earth remained motionless in the center with the fixed-star-heaven rotating around it. The sun and the moon still circled the earth, but the other planets were orbiting around the sun while it traveled in its earth-orbit. Tycho may also have been driven by the ambition to rank with the great cosmologists of the world. The wall of his circular observatory in Uraniborg bore the pictures of the legendary Timocharis, of Hipparchus, Ptolemy, Albattani, King Alphonse, Copernicus and Tycho himself. Tycho's geocentric and anthropocentric feelings were apparently basic to Christianity and had many adherents. His system seemed to reconcile the Copernican scheme with the Scriptures. Mathematically the Ptolemaic, the Copernican and the Tychonic models were roughly equivalent. Since all measurements and calculations were essentially based on triangulation it made little difference whether angular differences were measured from A to B or from B to A, or on which angle within the same triangle the trigonometric functions were based. But because Tycho's measurements were so much more accurate than those of his predecessors their descriptive and predictive validity was much greater. Tycho's other great service to astronomy was that he recognized Kepler's genius and left his largely still unpublished data in the hands of the one man whose vision and perseverance would discover their true significance

It is ironic that Tycho's efforts to defend the traditional system contributed to its demise. When he proved that the nova of 1572 was a star he dealt a severe blow to the Aristotelian belief in the divine eternally unchanging nature of the "heavens" beyond the moon. Similarly, his finding that the erratic comets were also following a translunar path and were not atmospheric phenomena, as had been believed, undermined traditional authority. Tycho's own system at first had the effect of delaying the acceptance of the Copernican theory by offering an alternative to the traditionalists, but in the long run it prepared the way for it. If the planets rotated around the sun, the earth was no longer the absolute center of the universe. He also exploded the assumption of the nested crystalline spheres to which all celestial bodies were attached, since in his model the orbit of Mars intersected the orbit of the sun. Incidentally, the ascription of the Platonic imagery of solid spheres by some secondary sources and a succession of historians of science to Aristotle, Ptolemy and Copernicus has no basis in fact and is contrary to their *ipsissima verba*, as the late Edward Rosen has so clearly demonstrated.[3] Tycho's data made the proof of the Copernican system possible, and when Kepler had achieved an honored position at the court in Prague he wrote in a letter in 1604: ..."the only honor I recognize as such is that bestowed by providence, which has allowed me to make use of Tycho's observations."[4]

Tycho provides a vivid example of the lack of justification for the artificial dichotomy that has been set up between the "antiquarianism" of the humanists and the empiricism of the scientists, who have turned from the "books of men" to the "book of nature." Tycho's main successes were achieved through his empirical methods of observation and his practical ingenuity in the design of his instruments, but it was his humanistic education and philosophy, "the books of men," especially Aristotle and Ptolemy, that had inspired and prepared him for his undertakings.

Before considering the major accomplishments of Kepler and Galileo during the 17th century, it may be well to review some other innovations that had been made during the 16th century which helped to advance mathematics and astronomy. In 1591 Francois Viète introduced algebraic notation. His contemporary Simon Stevin pioneered the study of falling bodies and the conditions of mechanical and hydrostatic equilibrium, and initiated the use of decimal fractions. John Napier developed the principle of logarithms in 1594 and began his computation of the logarithmic tables. Lens-grinding had become a specialized craft and spectacles were in general use from the beginning of the 16th century, extending the literate life of individuals by decades. Practical experience was gained with refraction and optics, which benefited astronomers. By the end of the century telescopes had made their appearance in Holland, probably for nautical use. Galileo, who had never seen one but had heard of them, constructed his own.

As mentioned above, the Copernican system had not found many adherents, but in 1576 Thomas Digges published a paraphrase of the *de revolutionibus*, book 1, in English, with a copy of Copernicus' simplified diagram of the concentric orbits of the planets around the sun. But he had made an important modification of his own: he had moved the fixed stars outwards beyond the outermost of Copernicus' circles and scattered them out to infinity. This was a logical consequence of the assumption that the fixed stars were standing still while the earth was moving. The stars no longer needed a sphere to hold them in place and to maintain their mutual relationship as had been necessary while they were visualized in eternal revolution. The concept of an infinite universe was in keeping with another classical current of thought which, after repeated rejection in ancient and medieval times, had resurfaced in the 16th century.

In 1417 the humanist Poggio Bracciolini had found a manuscript of Lucretius *On the Nature of Things* (*De rerum natura*) which was based on Epicurus' philosophy and Democritus' atomic theory. According to Lucretius, innumerable worlds in an infinite universe were continually being formed and dissolved by the whirling atoms without any divine intervention. Nicolas of Cusa had recognized, what Digges had not 125 years later, that an infinite universe cannot have any center. In 1564, the French scholar Dionysus Lambinus published the first printed edition of Lucretius. It must have been quite popular, as two more editions followed in quick succession. It remained for Giordano Bruno to combine Democritus' and Lucretius' atomic theories with the Copernican system.

Giordano Bruno (1547-1600), born near Naples, a former monk, made his living as a wandering teacher. He traveled from one university to another and wound up in England in 1584, where he published three booklets containing the philosophy he had developed. He had probably become acquainted with Digges' ideas and he also drew on Nicolas of Cusa. Bruno's world-view was a synthesis of Copernicanism, Lucretius' atomism and Neo-Platonism. The universe was infinite. The earth revolved around the sun. The sun was just another star and also moving, for nothing was ever at rest. Neither the sun nor the earth was in the center, since there was no center in an unlimited universe populated by many stars with their planetary systems and probably many inhabited planets. The earth and the sun were just infinitesimal specks in a universe infinite in time and space and permeated by an all-embracing world-soul. In 1592 Bruno was incarcerated by the Inquisition and burned as a heretic in 1600. The violent reaction of the Church against Bruno may seem puzzling at first, since there had been no previous condemnation of Nicolas of Cusa or of Copernicus. There might have been several reasons for the Church's changed attitude. Nicolas and Copernicus were both churchmen in good standing who never deviated from their profession of orthodox theology. The Renaissance popes usually had been sympathetic and tolerant towards scholarly activities. Even in Copernicus' time the Church still felt secure and confident that an accommodation with the Reformation could be reached; but in the second half of the 16th century the struggle between the Counter-Reformation and Protestantism had been joined in earnest.

It was at this critical juncture that Bruno carried the meaning of Copernicanism beyond astronomy into religion by marrying it to the antireligious atomic cosmology of Lucretius; every church doctrine was violated. In Bruno's pamphlet the personal biblical God and Trinity were replaced by a world-soul diffused to an infinite universe. Mankind, for whose benefit the world had supposedly been created, was lost on one of an infinite number of planets deprived of its uniqueness and importance. In this world without center filling infinity there was no longer room for a heaven or a hell. In the eyes of the Church the association with the ideas of Lucretius had dealt the Copernican system the death-blow. Kepler had no doubt about these reasons for Bruno's condemnation.[5]

Galileo Galilei

Galileo was born in Pisa in 1564. At age 17 he attended the University of Pisa to study medicine. He became interested in mathematics and so proficient in that field that he was appointed professor of mathematics at Padua in 1592. While he was teaching traditional Aristotelian physics, he was systematically testing them. He experimented with falling bodies, inclined planes and the pendulum. He used his pulse to time physical events, and a pendulum to measure increments as small as a ninth of a second. Galileo's great contribution to science was his realization that physical processes can be measured, quantitatively determined and experimentally verified. He studied uniform and accelerated velocities and was convinced that falling bodies fall with equal velocity regardless of weight, contrary to Aristotle's teaching.

In 1597 Galileo's reputation must have been well established as he was one of the authorities to whom Kepler sent a copy of his first major work, the *Mysterium Cosmographicum*. Galileo answered "within hours" as he said, on August 4, 1597, and he indicated in a veiled fashion that he shared Kepler's view of the validity of the Copernican theory, but that he was reluctant to propound it publicly.[6] Perhaps he was discouraged by the overwhelming majority of opponents and by a feeling of not having adequate proof or else the arrest of Bruno had told him something. Kepler in a reply of October 13, 1597 hoped for Galileo's support.[7]

Kepler spent the eight years after Tycho's death in futile attempts to work out "the true form of heavenly motion." He spent untold hours in tedious drudgery, not only in computing the positions of the planets from Tycho's tables, but also trying to fit theory after theory into the observed and computed data. All during this time he was under constant pressure from his royal patron, who wanted his *mathematicus* to provide solid results in the form of astrological predictions and advice instead of spending his time on valueless impractical speculations. Kepler was also in permanent financial distress because his salary kept being in arrears, as the imperial treasury was chronically broke.

Kepler himself never lost faith in astrology, since he was convinced, as Tycho had been, that in the grand cosmic harmony of the universe all phenomena including human fate were linked -- although he never believed that specific incidents in individual human lives were predictable. He once called astrology the foolish little daughter of the respectable reasonable mother astronomy.[8] As official court astrologer he rather functioned as psychological adviser to Rudolph. In spite of all the distractions he managed to write treatises on optics (1604), an eclipse of the sun (1605), and a new star (1606).

Finally in 1609 his most important work, *The New Astronomy or the Motion of Mars* (*Astronomia nova seu physica coelestis* or *De motu stellae Martis*) was published in Prague. It was dedicated to Rudolph and had been completed several years earlier, but had been delayed because the imperial printshop had been out of funds. In his long study of Mars Kepler had reached the conclusion that none of the existing systems from Ptolemy's to Copernicus' to Tycho's nor his own fruitless experimentations with compounded circles could be reconciled with Tycho's or his own observations. The very pattern of the discrepancies led him to his revolutionary solution that the planetary orbits were not circles at all, but, as he stated in what was to become Kepler's First Law of Planetary Motion, ellipses with the center of the sun constituting one of the two *foci*. His second and just as unprecedented discovery was that the speed of the planets in their course was not uniform. Since he considered the sun as the moving force (*anima motrix*) in the motion of the planets, he assumed that the sun's effect on the planets would be strongest at the closest approach to the sun (perihelion) and weakest at the greatest distance from the sun (aphelion). This was confirmed by his observations. Expressed in arithmetical terms, the speed of a planet varies in inverse proportion to its distance from the sun. This was a close approximation but not quite exact. He later expressed the relationship in geometric terms that he considered equivalent, but which were slightly different and fully exact: the orbital speed of a planet varies in such a way that a line from the planet to the sun sweeps through equal areas of its orbital ellipse in equal intervals of time. This is Kepler's Second Law. For the first time the true motions of the planets had been accurately defined.

Ever since antiquity it had been an article of faith that in the perfect divine heavens the celestial bodies revolved in perfect eternal circles. Since the circle was considered the perfect geometric form, no other path was conceivable. Nor was it conceivable that in a perfectly ordered universe-- a cosmos-- in which months, seasons and years followed each other with unchanging regularity, the speed of the heavenly bodies could ever vary. It is almost impossible today to realize the magnitude of the intellectual and spiritual upheaval wrought by Copernicus and Kepler. Yet it was the same classical conviction of the perfection of the universe which had inspired Plato and Aristotle that guided the investigations of Copernicus and Kepler.

Kepler's mathematical reasoning, however, just as Copernicus' earlier disquisitions, would probably not have penetrated beyond the small circle of mathematical astronomers if within a year of Kepler's publication of the *New Astronomy* Galileo's book, *The Messenger from the Stars* (*Siderius Nuncius*), had not appeared in 1610. This messenger was the telescope. Galileo triumphantly introduced the *Messenger* in these words:

Great are the findings which I offer in this small treatise ...Great...because of its unheard of novelty and especially because of the instrument by whose benefit these phenomena presented themselves to me.

It is something great to be able to add to the multitude of fixed stars which men to this day have been able to see with their natural faculty, countless others never seen before which exceed the number of the known ones more than tenfold.

It is something most beautiful to see the moon so that anyone may know with the certainty of his own eyesight that the moon is by no means covered by a smooth polished surface, but is rough and uneven, and like the face of the earth itself, full everywhere of enormous swellings, depressions and irregularities of all kinds.

What can be of greater importance than to put an end to the debates about the Milky Way and to reveal its true nature as a mass of stars? It will be a marvelous pleasure to show to any of the astronomers who called its substance a kind of a fog, how different it is from what has been believed until now.

But what surpasses all these wonders... is our discovery that four planets never seen before, are circling a certain one of the known stars [Jupiter] just as Mercury and Venus travel in their orbits around the sun. All this I have discovered and observed within a few days after I had first through divine grace devised my looking glass...

In addition to mapping the lunar landscape, describing the four moons of Jupiter, and locating more than five hundred new stars with less than two degrees of error, Galileo discovered that the fixed stars seen through the telescope, instead of appearing larger, were smaller. He ascribed this phenomenon correctly to the diffusion of light by the atmosphere; the telescope screened out the corona. This dispelled another of Tycho Brahe's arguments. Tycho had reasoned that if the stars were so far away that there was no parallax from even widely distant points in earth orbit, each star would have to be larger than our whole planetary system, in order to be visible at its apparent size. Galileo showed that the stars are smaller than they appear and thus not as large as Tycho made them out to be. Jupiter, circled by his own planets, seemed a perfect model for the solar system. Galileo now seemed to be confident that he had sufficient evidence for the Copernican system to convince everyone and for the first time declared in public his adherence to the heliocentric theory. He dedicated the *Messenger from the Stars* to his patron, the Grand Duke of Tuscany and named the moons of Jupiter in his honor the "Medicean Stars." The impact of Galileo's book was infinitely greater than that of Copernicus' or Kepler's writings, because it was based not on esoteric mathematics and astronomic tables but on reasoning everyone could understand and on observations that any owner of a telescope could verify. As a matter of fact Galileo's work, and even more so his subsequent trial, made telescopes fashionable and awakened interest in astronomy.

Galileo had sent one copy to the Emperor Rudolph and another through a courier to the Tuscan ambassador in Prague for delivery to Kepler, with a request for Kepler's comments. The ambassador conveyed his commission to Kepler on April 13, 1610, and the courier returned to Florence on April 19 with Kepler's reply. In his letter Kepler enthusiastically accepted and supported Galileo's findings. He pointed out that they confirmed his own views, which he had published at various times, and he was unstinting in his praise of Galileo's conclusions. Since the emperor and others were also asking for Kepler's opinion he decided to have his letter to Galileo of April 19 printed and published. He entitled the little booklet *Discussion with the Star-Messenger* (*Dissertatio cum Sidereo Nuncio*).

The official reception of the *Messenger* was totally negative; the members of the philosophy faculty at Padua refused to accept any of Galileo's findings. When he tried to induce them to see for themselves they refused to look through the telescope, stating that the instrument was a source of illusions. The prominent astronomer Magini at Bologna assembled a group of professors for a demonstration by Galileo. After looking through the telescope, they said that they had seen nothing of Galileo's claims. Magini wrote letters declaring that Galileo's discoveries were either fraud or self-deception. Galileo in dispair wrote to Kepler, "you are my only supporter." Kepler, who had bad eye-sight and lacked a good telescope, did not see the moons of Jupiter until September, when a visitor to the court lent him a more powerful instrument. At last they were seen also by other observers in Germany and Italy.

In December Galileo discovered that Venus had different phases like the moon. This confirmed a prediction by Copernicus that Venus, if it were indeed in solar orbit, would have a full range of phases, while if it were in earth orbit it would never present more than a narrow crescent to a viewer on earth. This had not been verifiable with the naked eye. Galileo considered this discovery further proof that the planets were dark like the earth and received their light from the sun, so that there was no fundamental difference between the earth and the other planets. He felt now sufficient confidence that he would be able to convince the papal hierarchy, and he went to Rome in 1611 to appear before the prelates of the Roman college. He was well received, he lectured and held discussions in the assembly. He did receive recognition for his observations but not for his theories. The Jesuit order had strict instructions to hold fast to the traditional system. Although his observed facts, such as the moons of Jupiter or the phases of Venus, were no longer disputed, they were not considered proof of the motion of the earth and the heliocentric system-- which strictly speaking they were not.

Telescopes had become popular and many new discoveries were being made. Galileo became involved with a Jesuit astronomer in disputes about priority of his discovery of the sunspots and later about their interpretation-- whether they were actually spots on the sun or smaller bodies obscuring the sun. Galileo attacked the whole traditional system and made the Jesuits his bitter enemies. The stream of new discoveries and the debates incited the imagination of the public. There was widespread speculation about the existence of other "worlds" such as Jupiter, and life on other planets. Kepler wrote in his *Discussion with the Star-messenger* that circular outlines (craters) on the moon might be walled cities. To the Church hierarchy it seemed that Bruno's ghost had been raised again and Galileo was denounced as heretic. In order to defend himself Galileo in 1615 in an open *Letter to the Grand Duchess Christina* tried to show that the Copernican system could be reconciled with the Bible: "... it is very obvious that it was necessary to attribute motion to the sun and rest to the earth, in order not to confound the shallow understanding of the common people and make them obstinate about believing the articles of faith, that this was wisely done in the divine Scriptures." (Stillman Drake pointed out the ironic fact that the Church in its encyclical *Humani Generis* of August 12, 1950, used the same argument of the need in the first 11 books of the Bible for the "naive, symbolic way of talking well suited to the understanding of primitive people.")

In 1516 Galileo went again to Rome in the hope of convincing the clerical authorities, and to clear himself of the accusation of heresy, but this time he found no disposition for scientific discussions. For the authorities the issue was now the prerogative of the Church in matters of theology, and to put an end to public discussions of doctrines of faith by priests and laymen. The verdict of the court was that the thesis that the sun is the center of the world and entirely unmoved while the earth was in motion was foolish, philosophically absurd, and formally heretic. Galileo was ordered to abandon these opinions and to abstain from teaching or defending or even discussing them. The Congregation of the Index ordered Copernicus' *de revolutionibus* suspended until it was "corrected" to present his theory not as a truth but as a mathematical hypothesis. Thus Osiander's wisdom in inserting his unauthorized preamble to the same effect in the first edition of the *de revolutionibus* was confirmed 75 years after its first publication and Copernicus' death.

These events show the enormous part played by printing and the independent printers in the survival and communication of ideas. A new, third, edition of Copernicus' book was printed in the following year (1617). The Protestant printers followed the *Index* to determine which books would be in demand. Thus the printing press had made attempts at censorship and thought control counter-productive.

While Galileo suffered the intolerance of the Catholics Kepler was persecuted by the Lutherans, and in addition suffered a painful blow in the death of his wife. The unrest preceding the Thirty Years War had reached Prague. When emperor Rudolph, who had more and more withdrawn from politics, could not even pay his soldiers, riots broke out in the city, and Kepler wanted desperately to return to his native Tübingen. Although the Duke of Wurttemberg was favorably disposed towards him the Lutheran theologians blocked his appointment because of his liberal views and accused him of being a secret Calvinist. Rudolph died in 1612 after being forced to abdicate by his brother Matthias. Although Matthias reappointed him court-mathematician Kepler found conditions in Prague unbearable. Eventually he obtained a teaching position in

Linz, in Austria, similar to the one he had held in Graz. But the influence of the Protestant Consistory in Wurttemberg reached even that far, and he found himself excluded from communion. With his mystical devotion to religion he suffered greatly under this exclusion. He nevertheless stayed in Linz from 1612 to 1626 because he had no other place to go. During all this time he continued his endless computations on the Rudolphine Tables and the related presentation of the Copernican system based on eliptic orbits of the planets. Finally he was able to publish his *Epitome Astronomiae Copernicanae*, the first coherent presentation of the revised Copernican system without all the complications of epicycles and deferents which Copernicus had inherited from Ptolemy. While working on the *Epitome* he received word that Copernicus' book had been banned in 1619 and that the first part of his *Epitome* had also been put on the *Index*. Kepler was now very much afraid that the censorship would be extended to Austria and that he would not be able to have any more books published.

In the same year Kepler published his *World-Harmony* (*Harmonice Mundi*), an exercise in unbridled mysticism in which he tried to relate every phenomenon in the world to every other one in a universal grand design. Yet it contained again a most ingenious mathematical insight that has become known as Kepler's Third Law of Planetary Motion. It states that the squares of the orbital time periods of the planets are proportional to the cubes of their mean distances from the sun. For Kepler this was the culmination of his lifelong quest: the simple mathematical harmony that revealed the creator's design of the universe. His first two laws had shown the principles underlying the motion of each planet, but the third law was the unifying principle of the world-system.

While Kepler was thus occupied from 1616 to 1620 his mother in a small town in Wurttemberg had been accused of witchcraft by a neighbor, and the proceedings against her had been dragging on for three years. Kepler had written several petitions on her behalf to the Duke of Wurttemberg, to no avail. When she fell victim to several assaults on her person, he went back and used his meager resources to hire lawyers for her defense. Despite his efforts she was imprisoned at the age of 73. As she faced torture and possible execution,-- another woman accused with her had already had her thumb torn out on the rack-- he traveled there again through the war-torn country, leaving his second pregnant wife and his children in Linz. Although he spent a full year there away from his family and his work he was unable to prevent her consignment to the torture chamber to make her confess. But when she dramatically fell on her knees, asking God for a miracle to show her innocence, and insisted that she would prefer death to an extorted confession she was finally acquitted after 14 months in prison. Half a year later she died.[9]

In 1626, just when Kepler had finally readied the Rudolphine Tables for print, he had to leave Linz before he was able to publish them. He was again under religious attack, and his library had been sealed up because it contained heretical literature. He managed to make his way on a wagon with the plates of his Tables to the free city of Ulm, where he had them printed and published in 1627. The accuracy of the Rudolphine Tables made all previous data obsolete and they remained the standard throughout the 17th century, until they were superseded by telescopic observations.

Kepler, who had by that time seven children from his two marriages, had been fighting poverty all his life. Although he had been court mathematician under three German rulers on a supposedly generous pension, he had never been able to collect the money except in fractional driblets. In 1630, when he was again in dire financial straits, he rode in winter in dismal weather to Regensburg to collect 11,817 *Gulden* which the emperor had promised to be paid by the German Reichstag. He arrived deathly sick, probably from pneumonia and died a few days later at the age of 59. Even then he was recognized as one of the greatest mathematicians who had ever lived. His work in astronomy and Galileo's in mechanics assured the eventual victory of the Copernican theory and provided the basis for Newton's laws of gravity. The Middle Ages, however, were still far from dead, as the trial of Kepler's mother by the Protestants and the condemnation of Galileo by the Catholics five years later demonstrated. No other force but the printed word could have weakened the spirit of obscurantism sufficiently to allow modern science to take root, and then it took until 1835 for Copernicus, Kepler and Galileo to be removed from the *Index.*

Galileo in the meantime had been using the power of print to the utmost. Since he had been prohibited from any further discussion of astronomy he had concentrated again on his studies of physics. To reach the largest possible audience he wrote some of his books in Italian instead of Latin. In 1624 he published *The Experimenter (Il saggiatore)*. It contained some concepts that had great influence on the nature of subsequent philosophic and scientific thought. Following initially Aristotle's categories he goes a step beyond Aristotle and distinguishes what might be called objective properties of substances from subjective ones. Subjective qualities or, as they were called later on, secondary qualities exist in (Galileo's view) only in the sense perception of the observer-- such as color, smell, beauty, etc. The objective or primary qualities are intrinsic in the substance-- such as size, shape, weight, motion etc.; in other words primary qualities are measurable and are the qualities that concern science. Galileo made scientific thought quantitative.

In 1630, the year of Kepler's death, Galileo wrote his literary masterpiece, his *Dialogue concerning the two chief world systems (Dialogo supra i due massimi sistemi del mondo, Tolemaico e Copernicano)*. Since Galileo was not allowed to discuss the heliocentric theory he took the subterfuge of writing a Platonic style dialogue in which three characters debate the merits of the Copernican versus the Ptolemaic systems: Salviano(a name which evokes the meaning of healthy or sound) advocates the Copernican system, Simplicio (whose name is the Italian form of Simplicius, at the time the most read ancient commentator on Greek philosophy, but whose name also means simpleton) defends the Ptolemaic-Scholastic views; Sagrado, (the consecrated one ?) is a neutral observer, perhaps a hint of what the position of the Church should be. Galileo elsewhere quoted a contemporary churchman that "The Holy Spirit intends to teach how to go to heaven, not how the heavens go." In an ostensibly objective presentation of the two theories Galileo in a bitingly ironic fashion makes the traditionalist Simplicio look obtuse and unable to deal with the Copernican's superior arguments. In the whole tongue-in-cheek composition Galileo not only shows total command of all the ancient sources, from the Presocratics, Plato and Aristotle to the Hellenistic writers and commentators, but also builds a solid case that the same causes produce the same effects everywhere, refuting the entrenched notion that the physics that apply in heaven are different from those on earth. Going beyond Copernicus he places the stars at vast, different distances from the earth. Because the book treated a contemporary controversy in Italian in an extremely readable satirical fashion it was an immediate success. By the time the book was banned all copies had been sold and had become hot black market items. A Latin translation was published shortly thereafter by a group of Protestant scholars.

Galileo, who was 70 at the time, was ordered to report to Rome regardless of his excuse of age and illness. The Inquisition forced him to abjure his heresies, put him under house arrest for the rest of his life, and forbade him to write. In 1638 Galileo went blind. He nevertheless dictated to his pupil Viviano his *Discourses on two sciences*, in which he systematized his lifelong studies in mechanics. Through his experiments with falling bodies, inclined planes, and projectiles he had disproved many of the fallacious traditional notions. He was the first to calculate accelerated motions caused by the steady action of a force and motions caused by combinations of forces such as the trajectories of missiles. It is interesting to note that in antiquity the speculation on conic sections which led to the construction of the ellipse, the parabola, and the hyperbola had been purely theoretical exercises. Since in nature no example of such curves had ever come to light, they were entirely abstract constructs of the mind. Now for the first time their actual presence in the phenomena of the physical world had been found, in Kepler's elliptic orbits and in Galileo's trajectories.

As Singer observes, the discipline of elementary mechanics, which had already been well treated by Stevin, exists today essentially in the state in which Galileo left it.[10] Galileo's last work was smuggled out to Holland and printed by Elseviers in Leyden in 1638. In the same year Galileo was visited in his prison by Milton, who in *Paradise Lost* alludes to the conflict of the two world-systems and to Galileo. Galileo died in 1642 at the age of 78.

In 1979 Pope John Paul II in a speech before the Pontifical Academy of Sciences declared that there were no irreconcilable differences between science and faith. As a symbol of accommodation he made the rehabilitation of Galileo a major goal. In 1980 John Paul appointed a commission of scientists, historians and theologians to re-examine the evidence and the verdict. In March of 1984 the preliminary report of the panel stated that: "The judges who condemned Galileo committed an error" (*Time*, March 12, 1984). To this date the Vatican has not acted on the recommendation and Galileo is still waiting to be rehabilitated.

Of all the pioneers of science in the 16th and the early 17th century, Copernicus, Tycho, Kepler, and Galileo have been singled out because they, within the timespan of a century, brought about the greatest change of man's picture of the world. It has been said that they destroyed Aristotelianism, but they would have been horrified at this thought. What they destroyed were the remnants of mediaeval pseudo-Aristotelian scholasticism which had been based on Latin and Arabic translations, handbooks, summaries and commentaries. From these distorted sources the scholasticists had arbitrarily selected those parts that could well be fitted in with Christian dogma. Through their humanistic studies Kepler the theorist and Galileo the empiricist had succeded in returning to the true Aristotelian method.

Aristotle had defined scientific inquiry as the investigation of causes. The inquiry must always start from sense-perception and experience and proceed in the inductive process from the particular to the universal (*An. post.* I. 71); only then can deductive reasoning begin. But any deductive conclusions that contradict experience are necessarily purely dialectic and futile (*De Anima* I. 402b.16-403a). Obviously many opinions of Aristotle were wrong because of inadequate means of observation, faulty assumptions, and wrong reports, but as long as his method was followed the errors would eventually be corrected, especially as the means of observation improved. Without new investigations the misconceptions had become fossilized during the Middle Ages. It was not until 1498 that a complete printed edition in the original Greek became available from the press of Aldo Manucio in Venice.

Galileo, the empiricist, was fully aware of the necessity of a theoretical education, and expressed contempt for those who tried "to read the book of nature without knowledge of the language in which it was written [i.e. mathematics]." Albert Einstein writes in his introduction to Stillman Drake's *Dialogue of the Two Scientific Systems*:

> "To put into sharp contrast the empirical and the deductive attitude is misleading, and was entirely foreign to Galileo. ...Empiricism vs. Rationalism does not appear as a controversial point in Galileo's work. Galileo opposes the deductive methods of Aristotle and his adherents only when he considers their premises arbitrary and untenable, and he does not rebuke his opponents for the mere fact of using deductive methods. In the first dialogue, he emphasizes in several passages that according to Aristotle, too, even the most plausible deduction must be set aside if it is incompatible with empirical findings. On the other hand, Galileo himself makes considerable use of logical deduction. His endeavors are not so much directed at 'factual knowledge' as at 'comprehension.' But to comprehend it is essential to draw conclusions from an already accepted logical system." Schmitt quotes a letter of Galileo to Liceti dated 9/15/1640, in favor of Aristotle's method of logic in which Galileo states: "... up to this point I am a peripatetic... I am sure if Aristotle returned to the world, he would receive me among his followers."[11]

At the other extreme, Kepler the humanist and religious mystic, who at times on the basis of preconceived assumptions engaged in the wildest flights of deductive imagination, had sufficient respect for Aristotle's scientific method that he was able to reject his most cherished theories when their predictions deviated by only a few minutes of arc from Tycho's observations.

After Kepler and Galileo it was only a matter of time till the revised Copernican system would be universally accepted. The publicity of Galileo's trial only served to popularize experimental science and to draw Europe's "natural philosophers" closer together and promote more organized research. In 1645, at first secretly because of the repressive attitude of the Puritan Government, an association was formed in England, later (in 1662) chartered as the Royal Society, for the purpose of discussions, experiments and communications with foreign scholars. In Italy the *Academia del Cimento* was formed in 1657 by Galileo's followers and conducted systematic experiments in physics until their activities were stopped by the Church.

In France an informal association of scholars interested in the natural sciences was officially sanctioned in 1666 as the *Académie des Sciences*. In the same year regular periodical scientific publications made their appearance. The *Philosophical Transactions* were issued by the Royal Society in London and the *Journal des Savants* by the *Académie* in Paris. A direct road smoothed with printer's ink led on to Newton and modern science. The civilization of Europe had been transformed within two centuries from the installation of the first printing press. Many events and innovations had combined to achieve this result. If any one of the other factors that played a part in the intellectual revolution had not occurred, the result would most likely have been the same, but the one force without which the transformation of the world picture could not have occurred was the effect of printed communications, the instant dissemination of knowledge by the mass-media of books, periodicals, maps, almanacs, etc., and the concurrent expansion of literacy.

Notes

1. The biographical details on Tycho Brahe rely heavily on J.A. Gade, *The Life and Times of Tycho Brahe* (Princeton 1947)

2. Edward Rosen, "Biography of Copernicus" in *Three Copernican Treatises* (3rd ed. New York 1971), 332

3. Edward Rosen, "Dissolution of the Celestial Spheres," *Journal of the History of Ideas* 46 (1985), 13-31

4. Carola Baumgardt, *Johannes Kepler: Life and Letters* (New York 1951), 91

5. Baumgardt, 77, Kepler's letter to Georg Brengger of 11/7/1607

6. Baumgardt, 38-39, letter Galileo to Kepler, 8/4/1597

7. Baumgardt, 41

8. Kepler, *Tertius Interveniens*, 1610, Baumgardt 27

9. Baumgardt, 157-162

10. Charles Singer, *A Short History of Scientific Ideas* (Oxford 1959), 249

11. C. B. Schmitt, *Aristotle and the Renaissance* (Cambridge, Mass. 1983), 28

14

The 18th Century

European literacy had reached a peak during the 17th century, but it is extremely difficult to generalize about its extent because of wide regional variations. Cipolla estimates the literacy rate for Western Europe as above 50 percent in the towns and below 50 percent in the country.[1] At the end of the 17th century about 75 percent of the people in France who made a marriage contract could not sign their names. By the end of the 18th century the number of those able to sign had increased to between 40 and 45 percent. In late 17th century England the evidence based on the ability to sign legal papers indicates a literacy rate of 25 to 40 percent, depending mainly on social status.[2] According to statistics gathered from marriage contracts in the years from 1754 to 1762 the number of signatures had increased to 54 percent.[3] Literacy seems to have been highest in the northern Protestant countries: in Amsterdam 57 percent of those getting married signed the register and in Sweden a law of 1686 stated that children in all parishes had to learn to read.[4]

The development of literacy during the 18th century seems to have been somewhat paradoxical. While the lower level of popular literacy seems to have suffered, or at least to have progressed very little, due to the religious wars and political disruptions, the higher levels of literacy flourished as never before.

The advances in mathematics, their applications to mechanics and physics by Galileo and Newton, the medical discoveries of Harvey, Boyle's pioneering work in chemistry, and systematic research in all the sciences gave impetus to a new look at the world and a literary movement that has become known as the *Enlightenment*. The thinkers of the 18th century, the "Age of Reason," tried to build their philosophy on the scientific insights of their 17th century predecessors.

Galileo is often named as the first. René Descartes (1596-1650) tried to grasp the realities of the world through quantitative reasoning. Through the logic of mathematics he sought to reconcile science, philosophy and religion. Thomas Hobbes (1588-1679), influenced by the logical pattern of Euclid's *Elements*, believed that starting from correct definitions the inductive process could be applied to the workings of nature and the mind. Every process could be understood in terms of mechanistic laws of cause and effect. Most important was his political theory as expressed in his *Leviathan* (1651). In it he develops a rational foundation for "natural law", which, evolved from Aristotelian and Stoic concepts in antiquity, was to become one of the fundamental tenets of the philosophers of the Enlightenment. Hobbes constructs a theory of absolute sovereignty which tries to substitute natural law for the divine right of kings. The body politic or commonwealth is the "great Leviathan" contrived by covenants of men to provide security, justice and peace. John Locke (1632-1704) was most influential in both England and France and eventually in America. In his *Essay Concerning Human Understanding* he accepted only sensation as a source of human knowledge; he denied the validity of abstract ideas and made empiricism the touchstone. Locke was especially sensitive to the role of language in the search for truth and made rationality the only guide. Locke followed Aristotle in his view of reason. Reason was the only faculty possessed by no other creature but man. Reason was the only attribute man shared with God. Reason had been given by God to man to rule between men.[5]

Among Galileo's, Descartes' and Locke's great contributions to literacy was that, in their acute consciousness of language, they shaped Italian, French, and English, respectively, into effective vehicles of intellectual discourse. Up until their time only Greek and Latin had had that capability in the West. Thus the Enlightenment, an international movement like the Renaissance before it, gave impetus to nationalism and to an outpouring of national literature-- not only works by scientists and *philosophes*, but also novels, satires, and literature of all genres permeated by the ideas of the age.

P.M. Spurlin, in *The French Enlightenment in America*,[6] names the following as the most influential thinkers of the Enlightenment: Isaac Newton, John Locke, David Hume, Adam Smith, Montesquieu, Voltaire, Rousseau, Diderot, Helvetius, Holbach, Condillac, Condorcet, Kant, Lessing, Beccaria, Benjamin Franklin, and Thomas Jefferson. Some people might want to add more names to Spurlin's list. The figures of the Enlightenment may differ on some views, and they did not all espouse all of them, but they shared certain main interests. They all enthroned reason and were humanitarians, concerned with the human condition and desirous of improving it. To quote Spurlin, "They opposed every form of tyranny and cruelty, did their best to depose blind faith, combat credulity, stamp out superstition." Something else the thinkers of the enlightenment had in common was their fascination with antiquity. As H. S. Commager says, "...they studied its history, read its literature, imitated its art and architecture, cultivated its philosophy, and, in theory at least, embraced its political principles."[7]

There are certain concepts that keep emerging from the various genres of Enlightenment literature. One is a firm belief in Natural Laws, which may or may not be of divine origin, can be recognized by reason, and transcend conventional laws. Another is a notion of the goodness of "natural" man unspoiled by civilization. With increasing frustration in the effort to institute the rule of reason the myth of the noble savage spawned a literature of escapism. Not necessarily consistent with the idea of the goodness of primitive man was a conviction of the unchangeable quality of human nature, which explains the never-ending fascination with the history of the ancient world, especially its biographical literature. And finally, the Enlightenment took a rational critical approach to religion that resulted in a spirit of tolerance. The same critical attitude which put all traditional institutions to the test of reason eventually caused violent reactions by the establishments in which it had instilled fear of discontent and rebellion. In recurring cycles throughout the 18th and 19th centuries the rulers, the churches, the universities and the military combined to suppress the ideas of the Enlightenment and their advocates. In the 18th century there was only one place in the world where the Age of Reason became a practical reality, and that was in America.

Colonial America in the later 18th century had probably the highest literacy rate of any country at that time. A statistical study by K. A. Lockridge of signatures *versus* marks on wills,[8] deeds and other legal documents showed the following: the number of men able to sign the documents increased from 60 percent in 1660 to 70 percent in 1710, 85 percent in 1760, and 90 percent in 1790. These figures do not seem unreasonable in the light of the social pressures for Bible reading and the legislation for support of public education. The study also showed a continuous narrowing of the literacy gap between the wealthier and the poorer classes. If at the time of the revolution 90 percent of the male population were literate, this was the highest rate since antiquity and at that time equalled or surpassed only by Sweden.

R.B. Davis,[9] on the basis of library holdings, book sellers' lists, pamphlets and advertisements, wills, and signature statistics, comes to the conclusion that the literacy rate in the South was comparable to that in New England and that the range of southern literacy was broader and more diversified. Although in the South, too, religious literature predominated, there was also great interest in law, history, politics, and the classics, whose contribution to all these fields was avidly absorbed. Southern colonial and early national education was predominantly based on the classics.[10]

The Founding Fathers were thoroughly familiar with the Greek and Roman classics. Current opinions on their influence have been split, with classicists usually emphasizing the ancient influence and Americanists discounting it, but it is only in the last few decades that this question has been thoroughly and objectively investigated by a number of scholars, notably by Meyer Reinhold.[11]

Higher education had been strong in the American colonies. In 1776 nine colleges were in existence: Harvard, William and Mary, Yale, New Jersey (which later became Princeton), Philadelphia (the future University of Pennsylvania), Kings (Columbia), Rhode

Island (Brown), Queens (Rutgers), and Dartmouth. In the grammar schools preparing students for college the curriculum, with slight variations, consisted of works by Cato, Aesop, Ovid, Cicero, Vergil, Horace, Terence, and (in Greek) Homer, Xenophon and Isocrates. These authors appeared on all bookseller's lists and James Madison referred to them as "the common list of school classics." In spite of their classical education and interest in antiquity the framers of the American constitution were no classicists. Most of their knowledge came from translations and histories which were popular in England at that time. For the thinkers of the Enlightenment, history was the source of knowledge of unchanging human nature and moral law. In the words of Bolingbroke, "History was philosophy teaching by examples."[12] Gibbon's *Decline and Fall* (1776-1788) provided the horrible example *par excellence*, the end of Rome because of ambition, luxury, greed, vice and corruption, as well as the shirking of patriotic duties. In addition to moral lessons the Founding Fathers sought in Greece and Rome practical guidance for their political institutions. Patrick Henry, who professed otherwise no interest in antiquity, said in 1775 in his speech to the Convention of Delegates: "I have but one lamp by which my feet are guided, and that is the lamp of experience. I know of no way of judging the future but by the past."[13]

Thomas Jefferson was the most familiar with the classical authors. He suggested the following "reading list" to Peter Carr: Oliver Goldsmith's Grecian History (1774), Herodotus, Thucydides, Xenophon and Quintus Curtius; later he added to the list Diodorus, Livy, Caesar, Suetonius, Tacitus, Dio Cassius, Arrian, Polybius, Sallust, Dionysius of Halicarnassus, Gibbon and a general history. Plutarch was Alexander Hamilton's favorite author. John Adams in 1765 exhorted the Founding Fathers: "Let us study the law of nature, search into the spirit of the British Constitution, read the histories of ancient ages, contemplate the great examples of Greece and Rome, set before us the conduct of our British ancestors who defended for us the inherent rights of mankind against foreign and domestic tyrants and usurpers . . . let every sluice of knowledge be opened and set a-flowing."[14] In 1774 John Adams

justified American revolutionary rights on the basis of "the principles of Aristotle, Plato, Livy, Cicero, and Sidney and Harrington,
and Locke; the principles of nature and eternal reason."[15]

Repeated references to Locke and Sidney show the influence of
English thought on the framers of the Constitution. Many of them
had received their knowledge of the Greek and Roman political
ideas through the British intermediary. All the Founding Fathers
seem to have been well aware of the theories on the "three forms
of government", their cyclical nature, the supposed advantages of a
"mixed constitution," and the separation of powers. These concepts
are reflected in all the historical and political writing from Plato,
Aristotle and Polybius in antiquity to Macchiavelli, Hobbes, Locke,
Montesquieu et al. Thus those of the Founding Fathers who did
not study the ancient originals were nevertheless well versed in
their political content. Meyer Reinhold states:[16]

> The records of the Federal Convention and the Federalist papers written by
> Madison, Hamilton and John Jay are dotted with parallels and lessons. It is
> discernible that some of these were extracted from translations of Plato, Aris-
> totle, Demosthenes, Polybius, Livy, Cicero, Sallust, Strabo, Tacitus and
> Plutarch, but most were from contemporary works on ancient political theory
> and history, such as Rollin, Vertot, Edward Montagu, Adam Ferguson, Wal-
> ter Moyle, Conyers, Middleton, Mably, Millot, Mitford, and Gillies.

It might be instructive to follow briefly the development of one of
the classical political concepts through several of the sources. Plato
discusses the possible constitutions in descending order of his preference thus:

> Approved by the majority of the people is the [aristocratic] constitution as in
> Crete and Sparta. Next to it and next in approval is the one called oligarchy,
> fraught with evils; next follows its opposite, democracy; and finally, tyranny,
> supposedly noble, but in reality, the outstanding and ultimate disease of a
> state. (*Republic* 8.544c, my transl.)

In Aristotle the idea takes the following form:

Of forms of government in which one is the ruler, we call that which regards the common interest, monarchy; that in which more than one, but not many rule aristocracy; and it is so called because the rulers are the best men, or because they have at heart the best interests of the state and the citizens. But when the citizens at large govern for the common interest, it is called constitutional government (*politeia*)...Of these forms of government the corruptions are as follows: Of monarchy - tyranny; of aristocracy - oligarchy; of constitutional government - democracy. For tyranny is a kind of monarchy which has in view the interest of the monarch only; oligarchy has in view the interest of the wealthy; democracy of the needy: none of them the common good of all. (*Politics* 3. 7. 1279b; translation after Benjamin Jowett).

Aristotle is the first to suggest the separation of powers:

There are three things which a careful legislator ought to consider ...The first of these is the element which deliberates about public affairs; secondly that concerned with magistracies - the questions being what they should be, over what they should exercise authority, and what should be the mode of electing them; and thirdly that which has judicial power. *Politics* 4. 13. 1297b41-1298a, tr. Jowett)

The separation of powers had already become a familiar theme in England and had been incorporated in several American state constitutions. The theory concerning the advantages of a mixture of the three forms of government goes back to Aristotle and was well known in England. Of all the classical literature Polybius' description of the Roman Republic had made the greatest impact on the Founding Fathers. Polybius (203-120 BC) lived at the time of the rapid expansion of Roman power over the Mediterranean area and the Roman conquest of Greece. He spent considerable time as hostage in Rome. In his *Histories* he tried to explore the reasons for the Roman successes. Without a doubt he extolled the excellence of the Roman political system not only to please the Romans but also to make the defeat of the Greeks more palatable to them. His description of the Roman "mixed" constitution was also known from Macchiavelli's *Discourses* and Montesquieu's *Laws*. The following are some excerpts from Hampton's (1811) translation of Polybius, which was well known to the Founding Fathers:[17]

Royalty degenerates into tyranny; aristocracy into oligarchy; democracy into savage violence... Lycurgus [the Spartan law giver], therefore foreseeing this necessity , instead of adopting either of the single forms of government, collected what was excellent in them all; and so joined together the principles that were peculiar to each several form, that no one of them might be extended beyond proper bounds, and slide into the evil to which it was inclined by nature, but that each separate power, being still counteracted by the rest, might be retained in due position, and the whole government be preserved in equal balance; as a vessel impelled to either side by the wind is kept steady by a contrary force...The three kinds of government, of which we have been speaking, were found all united in the commonwealth of Rome. And so even was the balance between them all, and so regular the administration that resulted from their union, that it was no easy thing, even for the Romans themselves, to determine with assurance, whether the entire state was esteemed to be an aristocracy, a democracy, or a monarchy. For if they turned their view on the power of the consuls, the government appeared to be purely monarchical and regal. If again the power of the senate was considered, it then seemed to wear the form of aristocracy. And lastly, if regard was had to the share which the people possessed in the administration of affairs, it could then scarcely fail to be denominated a popular state...(Polybius 6. 10-11; Hampton 279-280).

Niccolò Macchiavelli (1469-1527), a practical politician and one time Secretary of State of the Republic of Florence, revived the classical theoretical speculations on government and politics. The following are brief excerpts from Ellis Farneworth's translation of 1762, which circulated in the American colonies:

But as I propose to treat more particularly of the laws and constitution of the Roman Republic and shew what accidents contributed to bring it to perfection, I must observe in the first place, that according to some authors, there are but three sorts of government , viz. Monarchy or Principality, Aristocracy, and Democracy; and that those who intend to erect a new state, must have recourse to some one of these which he likes best... Monarchy often degenerates into Tyranny, Aristocracy into oligarchy, and Democracy into licentious anarchy and confusion... The wisest legislator therefore being aware of these defects, never established any one of them in particular, but contrived another that partakes of them all, consisting of Prince, Lords, and Commons, which they looked upon as more firm and stable, because every one of these members would be a check upon the other: and of those Legislators, Lycurgus certainly merits the highest praise, who constituted an establishment of this kind in Sparta, which lasted above eight hundred years, to his own great honour and the tranquillity of the Citizens. (Machiavelli, v. 2 *Discourses on Livy*, 6-7)

In Thomas Hobbes' *Leviathan* (1651)[18] the ancient concept appeared thus:

The difference in commonwealths consists in the difference of sovereign, or the person representative of all and every one of the multitude. And because the sovereignty is either in one man or in an assembly of more than one, and into that assembly either every man has right to enter, or not every one but certain men distinguished from the rest, it is manifest that there can be but three kinds of commonwealth. For the representative must needs be one man or more, and if more then it is the assembly of all or but of a part. When the representative is one man, then is the commonwealth a MONARCHY; when an assembly of all that will come together, than it is a DEMOCRACY or popular commonwealth; when an assembly of part only, then it is called an ARISTOCRACY. Other kind of commonwealth there can be none, for either one or more or all must have the sovereign power, which I have shown to be indivisible, entire.

John Locke, too, in 1690, makes the classical definition of the three forms of government the starting point for his discussion of the Separation of Powers:[19]

The majority having, as has been shew'd, upon mens first uniting into society, the whole power of the Community, naturally in them, employ all that power in making Laws for the Community from time to time, and Executing these Laws by Officers of their own appointing; and then the *Form* of the Government is a perfect *Democracy*: Or else may put the power of making Laws into the hands of a few select Men, and their Heirs or Successors; and then it is an *Oligarchy*; Or else into the hands of one Man, and then it is a *Monarchy*...

Locke then proceeds to his definitions of the legislative, executive, and "federative" power (by "federative" Locke means the power to make foreign policy). He develops the thesis that without separation of the legislative and executive powers liberty is not possible. By the fundamental law of self-preservation, however, the community as a whole has a "supreme power" to defend itself against encroachments by the governing bodies against their persons or properties. But there is a catch: the supreme power of the people cannot be exercised so long as the government exists. Therefore in Locke's theory the supreme power must rest with the legislative power (par. 149-150).

Montesquieu in his *Spirit of the Laws* (1748), after giving the traditional definition of the three forms of government, discusses the constitution of England.[20] In this context he makes the most lucid case for the separation of the legislative, the executive and the judicial powers, as the basis of a free country. He emphasizes the necessity that none of the three branches of government may have sovereignty over the other two. Since his presentation supposedly reflected conditions in England, where no such equality of the three powers existed, there has been much debate on this point. But the important fact is that his specification of the separation of powers is the one that became most influential in America.

The authors from Plato to Montesquieu have been quoted in their almost identical citations in order to illustrate the unbroken survival of some of the ancient political concepts; the continuity of other ideas could be demonstrated in the same fashion. All these modern authors studied history intensely, used examples from classical history to prove their points, and applied ancient parallels to explore the present. Their books were in all the public and many private libraries in the original or in translations, and often in both. They were continually quoted and discussed in the gazettes and speeches, so that the views and concepts were widely known also by those who had no firsthand knowledge of the classical sources. As P. M. Spurlin states: "By the opening of the Constitutional Convention in 1785 *The Spirit of the Laws* had become an 'American' Classic."[21]

The reference to ancient models was of utmost importance to the Founding Fathers for several reasons. The autopsies into republics that had failed provided warnings for the present. Thus the writers of the constitution attributed many of the failures in antiquity to direct democracy and sought to prevent them by the delegate system, which would isolate the lawgivers from the emotions of the populace. Most of the system of checks and balances was intended to avoid the pitfalls of popular government. Another reason for the reaching back to the republics of Greece and Rome was to justify and legitimize the American revolution through precedent and natural law. The American secessionists saw themselves following the footsteps of famous Greek and Roman patriots and heroes, while England was cast in the role of the decadent late Roman empire in Gibbon's *Decline and Fall*. As Meyer Reinhold put it,[22]

> The Founding Fathers were, however, not classical scholars but humanistic statesmen, and the uses to which they put the classical heritage were a function of their quest for political freedom, not of a search for the truth. Insecure and inexperienced they looked for guidance to the 'perfect Models of Antiquity,' and plundered the classics for instant history - uncritically, selectively, opportunistically - constructing timeless models, political abstractions, stereotypes, ideals.

An exchange of letters between Thomas Jefferson and John Adams offers an illuminating insight. Jefferson had written about Plato's *Republic*:

> It was the heaviest task-work I ever went through... while wading through the whimsies, the puerilities and unintelligeable jargon of this work, I laid it down often to ask myself how it could have been, that the world should have so long consented to give reputation to nonsense as this?

John Adams, who in 1787 had used extensive quotations from the eighth book of Plato's *Republic* in his *Defense of the Constitutions of Government of the United States*, answered Jefferson as follows:[23]

> I am very glad that you have seriously read Plato; and still more rejoiced to find that your reflections upon him so perfectly harmonize with mine. Some thirty years ago I took upon myself the severe task of going through all his

works. With the help of two Latin translations, and one English and one French translation, and comparing some of the most remarkable passages with the Greek, I labored through the tedious toil. My disappointment was very great. His Laws and his Republic from which I expected most, disappointed me most. I could scarcely exclude the suspicion that he intended the latter as a bitter satire on all republican government...

Thus John Adams as practical politician did not hesitate to gather material and marshal arguments from an author with whom he as a philosopher violently disagreed. Nobody can blame Jefferson and Adams, two outstanding representatives of the Age of Reason, for being antagonized by Plato's mysticism and, especially, by the authoritarian state proposed in the *Republic*. Still, subconsciously they were imbued with the Platonic spirit, which put the highest value on virtue as its own reward and as the basis of all community life. And they knew well and tried to live up to Plato's dictum that, "the human race will never see the end of troubles until true philosophers should come to hold political power, or the holders of political power... should become philosophers" (*Seventh Letter*).

The common objectives of the apostles of the European Enlightenment were to return to the laws of nature and to reason, to liberate human minds from outside constraints and superstitions, and to abolish torture, cruel punishment, slavery, and slave-trade. But nowhere in Europe was there a way to accomplish these objectives without the help of the existing establishments; thus the *philosophes* had to try to remodel the kings into philosophers. At first the various monarchs pleased themselves in the role of prospective philosopher kings and they welcomed the prominent figures of the Age of Reason to their courts. Voltaire and Diderot visited Frederick of Prussia, while Catherine of Russia surrounded herself with Diderot, Baron Grimm and other *philosophes*. For a while the rulers and their intellectuals formed a mutual admiration society, but after the French revolution the reaction set in. As H. S. Commager has pointed out,[24] while the Americans elected their philosophers as kings (Adams, Jefferson and Madison in succession), Catherine the Great of Russia threw out the busts of Voltaire and Diderot and shipped her stable of house philosophers to Siberia. In Vienna the reforms of Emperor Joseph were rescinded. The Inquisition returned to Spain. Diderot went to jail, Voltaire into exile. King Gustavus III of Sweden, who had ended torture and established freedom of the press, had been murdered. France after its bloody revolution turned to Napoleon.

In America during the same period an assembly of exceptional men made many of the ideas of the Enlightenment a reality. They had originated none of the concepts, but they were truly literate and had absorbed the ancient and contemporary literature on government, politics and history. With indefatigable zeal they had gathered all the available information they considered pertinent, then after much private and public discussion they used their own judgment to create the institutions that would put the ideals into practice. In the words of H. S. Commager:[25]

> The speedy creation of a national government was perhaps the most astonishing achievement of that generation of nation-makers, and the most enduring. It required a higher degree of political wisdom and resourcefulness than any people had heretofore displayed... In a single generation they invented - it is possibly the most original invention in the history of democracy - the institution of the constitutional convention; drew up the first written Constitutions for State and Nation; created the first workable federal system in history and endowed it with power to grow and expand without serious difficulty by substituting the principle of the coordinate state for the practices of Old World colonialism; and fixed effective limits on government thus created - separation of powers, checks and balances, bills of rights, and judicial review. Thus they solved, at one stroke as it were, those problems of government that had perplexed statesmen and philosophers since Pericles.

While established churches played a powerful role in most European states the Founding Fathers separated state and religion; it was one of Jefferson's greatest achievements as governor of Virginia. In 1776 Mason's Bill of Rights had declared religious freedom; in 1779 Jefferson disestablished the Anglican Church and proposed the separation of church and state. Patrick Henry tried to neutralize the bill by proposing aid to all denominations, but Madison rallied to the support of Jefferson's side for complete separation, and in 1785 and 1786 Jefferson's statute of religious liberty was enacted. Because of his long fight for religious freedom he was subject to repeated scurrilous attacks.

Under John Adams' guidance the Founding Fathers institution-alized the principle that government derived its power from the consent of the governed, and provided a peaceful means to change the Constitution through amendments, a possibility that had not existed anywhere heretofore. They upheld the freedom of the press and through support of public instruction fostered a broader liter-acy than existed anywhere in their contemporary world.

All this was accomplished by an elite that combined intellectual with practical genius. Most of them-- not all-- belonged also to the economic elite, yet they could have attained none of their objec-tives without the support of the great majority of the common peo-ple. They obtained that support because there was no literacy-gap between them and the people. All the issues were continuously de-bated in public and in the burgeoning press.

There was only one great betrayal of the ideals of the enlight-enment. That was the failure to abolish slavery. Jefferson's rather modest bill to the effect that everybody born after 1800 would be free died in committee. This failure would have to be paid for later.

The other principles of the Enlightenment that had become re-ality in America remained a reminder to the rest of the world, where they had been suppressed. They inspired another unsuccess-ful series of revolts in 1848, and were not generally accepted throughout the West until the late 19th and early 20th centuries.

Notes

1. Carlo Cipolla, *Literacy and Development in the West* (London 1969), 60

2. David Cressy, *Literacy and the Social Orders, Reading and Writing in Tudor and Stuart England* (Cambridge 1980)

3. Cipolla, 62

4. Cipolla, 54

5. John Locke, *Second Treatise*, par. 172; Aristotle, *Eth.Nic.* 177a7-177b31

6. P. M. Spurlin, *The French Enlightenment in America* (Athens, Georgia 1984), 7

7. H. S. Commager, *Jefferson, Nationalism and the Enlightenment* (New York 1975), 130

8. K. A. Lockridge, *Literacy in Colonial New England* (New York 1974), 13

9. R. B. Davis, *A Colonial Southern Bookshelf, Reading in the 18th Century* (Athens, Georgia 1979), 15

10. Davis, 23

11. Meyer Reinhold, *The Classick Pages: Classical Reading of Eighteenth Century Americans* (University Park, Pa. 1975), and *Classica Americana: The Greek and Roman Heritage in the United States* (Detroit 1984)

12. Commager, 125

13. Reinhold, *Classick Pages*, 97, n. 1

14. *The Works of John Adams* (Boston 1850-1856]), vol. 3, 462, as quoted by M. Reinhold, *Classica Americana*, 96

15. *Works of John Adams*, vol. 4, 15

16. Reinhold, *Classica Americana*, 102, with a score of references on p. 113, n.43

17. Reinhold, *Classick Pages*, 122-123

18. *Leviathan, Parts one and two*, H. W. Schneider (ed.), (New York 1958), 152-3

19. John Locke, *Two Treatises of Government* (London 1698), Second treatise, par. 132

20. *Montesquieu - Oevres complètes*, Roger Caillois (ed.), (Paris 1949), vol. 2, livre XI, chap. 6, 396-407

21. Spurlin, *Montesquieu in America 1760-1801* (New York 1969), 177

22. *Classica Americana*, 175

23. Jefferson, *Mem. Ed.* XIV, 156-157, as quoted by M. Reinhold, *Classick Pages*, 114

24. H. S. Commager, *Jefferson, Nationalism, and the Enlightenment*, 8, 72, 132

25. Commager, 183

15

The Nineteenth Century: Supremacy of the Printed Word

Culturally, the 19th century really extended from 1815 to 1914, from the end of the Napoleonic era, which spiritually was still an extension of the 18th century, to the beginning of the first World War. In America the end of Madison's second term as president at the end of 1815 marked the end of the time of the Founding Fathers who personified the 18th century Age of Reason. It remained for the outbreak of World War I to end the gentility and pride, the smug confidence and optimism of the 19th century. The period from 1815 to 1914 generated an accelerating process of transformation that changed the human environment more than all of previous history. It would be futile to try to enumerate all the changes that had their beginnings then and are still going on, but here are a few of the most significant:

- Literacy became universal in most of the western world and an effort is now under way to make literacy globally universal.

- More scientific knowledge was discovered than in all previous human existence, and it is still accumulating at an ever increasing rate.

- The population of the earth, which had been fairly stable at about 500 million, increased to about one billion by the end of the 19th century. It stands now at five billion and, if present trends continue, will double every twenty years.

- Primeval forests, which early in the 19th century covered four fifths of the earth's land mass, were beginning to be cut down and are now disappearing at an exponential rate.

At the time when these and many other ecological changes had their beginnings in the last century, nobody suspected their future consequences. Although these are now well known, most of the pernicious trends are still continuing.

Towards the end of the 18th century the Industrial Revolution in England with its dislocations, migration to the mining and mill towns, and increasing use of child labor had a decidedly retarding effect on schooling and the spread of literacy. Education stagnated and the progress in literacy in the first half of the 19th century was negligible.[1] By 1850 the literacy rate, according to most estimates, was still between 50 and 60 percent for men and around 40 percent for women.[2] Fear of popular literacy among the upper classes in the aftermath of the French Revolution had probably also dampened enthusiasm for widespread literate education. In 1807 a bill to provide elementary schools throughout the country was defeated in the House of Lords. The president of the Royal Society spoke in opposition to the bill:[3]

> However specious in theory the project might be of giving education to the poor, it would in effect be found prejudicial to their morals and happiness; it would teach them to despise their lot in life, instead of making them good servants in agriculture, and other laborious employment to which their rank in society has destined them; instead of teaching them subordination, it would render them factious and refractory, as was evident in the manufacturing counties; it would enable them to read seditious pamphlets, vicious books, and publications against Christianity; it would render them insolent to their superiors...

It was not until 1870 that the Elementary Education Act was passed, which, with supplementary laws, established universal compulsory education. Between the mid-century and 1870, however, schools in the factories, charitable instruction, the beginnings of labor organizations, and self-instruction had raised the literacy level already to 80 percent for men and 73 percent for women.[4]

In the meantime, by 1850, in the Scandinavian- and German-speaking countries of continental Europe, adult illiteracy had been reduced to less than 30 percent. In Belgium, Ireland and France, as in England, adult illiteracy remained at 30 to 50 percent.[5] From 1850 on, most western European countries, following Germany's, Holland's and Switzerland's examples, made elementary education free and compulsory, and thus literacy became near-universal. Because industrialization came to the Continent considerably later the advanced countries were able to profit from the lessons of England and to avoid the worst social disruptions, especially since the European governments were more prone than the British or American to intervene in economic and social developments. Ever since Napoleon had discovered that recruits who knew how to read and write were easier to train than illiterates the military in the various countries had been exerting pressure for general education. Empress Maria Theresa of Austria had ascribed the defeat of her armies by Frederick II of Prussia to "the Prussian schoolmaster," and instituted obligatory schooling in 1774. From the 1870s on most western and northern European nations tested their recruits for literacy and kept accurate statistics on their competence. In many southern and eastern European countries comparable levels of literacy were not reached until the twentieth century.

While literacy was high in the United States at the time of independence, because of the resistance to any interference by the Federal government there was a hodgepodge of private, state-supported, and denominational or private schools with more or less state support. With the great volume of immigration, the westward expansion and the gathering momentum of industrialization, especially in the cities where population was increasing rapidly, the old system (or lack of system) became inadequate. The population which had been 4 million in 1790, grew to 30 million by 1860, 50 million by 1880, and 100 million by 1920. In the 1830s two fifths of the work force in Boston were children under sixteen years of age, some as young as eight.[6] There was growing demand for free tax-supported schooling, and in most states free education became public policy, even if it was not fully implemented everywhere before the outbreak of the Civil War. Slavery, the Civil War, the Reconstruction period, and the ensuing segregation had the well-known disastrous consequences on education, especially of blacks, in the Southern states.

The first high school, the English Classical School, was established in Boston in 1821, and in 1827 the state of Massachusetts required the establishment of a high school in all cities with more than 500 families. The idea of the high school was gradually accepted by other states; the first coeducational high school opened in 1856. At the same time many private Latin grammar schools and academies continued to operate. The first state universities had existed since the days of the Founding Fathers-- the University of North Carolina since 1789, Vermont 1791, Georgia 1800, South Carolina 1801, and Jefferson's University of Virginia since 1818.

A most important type of school, the Normal School, was inaugurated in Massachusetts in 1835 for the training of teachers. Three schools were authorized, and New York followed suit with a Normal School in Albany. By the beginning of the Civil War twelve Normal Schools were in operation. As mentioned above, the population increased by seventy million between 1860 and 1920. It was the time when industrialization hit its full stride. In the large cities of the northeast, most of the population increase resulted from immigration. Many of the immigrants during the latter part of the 19th century came from southern or eastern Europe, and most were illiterate. The tremendous task of the big-city schools was to teach the children of the immigrants to understand, speak, read and write English, and to instill a patriotic American spirit in them -- to Americanize them. In this the teachers produced by the Normal Schools were spectacularly successful; the schools were truly the melting pot, and played that part until the 1920's.

By that time the idea of the American high school and its free tax-supported status was well established. In 1858 in Kalamazoo, Michigan, a group of taxpayers had sued the state to prevent tax use to support a high school. In 1872 the Supreme Court decided the case in favor of the school, reasoning that the high schools were a necessary link between grade schools and universities. This ruling set the pattern for the growth of high schools throughout the country, with widely varying curricula. Latin and algebra had the highest enrollment, and the classics curriculum was the most popular. Some schools offered the choice of an English or a science major; some offered also teacher training or vocational and commercial programs.[7] Then as now there was pressure to make the high school programs more utilitarian and vocational. In 1892 the National Education Association appointed a committee to investigate the high school curricula and to make recommendations on methods, standards and programs. The committee resisted the pressures and recommended academic courses: Latin, Greek, English, modern languages, mathematics, physical sciences, biological sciences, history, and geography. By holding that the purpose of studying any subject was mental discipline and exercise of the powers of the mind, the committee preserved the academic subjects.[8]

This debate, vocational versus academic, has continued until the present. The opponents of the traditional academic subjects attacked them mainly by labeling them "college preparatory" and arguing that these subjects were not appropriate for the vast majority of the students (90 percent in the 19th century) who were not going to enter college. This argument is fallacious, because a liberal education is a most important preparation for life, not just for college; in fact it is much more essential for students who will not go on to college, since it is their last chance for a general education, while the students who enter college will have ample opportunity to study the liberal arts and sciences. The pressure for a more "practical" curriculum in high schools and colleges has persisted despite repeated surveys of industry and business showing that most employers prefer workers with a solid all-round educational background to applicants who have received a smattering of job skills in school. The employers maintain that they have to train all employees for their particular jobs, which they are well able to do, while they are not able to to teach them mathematics or the ability to express themselves orally or in writing or to follow written instructions, which are important aspects of most jobs.

During the second half of the 19th century literacy became universal in the Western world. In England and the United States the spread of literacy initially had been hindered by the social disruptions of industrialization. But as industrial development progressed it created a need for supervisory, clerical and other service personnel who had to be literate. New positions opening required literacy and made it a marketable skill. Literacy became a status symbol and thus created a demand for elementary schooling everywhere, while the classical curriculum in selective secondary schools prepared the elite for the colleges and universities.

The results of continuing research in the sciences in Britain, France, Germany, and increasingly in the United States were translated into growing new technologies serving new industries, while industrial competition in turn stimulated more research. Refined manufacturing methods and skills produced new extensions of human capabilities in the form of ever more sensitive instruments, from telescopes to microscopes, barometers and chronometers, thermometers, photographic equipment, etc., which in turn not only stimulated and facilitated research, but which themselves became the products of new industries.

Newspapers became a part of daily living, while novels from the level of trash to those representing a sophisticated art form provided mass entertainment. The telegraph opened the world to instant communications. The typewriter and the invention of shorthand brought a minor revolution not only in the technique of writing but also in female employment. The printed word dominated all aspects of life. As literacy reached its highest quantitative and qualitative levels and technology proliferated the sum total of knowledge began to increase at an exponential rate.

Literature at the beginning of the 19th century had still been inspired by the classical revival and the liberalism of the Enlightenment and the American and French revolutions. In England the revolutionary spirit produced the classicist poetry of Keats, Shelley and Byron, whose physical participation in the Greek war of liberation caused his death. In Germany the enlightened work of Winkelmann, Lessing, Herder, Schiller and Goethe had created a classical literary Renaissance which Germany had missed in the 17th century because of the religious conflicts and the Thirty Years' War. Liberal literature contributed to the unsuccessful revolts of 1848 in many German principalities, the provinces of Austria, and Italy; the repression of these rebellions brought a new wave of immigrants to the Americas.

The second half of the 19th century also became the Golden Age of the novel. This time the influence moved from east to west. Tolstoy's (1820-1910) *War and Peace* and Dostoevsky's (1821-1881) novels created realistic characters and delved into their psychological motivations. In France, Gustave Flaubert (1821-1880) broke new ground with highly polished, logically crafted artistic novels and Emile Zola (1840-1902) led in the development of the naturalistic novel. Victor Hugo (1802-1885) in *Les Misérables* painted the stark realistic picture of the dispossessed proletariat of Paris. At the same time the novels of Charles Dickens (1812-1870) were an anguished protest against the inhuman effects of the industrial revolution in England, especially London. These works, for the moment, were probably more effective in mitigating the worst abuses than the contemporary writings of Karl Marx (1818-1883). In America, Harriet Beecher Stowe's (1811-1896) *Uncle Tom's Cabin* helped create anti-slavery sentiment.

Marx's greatest merit consisted in pointing out that the laws of economics were not "natural laws" like, for example, the laws of gravity, but the result of human action, and consequently could be changed by changing the human actions that caused them. Thus he placed the responsibility for the abysmal misery of industrial workers and miners on a society which had shrugged off its callousness under the pretext that the Malthusian "natural laws of economics" were God-given and inalterable. The conflict between Marxism and the *laissez-faire* economics of Adam Smith's *Wealth of Nations* has never stopped. Nor has Charles Darwin (1809-1882) ceased to upset American fundamentalists.

Despite the new socio-economic problems created by industrialization it seemed to the majority of the inhabitants of Britain, the United States and Europe of the late 19th and the early 20th centuries that they were living in an eminently sensible and satisfying period of progress. They had limitless trust in the ability of science to solve all problems. In the security of the *Pax Britannica* wealth was being created continuously. Progress was being made in the technologies of travel, communications and the convenience of daily living. Political debates were carried on through the dispassionate medium of print in newspapers, books and pamphlets addressed to a public endowed with a minimum of literacy and rationality which universal schooling was supposed to provide.

Together with free compulsory education and literacy the 19th century had produced piped hot and cold water, flushing toilets, central heating, railroads and ocean-going steamers, bicycles and automobiles, the telegraph and wireless, gas and electric lights and heating, streetcars and subways, immunization against some diseases and antiseptic surgery, and safer travel than ever before. The first airplane flew in 1903.

Just when it seemed that every problem that was not solved today would be solved the day after tomorrow, the complacency was suddenly shattered. The disaster of the first World War brought the senselesss slaughter of tens of millions of men and, in its aftermath, a world-wide depression and a general disillusionment with rationality. The new media of radio and cinema began to compete with reading as leisure time activities and means of gathering information. Amid widespread unemployment literate education seemed irrelevant. Radio and film with their ability to attract mass audiences exposed the public to the appeal of the impassioned orator, so that the demagogue had now the means to manipulate the emotions of millions: oratory regained its ancient power. Communism threw its mantle over Russia and fear over the rest of the world, a fear that was exploited by Mussolini in Italy to establish his dictatorship which would be the beginning of a new Roman Empire. Soon Hitler in Germany and Franco in Spain followed in Mussolini's footsteps. Mysticism, anti-intellectualism, book-burnings, and a ruthless will to exterminate all opposition reduced formerly civilized nations to savagery and brought the Second World War twenty years after the First.

Notes

1. Carlo Cipolla, *Literacy and Development in the West*, 69, 78

2. Kenneth Levine, *The Social Context of Literacy* (London 1986), chart A2.1

3. Cipolla, 65

4. K. Levine, 93

5. Cipolla, 113-114, Chart 23

6. J. D. Pulliam, *History of Education in America* (Columbus 1976), 56

7. Pulliam, 87

8. Pulliam, 88

Epilogue: Present and Future

Our review of the important innovative periods in Western history suggests a correlation between intellectual achievement and literacy in one or more languages. Obviously most historical developments result from complex interactions of many frequently conflicting internal or external forces-- economic, social, cultural or psychological. Even if it is therefore almost impossible to assert specific cause-effect relationships, events or processes may occur that have a clearly distinguishable impact or create the prerequisites that make certain developments possible and thus directly or indirectly set a historic evolution or chain of events in motion. Our study of important innovative eras of ancient history has tried to show that an association of expanded literacy with cognitive advances appears so consistently that it does not seem unreasonable to assume a causal connection.

Even on the lowest level of literacy the process of learning to write develops new abilities. Just to form the characters requires better hand-to-eye coordination than most day-to-day tasks. The shapes, names and sound-values of the characters have to be remembered. In the ideographic and syllabic scripts with their hundreds of signs this required a much greater effort than in alphabetic writing. In alphabetic writing, however, the learner must combine many different letters to produce the appropriate word while remembering the sequence forming the sentence. The activity of writing requires a continuous interplay between memory, the speech center, the visual, the audio, and the motor centers of the brain. Reading reverses the problem; the reader must retain the context in memory while deciphering each additional word. The mental concentration necessary for all this exceeds that required in most other activities and is in itself a valuable exercise. The exercise becomes even more complex if it involves translation from one language into another.

On a higher level of literacy, where reading and writing have become a habitual mode of dicourse, the rules of language change.
The hearer is no longer face-to-face with the speaker. The reader
cannot ask the writer to clarify his meaning, nor can the writer expect any feedback telling him whether he has been understood.[1]
Therefore much greater precision in expression becomes impera-
tive; definition of terms and causal connections must be stated.
Written communication has to follow certain mutually agreed-on
rules of logic and organization and, when the study and practice of
these rules becomes part of education in childhood and youth, their
application becomes a subconscious part of thought processes
which then also shape the spoken language. The transformation of
the spoken language through literacy has both positive and negative effects. On the one hand it accentuates class differences between the educated and the less educated or illiterates; on the
other hand the standardized written languages have served to unify
the nation states like Germany and France in spite of their many
regional dialects.

Literacy is much more than a means of communications. It is a
tool for clarifying one's own thoughts. When you "put your
thoughts on paper," you are able to analyse their logic, to follow
their ramifications and consequences. Thinkers from Plato to Marcus Aurelius to Leonardo da Vinci have used the device of "writing
to themselves." Ian Winchester[2] sees a

> ...threefold impact of high-grade literacy on the thought of an individual: It
> frees the mind to dwell on generalities by freeing it from remembering neces-
> sary but encumbering details; it enables the simultaneous consideration of
> numerous connections; and it permits the indefinite extension of argument.

Frank Smith, opposing the current metaphor for the brain as an information processor, put it thus:[3]

> ...the primary, fundamental, and continual activity of the brain is nothing else
> than the creation of worlds, both 'real and imaginary', learning is their elabo-
> ration and modification, and language - especially written language - is a par-

ticularly efficacious but by no means unique medium by which these worlds can be manifested, manipulated and sometimes shared.

From the beginning of history-- and without writing there would be no recorded history -- writing has been used to codify laws. The formulation of written law raises concerns from the specific to the general. The anthropomorphic projection of human law to the religious and cosmic spheres gave rise to concepts of divine law and later natural law which marked the beginning of scientific thought.

Many of the advantages of literacy are obvious and have been recognized since earliest times. Human knowledge stored in literature became permanent and cumulative. Writing as a tool of administration made large communities and complex socio-economic systems possible. Ever since classical Greek antiquity the training for literacy in childhood and adolescence, including the symbolic language of mathematics, has been considered a most important factor in the development of the individual. Its value as "training of the mind" was uncritically accepted.

Therefore it is not surprising that in the aftermath of World War II, the governments of the newly independent nations of the "Third World," facing the necessity of development, identified illiteracy as their main problem. In 1964, after UNESCO testified to "a growing awareness in the international community of the political, intellectual and economic consequences stemming from the illiteracy of a large proportion of mankind," the Secretary General of the U. N. presented the proposal for the "Eradication of Mass Illiteracy."[4] Since 1964 UNESCO has been coordinating successive projects in many countries with cooperation of local and other international agencies and has issued progress reports in 1970, 1972, 1976, and 1980. The overall impression one gains from these reports is that, regardless of their effectiveness or ineffectiveness, the efforts are being overwhelmed by the population explosion, especially in Africa, South Asia (including the islands) and South and Central America. While the percentage of illiterates decreased, their total number steadily increased.

In addition, since the 1970's there has also been growing concern with deteriorating literacy in the industrialized countries, especially in Great Britain and the United States.

In the United States a *Report of the National Commission on Excellence in Education* (Government Printing Office, Washington, D.C. 1983), describing the collapse of literacy standards in the secondary schools and colleges, declared that "the Nation is at risk." In June of the same year, 1983, the Office of Vocational and Adult Education, U.S. Department of Education, reported 74 millions of adults functioning on a "marginal level" of literacy. A press release by the White House on September 9, 1983, put the number of functional illiterates at 72 million. On January 18, 1984, the National Institute of Education, Department of Education, estimated the number to be 60 million. The general consensus seems to accept this last figure, which amounts to about a third of the adult population.[5]

Ever since the sixties, when UNESCO made the propagation of literacy one of its priority goals, literacy and its cultural effects have been a subject of much discussion, and the debate has intensified even more with the realization of the decline of literacy in industrialized countries.

During these same decades from the sixties to the eighties, several books have appeared which on the basis of historical and anthropological research defended the tacitly accepted concept that literacy, especially the use of the phonetic alphabet, had profoundly influenced cultural and intellectual developments in the Western world.[6] In the absence, however, of any hard and fast "proof" of direct causal effects of literacy on economic and cultural development, the authors had to support their conclusions with inferences drawn from history and some contemporary parallels. These works, as well as the various literacy campaigns, have triggered a very avalanche of opposing articles and books. Their general assertion is that throughout history literacy has been used by the ruling class as a tool to dominate the masses; that the emphasis on literacy is an "elitist" and capitalist plot to create cheap labor pools and markets for multinational corporations while in fact most of the population in developed as well as in developing nations have no need for literacy, and oral cultures are in no way inferior to literate ones.[7] As Robert Pattison puts it, a whole new generation of social historians is now busily engaged in proving that no such relation (viz. between literacy and development) exists."[8] If it is difficult to prove a positive causal relationship between historical events, however, it is even more difficult to prove the absence of such a relation. Thus the debate, fought mainly along ideological lines, may seem moot and unproductive. Still, in the present precarious condition of human survival, threatened by overpopulation, widespread warfare and famine, pollution of the environment, ozone depletion, the new plague of AIDS, and nuclear destruction, the stakes are much too high to dismiss a problem whose solution might possibly contribute to a raising of the general level of intelligence and rationality.

The denial of the cultural value of literacy, like the denial of all comparative values in societies, is typical of the approach of some sociologists. There are several causes for this fear of value judgments. One is the misguided attempt to represent their fields as equal to the exact sciences in objectivity and precision, which, as already Aristotle observed, is neither appropriate nor attainable outside of mathematics and physics; indeed, as Kurt von Fritz has suggested, there is need and room for value judgments even in the hard sciences. One solution of a mathematical problem may be simpler and more elegant than another. Copernicus, Kepler and Newton made their discoveries because, inspired by the Greek tradition, they were looking for the values of order and beauty (cosmos) in the universe. Without the values of truth and integrity no science would be of "value."

Another reason for the fear of value judgments is the justifiable reaction against 19th century European chauvinism. The guilt-feelings after the dismantling of the "white man's burden" caused anthropologists to treat all cultures as equal, considering only their utilitarian effects. By euphemism any primitive culture became "traditional;" so long as it seemed to assure survival of the tribe, it was considered successful even if it was based on such customs as cannibalism, slavery, human sacrifice, female circumcision, or total oppression of a certain group, sex, caste or race. A misplaced egalitarianism confuses the equal worth of human beings or human races with the relative values of different cultural systems. By some stretch of the imagination one might consider the Mayan or Aztec civilizations as equal to the Sumerian on a material level, but the Central American practice of mass human sacrifice certainly places them on a much lower level as far as human values are concerned. No civilization outside the Western orbit has ever formulated the ideas of government subordinated to the governed or of inviolable human rights, or has developed the experimental sciences and their systematic application to extend the human life-span and to ease human life. Today these principles have become the aspirations of all men and women. Even the governments who pervert them to maintain themselves in power proclaim these ideals. Practice may often fall far short of the theory, but as long as the ideal is restated again and again and remains the ultimate objective there lives hope of approaching it.

The Third World rightfully has made literacy one of its goals and the United Nations Assembly has debated whether literacy itself is a human right. While literacy per se, as its detractors are wont to proclaim, obviously cannot procure instant development and prosperity, it is also obvious that it will be easier to instruct a literate rather than an illiterate population in hygienics and birth control practices, new conservation and farming methods, and the use of tools and basic machinery. No one even mentions values beyond mere utilitarianism.

The consensus for the cultural and economic benefits of literacy has been gaining lately, while dissenting positions are becoming less and less defensible in the light of steady progress in neurophysiology. While sociologists argue over the interpretation of ambiguous circumstantial evidence, neurological research has been accumulating many indications of the cognitive benefits of the exercise of the language capability, of which literacy is the most intense.

The late Norman Geschwind noted that because of the long dominance of behaviorism a long gap in neuropsychological studies has delayed the biological understanding of cognitive processes by many decades and that only recently has the importance of the knowledge of the underlying neurological structures again been recognized.[9] Many more explorative methods as well as experimental results have become available. D. F. Benson (Director of the Neurobehavioral Center at the V.A. Hospital in Boston, and a collaborator of Geschwind) has enumerated the following approaches for study of the neuropsychological processes involved in reading.[10] He discounts psychometric models based on the study of healthy mature individuals as hopeless, because too many variables are involved. More informative is

> the probe of the incompletely acquired language functions seen at various stages of childhood. Most of our knowledge of the acquisition of language must be sought in this manner including the acquisition of reading.

The most important source is the study of language and reading disorders. Information is gained mainly from the study

> of brain damage, brain surgery, stimulation of the brain during surgery, the effects of drugs on the brain. Of these most fruitful has been the study of language disorders followed by post mortem analysis of the brain. From these studies has emerged a model of how language areas of the brain are interconnected and what each area does. (Benson and Geschwind, "The Alexias", 72).

In addition many non-pathological techniques have been perfected to explore and measure brain activities; for example, measuring the bloodflow to various areas of the brain, Electroencephalograms (EEG), Event Related Potential (ERP), Electromyographic Potentials (EMG), all measuring electric activities, provide new insights.

The brain is the most complex piece of matter in the universe, more complex than the universe itself. The brain contains some ten billion neurons, each of which has many connections (axons and dendrites) linking it to other neurons, forming a network of a quadrillion (1 with 18 zeroes) potential connections (synapses). The synapses are activated by electrochemical impulses, millions at any one instant. Every mental activity is caused by activation of a pathway of a series of connections in the three-dimensional network of neurons, and in turn causes new connections to be activated. Thus, the learning process continually changes the structures. The infrastructure of the brain has developed over the millions of years of evolution, with new structures and new functions accruing to the older ones without ever discarding any. The human brain still shares its older components with the animals, such as the limbic system, which regulates such unconscious activities as the heartbeat, breathing, sweating and many others. In animals most actions are automatic: as the nerves bring in information from the senses or internal organs of the body the brain transmits its programmed responses to the motor centers, which initiate the body's reactions. In the higher animals, however, the outer cortex is superimposed on the older parts of the brain. The cortex provides additional memory and thus learning ability and capability to overrule the programmed system and to substitute learned responses for the automatic stimulus-response reactions.

While humans share the cortex with the other mammals theirs is proportionately much larger and more complex. Not only did human brain-size increase by fifty percent during the two million year transition from *homo erectus* to *homo sapiens*, but the human brain also differentiated itself from that of all the other animals (except perhaps chimpanzees and orangutans) by lateralization. While in other animals all functions are equally distributed in both hemispheres, in humans the locations of some functions are asymmetrical. While language in right-handed individuals is mainly centered in the left hemisphere of the cortex, spatial concepts seem more controlled by the right cerebral hemisphere. It has to be understood, however, that in all the activities that seem localized in mainly one area or center a whole network of other structures is generally involved.

The outstanding quality of the human brain is its plasticity-- the capability to change, and for some parts to assume new functions. Although both halves of the brain are involved in the language function the left hemisphere's domination increases with maturation of the spoken as well as the written language activity. Any loss of speech (aphasia) due to injury of the language area before puberty is usually compensated by development of language function in the right hemisphere. A person young enough can relearn to speak even after loss of the whole left hemisphere. Furthermore, the fact that illiterates are less affected by aphasia after left hemisphere injury indicates that learning to read and write contributes to left brain specialization, and thus to language capabilities.[11]

M.L. Albert and L.K. Obler find that:[12]

particularly strong is the evidence that different orthographic systems (e.g. phonemic vs. logographic, left to right vs. right to left) may encourage different cerebral organization... Evidence from study of bilingualism suggests that the brain is a plastic, dynamic organ which continues to change throughout life as environmental, e.g. educational, stimuli impinge on it... The brain ...may be modified by the process of learning.

The modification of cerebral stuctures in the language area through learning seems confirmed by experiments conducted with bilinguals by G. A. Ojemann at the University of Washington.[13] He reports that:

Sites in the center of the language area in each patient were involved in both languages. Peripheral to this, in both frontal and parietal cortex, were sites involved in only one of the languages. In each patient, each language in part used different areas of the brain.

Thus learning a second language seems actually to have caused an expansion of the language area. Ojemann thinks

that anatomic alterations might occur in neurons following learning. ...A given memory may involve changes in many neurons, perhaps involving a number of different specialized regions of the brain.

Measurements of the bloodflow show that reading actuates the visual association area, the frontal eye field, Broca's speech center, the supplementary motor area, the motor area for the mouth and the auditory and the visual cortex. Thus the act of reading aloud causes simultaneous activity in seven discrete cortical centers in both hemispheres.[14] Learning to read thus involves more parts of the brain than most other activities. This is not surprising as reading requires the analysis of visual symbols whose meanings are recalled from memory and then converted to audio-symbols, assembled into words and sentences, and finally examined for their meaning until through prolonged practice the network of synaptic pathways becomes so well established that the process becomes subconscious and almost automatic. There can hardly be any doubt that such continuous intensive exercise of the brain during its time of greatest plasticity in childhood and youth develops new neural structures and thus cognitive abilities. Arnold Scheibel, a psychiatrist and anatomist at the University of California Medical School at Los Angeles, in his study of human brains has found that brain cells change in size and structure under constant intellectual stimulation. Specifically it appears that in areas most closely involved in complex tasks like language and information-processing, the size of neurons and the number of supporting glial cells increases, and the dendrite system becomes more thickly branched. From all this it appears that the intensive efforts involved in learning to read and write, and in the further education in literacy, actually may develop new brain circuitry and thus "improve the mind."

The proliferating sociological literature on literacy misses what is probably its most important benefit to the learner: the learning process itself, which creates new neural pathways supporting new linguistic and cognitive abilities. The enhancement of the mental development of the individual through the acquisition of literacy may well outweigh the practical economic benefits which seem to be the only concern of the literacy debate on both the national and the international level. The adverse critics assert that the promotion of literacy is elitist because the majority of the people make no use of writing and do only a very limited amount of utilitarian reading. Only small minorities have ever become truly literate and have used their prestige for political control.[15] Even if this allegation were true the great number of people who never use their literacy after leaving school will have reaped an advantage through the cognitive benefits gained in the learning process. But the greatest benefit is that basic literacy increases the pool of those that have access to higher learning and thus to the literate elite, the ones who contribute most to the advance of knowledge and a better life.

The debate has been greatly intensified by the appearance of a number of books on the subject of literacy in the last two years. Some of them, addressed to the general public, have become bestsellers, while others are academic publications by members of various disciplines. Although their approaches and content at first seem quite disparate a closer examination will reveal that by presenting different aspects of the current literacy problem, taken together they form a quite coherent picture.

R. K. Logan, *The Alphabet Effect: The Impact of the Phonetic Alphabet on the Development of Western Civilization* (New York 1986) is essentially a restatement of Marshal McLuhan's ideas, with whom Logan had collaborated for several years. One major point of his book is that the Chinese during the Middle Ages had been ahead of the West in various sciences, such as astronomy, and especially in technology, and had invented paper and printing with moveable type several centuries before these technologies became known in Europe. Yet while in the West the

> alphabet has contributed to the development of codified law, monotheism, abstract science, deductive logic, and individualism. . . and through the printing press reinforced and encouraged many of the key historical events of modern Europe including the Renaissance, the Reformation, the Industrial Revolution, and the rise of democracy, mass education, nationalism and capitalism,

no such thing happened in China because of the complexity of the Chinese logographic writing system, while the alphabet "has provided us with a conceptual framework for analysis and has restructured our perceptions of reality" (18, 113-114). Like McLuhan, Logan credits the sequential nature of the alphabet with many of its beneficial effects (234-5).

Eric A. Havelock rejoined the fray with *The Muse Learns to Write: Reflections on Orality and Literacy from Antiquity to the Present* (New Haven and London, 1986). While conceding the validity of some sociological and anthropological approaches Havelock reasserts the Greek uniqueness in what he calls "The Special Theory of Greek Orality" and its concomitant "The Special Theory of Greek Literacy:"

Havelock contrasts the total control of the Greeks over the transition from oral to written culture with the models of literacy acquisition frequently derived by anthropologists from modern non-literate societies from Tahiti to South America to Africa, where the conquest by literate foreigners imposed literacy from the outside and instantly all but wiped out the oral tradition and supplanted the oral practices of government with written procedures; whereas in ancient Greece, the process of transition remained completely under Greek initiative and control:

> The main shift began to occur with the invention of writing itself, and it came to a crisis point with the introduction of the Greek alphabet. An act of vision was offered in place of an act of hearing as the means of communication, and as the means of storing information. The adjustment it caused was in part social, but the major effect was felt in the mind and the way the mind thinks as it speaks. The crisis became Greek, rather than Hebrew or Babylonian or Egyptian because of the alphabet's superior efficiency (p. 100).

Jack Goody, *The Logic of Writing and the Organization of Society* (Cambridge 1986): This book is a follow-up on the seminal article by Goody and Ian Watt "The Consequences of Literacy" in Jack Goody (ed.), *Literacy in Traditional Societies* (Cambridge 1968) in which the authors tried to credit alphabetic literacy with a large part of the Greek classical achievement. In *The Domestication of the Savage Mind* (Cambridge 1977), Goody had tried to analyse "the effects of writing on modes of thought (or cognitive processes)," and promised a further investigation of the effects of liter-

acy on the institutions of society (ix). His present book is the fulfillment of this promise. Goody, who calls himself a "social anthro-
pologist," investigates the changes that evolve in the religious, economic, political, and legal (judicial) institutions when societies
make the transition from oral to literate cultures (xvi). He meticu-
lously documents the changes caused by writing in almost all conceivable, even trivial, everyday transactions with a wealth of examples from ancient and modern Near-Eastern, mediaeval, and West
African societies where Goody has done extensive fieldwork. The
book is also a response to the concentrated ideological attacks of
sociologists against his previous works. He carefully tries to disarm
their charges of an "ethnocentricity" which establishes a dichotomy
between oral and literate, and of an "evolutionism" which implies
progress and a value system.

Harvey J. Graff, *The Legacies of Literacy: Continuities and Contradictions in Western Culture and Society* (Bloomington and Indi-
anapolis 1987), exemplifies the opposition to Havelock's and
Goody's views. It is a sequel to Graff's earlier *The Literacy Myth*
(New York 1979) in which he denied the cognitive benefits such as
greater objectivity and logic, as well as enhanced ability for abstract
reasoning, that are ascribed to literacy by such authors as Havelock
and Goody. He considers schooling and literacy as tools of the ruling elite to maintain their hegemony over the lower classes (11-12,
264). In his new book Graff is in conflict with himself. As it is a
comprehensive and scholarly work, many of his findings contradict
his ideology. Thus the "contradictions" seem to be in Graff rather
than in Western civilization.

For example, Graff acknowledges that "Elisabeth Eisenstein's
The Printing Press as an Agent of Change is a monumental work
dealing with the impact of printing" (115); taking up her conclusions one by one he cannot help but concede the validity of her
overwhelming documentation for them, but he goes out of his way
to downgrade their importance as he has consistently minimized
the effects of literacy throughout his review of literacy in Western
history. He concludes:

> Literacy is held to be not only important and useful but also an unambigu-
> ously positive thing, associated closely with the vital necessities of 'modern',
> 'developed' persons and societies. In addition, scholars, writers, and other
> constant users of literacy are referred to as examples in support of generaliza-
> tions. Especially curious is the scholarly reification at the core of such intellec-
> tual acts, as men and women of the book project their presumed advantages
> and disadvantages on others (382).

In fine, since the benefits of literacy for society are vastly over-
rated, there is no literacy crisis, but rather a social crisis:

> The relationship between schooling and success, and the importance of
> achievement over ascription constitute two of the most profound issues in
> modern social science and social theory... recent Western data contradict as-
> sumptions or expectations of direct links between school achievement and
> job, wealth, or status achievement (384).

The book that has drawn the most attention is Allen Bloom, *The
Closing of the American Mind*, (New York 1987). It is one of three
recent books that voice concern with the steady decline of American literacy in the widest sense, which includes the knowledge of
the American heritage in the context of the Western historical, political, literary, and intellectual tradition. The other two are E.D.
Hirsch Jr., *Cultural Literacy: What Every American Needs to Know*,
(New York 1987) and Diane Ravitch and C. E. Finn, Jr., *What Do
Our 17-Year-Olds Know? A Report on the First National Assessment
of History and Literature* (New York 1987).

The three authors agree that the ignorance of history and literature among the present college population is unprecedented.
Bloom concentrates mainly on the failure of the universities to
provide a coherent liberal arts education. While his findings are
impressionistic, based on the experience of a lifetime of teaching at
various prestigious universities, Hirsch and Ravitch confirmed their
similar experiences and findings through systematic testing of students. With funding provided by the National Endowment for the
Humanities Diane Ravitch commissioned the design and administration of tests in American history and literature by a government
agency, the National Assessment of Educational Progress, which

has been testing high-school students regularly since 1969. The history test was given early in 1986 to a sample of 8,000 seventeen year old students taken from widely different regions and social and ethnic environments. By applying normal high-school grading standards to the history test 75 percent of the students flunked and the top quartile was only in the "C" range. The test was given at the end of the year when 78.4 percent of the tested students were enrolled in American history. Results of the literature test were even more dismal.

The three authors are also generally in agreement about the many interacting causes of the decline in literacy. Besides the well publicized decrease of time devoted to reading because of the competition from television and electronic music there is the relentless pressure by business and the general public for practical job-oriented courses and ever-increasing technological specialization on the college level. The main causes of the decline in literacy, however, stem from the combination of an ideological sociology and educational policies which, unsupported by any empirical justification, were introduced by well-meaning theorists following in the footsteps of John Dewey (Bloom 25-7, Hirsch 110-12,120-5, Ravitch 110).

Sociologists, striving to gain recognition for their fields as true sciences, went overboard in denying the admissibility of values and paradoxically supplanted the traditional values of American civilization with their own values, a total relativism and egalitarianism. They downgraded the Western heritage which had created the modern world, to just one of many civilizations. Thus they removed the interest in searching into our past for the answers to the timeless questions: who we are, what makes humans civilized, and how the great minds of the ages judged what our objectives should be (Bloom 25-43; Hirsch 116-133).

Educational theories and "reforms" manifested themselves in several fallacies:

> Some in the social studies field believe that concepts matter more than facts...The power of the facts versus concepts dichotomy has grown so great within the social studies field that some professionals now harbor an instinc-

tive distrust of facts per se ...it is fatuous to believe that students can think conceptually when they are ignorant of the most basic facts of American history. (Ravitch 15-16).

In the quest for concepts History became *Social Studies*, a salad of social concepts dressed in jargon, and lost its content of historic facts. A similar dichotomy transformed English into *Language Arts*:

> There is a tendency in the education profession to believe that *what* children learn is unimportant compared to *how* they learn; that skills can be learned without regard to content; to believe that content is in fact irrelevant... (Ravitch 17).

The coalition of sociologists and educational psychologists succeeded in removing the traditional reading matter from schooltexts of the lower grades. The stories that form part of the Western and American heritage, taken from ancient mythology and folklore, from the heroes of history, the discoverers and the founding fathers were banished from the classroom. In their place what is known as the K-3 curriculum was introduced in the thirties and was reaffirmed by the National Council of Social Studies in 1984:

Kindergarten - Awareness of self in social setting

Grade 1 - The individual in primary social groups: understanding school and family life

Grade 2 - Meeting basic needs in nearby social groups: the neighborhood

Grade 3 - Sharing earth space with others: the community. (Diane Ravitch, "Tot Sociology: What happened to History in Grade Schools" *The Key Reporter* 53-1 (Autumn 1987).

Thus instead of the exciting common national folklore children were fed Dick and Jane or similar fare for four years. In the higher grades deadening readers, workbook exercises, and books catering to the teen-age milieu took the place of the literary classics. Thus

English, watered down into Language Arts, and History, now a neglected part of Social Studies, had lost their content.

The lost content was the important cultural background that students should acquire in school. This common knowledge is what is meant with the term cultural literacy. The three authors, each in his own way, point out that every piece of writing-- textbook, literature, news report, propaganda or position paper-- presupposes some level of knowledge by the public to which it is addressed. Therefore reading comprehension depends to a large degree on the reader's knowledge, and literacy consist of much more than the skill of decoding written or printed letters. What puts the information into context and perspective is a process of combining the information on the page with the knowledge that the reader brings with him that puts the information into context and perspective. Every writer assumes or tries to gauge the expected degree of knowledge of his readers and subconsciously tries to make his points by images and references which he assumes to be known. Without such a common background there is no common language, no effective communication, and the democratic process is endangered. Therefore literacy that consists only in the skill of decoding letters on a page is meaningless (Bloom 34-6, Hirsch xii, 8-13, 18, 21, Ravitch 8-21).

Thus it is the consensus of the three authors that the illiteracy of the present generation is real and that there is an urgent need to put content, the teaching of the common national heritage, back into education from Kindergarten through University.

A book which is peripheral but connected to the central theme of literacy is Gertrude Himmelfarb, *The New History and the Old* (Cambridge, Mass. 1987). The author describes the current trend in the history departments of the universities where "Social History" is threatening to overwhelm the traditional way of teaching and writing history. Social history, too, is a product of egalitarianism. It is concerned with the history of the "common man" rather than the "elite." Instead of concentrating on the events and personalities which shaped the world we live in, it is concerned with the trivia of daily life. Social history explores what people in 18th century America ate for breakfast rather than what forces led to the Declaration of Independence. Himmelfarb does not deny a certain value of such investigations into the material living conditions of the ordinary people, but if the new history gains dominance and exclusivity she is afraid of losing not only the unifying theme that has given coherence to history, not only the notable events, individuals and institutions that have constituted our historical memory and our heritage but also the importance of man as a rational, political animal. Social history strips historiography of its drama and literary value and is contributing to the students' lack of interest and to their ignorance. The popularity of historical novels indicates how much attraction the true adventures and personalities of history have to offer.

There are, of course, much deeper-seated social, racial, and economic reasons that underlie the purely educational problems. The stubborn persistence of poverty and related racial tensions, the insecurity of the nuclear age, the population explosion and its ecological consequences, an ever widening gap between the ability to gain new scientific knowledge and the wisdom to control its application, have undermined confidence in human reason. Drug use and mystical cults have proliferated, religious fundamentalism and pseudo-sciences have revived while popular literacy and humanistic education have declined. The only hope for humanity lies in a sustained effort to create a climate of dispassionate rationality. Such an environment has never existed on a global scale and the attempt may be utopian, but both the international literacy programs, as well the "back to basics" program in the U.S., deserve every possible support for whatever contribution to literacy and education they might be able to make.

The best hope, however, seems to lie in the latest advance in the evolution of literacy: the microchip revolution. The compact computer, combined with instant data transmission and practically unlimited storage facilities, seems to offer equally limitless possibilities. One could imagine a country-wide and perhaps later a worldwide satellite-connected computer network, including all university libraries, accessible by everyone with a personal computer. The non-mathematical, mature field of classical studies offers a striking example. At the University of California at Irvine a cooperative international project has been completed, storing the total corpus of ancient Greek literature to AD 600 (58 million words) in computer language on one single laser disk. This means that anyone with the appropriate desk-top computer and the disk can immediately print out any work of ancient Greek literature. A researcher can instantly find every Greek word in the entire literature in all its contexts and uses by each author. Until now the only corresponding reference work was the Thesaurus compiled by Henri Étienne II (Stephanus) in the 16th century and re-edited in the 19th century. The work took Étienne almost a lifetime and ruined him financially.

On the most basic level, small personal computers and word processing programs have made writing and editing much easier and less time consuming, and have added a playful enjoyment. Children love computers and with the right programs should easily take to writing as just another computer game. Past disappointments with the electronic media, such as teaching machines and programmed instruction, however, should raise warning signs about the use of computers. They should not be allowed to replace traditional instruction in the three R's, but only to supplement it. Computers will be effective in education only if children are allowed to use them freely on their own. If word processing falls into the hands of the methodologists and becomes part of the teaching routine it will lose its appeal to the students and contribute nothing except competition for their time and for scarce funds. A further danger is that computers will widen the gap between the reasonably affluent and the poor. Just as children from an environment full of books tend to become readers, those who can afford computers will have an advantage over those who cannot. Learning to program a computer is probably effective mental training, as it requires the exercise of explicit unambiguous logic, but it can soon become a purely mechanical skill. In view of the continual pressure for vocational training computer education can easily deteriorate into just another job apprenticeship at the expense of academic subjects. On a more advanced level computer programming becomes the stock-in-trade of the professional programmer and system designer, but computer users in other professions need only a short familiarization with their machines, since canned programs perfected by software designers will do the work for them. The U.S. Department of Education should sponsor an intensive interdisciplinary study, including biologists and neurologists, to determine and evaluate the comparative effects of traditional studies in the three R's and computer use and programming on the cerebral and cognitive development of children.

Nobody can doubt that the computer has immeasurably multiplied the capabilities of human understanding. It has opened the door to more scientific knowledge in the last fifty years than in all of previous existence. The question is how to make the best use of computers in education. Just as the importance of literacy has been downgraded on the grounds that the electronic media were making written communications and printed information obsolete it is now asserted that electronic calculators and computers make the learning of the basic arithmetic skills and memorization of the multiplication tables just a waste of time. Educators have depreciated memorization for a long time. They denied the value of "cluttering up the mind" with facts that could be easily looked up when needed. This kind of reasoning is based on the erroneous assumption that the brain is a small storage closet with limited shelf space. We know now that the brain circuitry has almost infinite capacity. In the face of steadily declining results on aptitude tests educators claimed that their objective was to teach pupils how to think rather than to remember facts. The premise that thinking and retention of information are somehow in conflict is absurd. What is thinking other than relating known facts to each other and drawing conclusions from known pieces of information? Without experience and information in memory one can relate only nothing to nothing as there is no direct wire from the brain to the public library or the data base. Furthermore it is another misconception that thought processes are systematic and always conscious, and that the thinking person knows in advance what information will be needed.

Most often the random stream of consciousness reveals unsuspected connections between seemingly unrelated facts.

"Association is not a logical process; rather associations are formed of contiguity, happenstance, similarity, or capricious events external to the association that is formed."[16] Some famous flashes of genius materialized in this way, such as Newton's (perhaps mythical) apple and Einstein's concept of relativity (from an encounter of two streetcars). The computer substituting for the library, bound in its relentless logic, cannot substitute for the haphazard spontaneous fireworks of the brain.

The computer has been commonly used as a metaphor for the brain, and the quest for artificial intelligence conversely has tried to imitate the brain by programming strictly sequential operational steps. A survey of prominent scientists in the field conducted by the *Economist* (June 29, 1985) found that these models are almost certainly wrong:

> The human brain contains 10 billion neurons, but they are tortoises: a transistor in a micro-processor can...process a single bit of information in a billionth of a second. The generation of an electrical impulse in a neuron takes about a millisecond - about a hundred thousand times longer. So where does the brain's remarkable power come from?... scientists believe it comes from from the dense network of connections among the neurons. Each neuron is connected to as many as 10,000 others. Most computers built so far use a single processor to work on information in a sequential stream one piece at a time. Not the brain: its neuron connections make it a massively parallel processor whose ability to handle large amounts of data at the same time makes up for its slowness.

Thus an infinite amount of random thought associations is probably occurring at any one time.

A fundamental question is whether the computer will be used as an additional tool of the mind or as a sustitute for it. The miraculous mathematical capability of computers offers the temptation to apply statistical techniques and quantitative solutions to non-measurable human qualities and questions of ethical values, thus abdicating moral and philosophical considerations to sociological statisticians or religious dogmatists.

Computers should not be expected to replace books. One cannot browse in a computer memory, nor is it practical to take a monitor screen on a commuter train or to the beach. Where computers might help the cause of literacy most is in the field of book publishing. The current exorbitant cost of books is a severe threat to literacy. From 1960 to 1980, 300 publishing houses have been acquired by conglomerates whose shareholders have no interest in literature; their main objective is the edition of a million copies. Since the public seems to be too often interested in the lurid details of the private lives of notorious personalities, these are the subjects preferred by publishers who in turn blame the public's taste and the high cost of printing. Not so long ago runs of 10,000 copies of quality books were considered quite respectable and paid for themselves, but now the tax structure is such that some publishers scrap books that are expected to sell 10,000 or fewer copies within a year's time.[17] Computer operated laser printers, however, have so lowered printing costs that small entrepreneurs may be able to enter the publishing field and to operate with lower prices without having to enter the mass marketing field where the publishing conglomerates also control the outlets.

Another recent development in literacy to which computers and telecommunications continue to make important contributions is the spread of English as a world-language. English as a second language is now taught, spoken and read by more people than live in all the countries where it is the native tongue.

In an attempt to sum up, two points seem to emerge as the most important, the greatest benefit of literacy may well be that it creates and strengthens cognitive abilities. Although much circumstantial evidence in the intellectual history of the West and in recent biological findings seems to point in that direction, this cannot be considered as proven. Therefore additional research in the neurophysiological field is of the utmost importance and should be supported by the government.

Secondly literacy is the basis and prerequisite of all learning and intellectual growth. For the individual the printed book is still the most practical and convenient vehicle of information, knowledge, ideas, and intellectual enjoyment. Electronic technology has enormously multiplied the capabilities of the literate human mind, but it can substitute neither for literacy nor for the mind.

Notes

1. Jack Goody and Ian Watt, "The Consequences of Literacy" in *Literacy In Traditional Societies*, J. Goody (ed.) (Cambridge 1968), 51

2. Ian Winchester in D.R. Olson, Nancy Torrance, and Angeline Hildyard (edd.), *Literacy, Language, and Learning* (Cambridge 1985), 45

3. Frank Smith, in Winchester et al.

4. *Report of the Secretary General on the World Campaign for Universal Literacy* (New York, N.Y., U.N. 1964), A/530

5. Jonathan Kozol, *Illiterate America* (New York 1985), 8-9

6. E.A. Havelock, *Preface to Plato* (Harvard 1963); *The Muse Learns to Write* (New Haven and London 1986); I. J. Gelb, *A Study of Writing* (2nd edition, London and Chicago 1963); J. Goody and I. Watt *Literacy in Traditional Societies*, (Cambridge 1968); Carlo Cipolla, *Literacy and Development in the West* (London 1969); J. Oxenham, *Writing, Reading and Social Organization* (London 1980); Elisabeth Eisenstein, *The Printing Press as an Agent of Change* (Cambridge 1979)

7. E.g., C. & L. Berggren, *The Literacy Process: A Practice in Domestication or Liberation* (London 1975), 13 and *passim*; H. J. Graff, *The Literacy Myth* (New York 1979), 11-12, 264; B. V. Street, *Literacy in Theory and Practice* (Cambridge 1984), 2-3

8. Robert Pattison, *On Literacy: The Politics of the Word from Homer to the Age of Rock* (Oxford 1982), 120

9. In David Caplan, A.R. Lecours & Allen Smith, (edd.), 411 *Biological Perspectives on Language*, MIT Studies in Neuropsychology and Neurolinguistics, (Cambridge Mass. 1984), 32

10. In J.T. Guthrie (ed.), *Aspects of Reading Acquisition* (Baltimore and London 1976), 7-8

11. Lecours et al., in *Biological Perspectives* (note 9) 230-231

12. M.L. Albert and L.K. Obler, *The Bilingual Brain: Neurolinguistic Aspects of Bilingualism* (New York and London 1978), 243-254

13. *Archives of Neurology* 35 (1979), 409-412

14. N.A. Lassen, D.H. Ingvar, and Erik Skinhoj, "Brain Function and Blood Flow", *Scientific American* 239 (October 1978), 68-71

15. E.g., Robert Pattison, *The Politics of the Word*, 83

16. David Caplan, et al., *Biological Perspectives*, 366

17. Jonathan Kozol, *Illiterate America* (Garden City 1985), 152

Appendix

The Hellenistic Textbooks[1]

Perhaps the outstanding achievement of the Hellenistic age was the systematization and the codification of existing scientific knowledge in well organized textbooks. These works, copied and recopied and translated into Latin, Syriac and Arabic, preserved the legacy of ancient science through the vicissitudes of the Middle Ages. In some cases these books, rather than the original works on which they were based, survived because of the logic and lucidity of their presentation. The following is a recapitulation of some of the most important of these compendia which became the foundation of Byzantine, Arab and, after the introduction of the printed book, of renewed Western European scientific inquiry.

Euclid's Mathematics

Probably the longest-lived textbook of all times was the *Elements* (*stoicheia*) of mathematics by Euclid of Alexandria (c. 330-275). It encompassed all the mathematical knowledge of his Eastern and Greek predecessors: six books on plane geometry; three books on arithmetic; one on irrational numbers and their determination by the method of exhaustion, including the derivation of the constant *pi* for the calculation of the circumference and area of circles; finally three books on solid geometry. The *Elements* set a standard for logical reasoning and clarity of expression. Beginning with a few self-evident axioms it develops its theorems and their corollaries step by step with irrefutable logic, building each new theorem on those previously proven. The *Elements* remained the Bible of mathematics well into modern times.

Translated into Arabic in the 9th century the *Elements* formed the basis of Arab mathematical learning and research. In the Western world only a few parts translated into Latin by Boethius in the 6th century survived until Arab versions became known in the 12th century. The first complete translation from Arabic into Latin known with certainty was by Abelard of Bath. This translation, revised by Giovanni Campano in the 13th century, became the first printed edition of Euclid; it came off the press of Radolt in Venice in 1482. The first translation from the original Greek into Latin by Bartolomeo Zamberti was printed in Venice in 1505 and was soon followed by others. The first edition of the Greek text was edited by Gryneus and printed in Basel in 1533; this was the text that served Copernicus. John Billingsley, Lord Mayor of London, made the first English translation (John Day, London 1570). Euclid and geometry have remained almost synonymous; it was not uncommon in 19th century England to ask a schoolboy whether "he had done his Euclid today." Only in the last one hundred years has "Non-Euclidean Geometry come into its own.

Ptolemy' s Astronomy

Another book that commanded the same authority as being the all-encompassing text in its field was Ptolemy's work on astronomy. Claudius Ptolemaios lived in Alexandria in the 2nd century after Christ. The Greeks named his book *The Greatest Mathematical Composition (he megiste mathematike syntaxis)*. In the Middle Ages it became better known as the *Almagest*, the Arabic transformation of its title derived from the Arab quasi-article *al* and the corruption of *megiste* in its Greek name. Like Euclid, Ptolemy incorporated the work of all his predecessors in his book from Eudoxus in the 4th century BC to Hipparchus in the second. Ptolemy often acknowledges his indebtedness to Hipparchus; despite the 300 year gap between them, apparently very little was added, and Ptolemy gives the impression that he considers himself an immediate successor to Hipparchus.

Aristotle's view of the world as a system of concentric spheres rotating around a central earth was based more on aesthetics than on exact observations. This mental image was part of Plato's and Aristotle's quest for divine perfection in the cosmos. Aristotle was well aware of reservations by practicing astronomers and mathematicians; his purpose, however, was not to construct a model realistic in every detail, but rather to determine the *telos*, the ultimate purpose, of the world. Therefore he considered the objections of Eudoxus, his colleague and mathematician at Plato's Academy, as minor and irrelevant (*Met*.12.8.107.3b17), especially since the general theory of nested concentric rotations was never questioned even by conscientious observers such as Eudoxus and Callippus. They, however, noted contradictory indications and irregularities, such as seeming retrograde movements of the planets, and tried to reconcile them with the overall theory. They called these efforts "saving the apparent facts (*sozein ta phainomena*)." The system, worked out by a succession of astronomers and approaching completion by Hipparchus in the second century BC, explained the deviations in the movements of the planets from their expected circularity in two ways: (1) a slight eccentricity of the orbital circles around the earth; (2) the so-called epicycles. According to this second theory, the planets moved not in simple circles, but rather in a series of smaller circles whose centers traveled along the basic circular orbital paths. This was the design of the universe which Ptolemy presented fully developed in the *Almagest* three hundred years later. Where Hipparchus ends and Ptolemy begins cannot be determined with certainty. Ptolemy's system was as accurate a mathematical model of the movements of the planets observed from the earth as could be devised with the instruments available in his time.

The presentation of the system, however, is only the final culmination of the book. Like Euclid's *Elements* the *Almagest* is a structure ascending from the most basic assumptions step by step to the completion of the intellectual edifice. Ptolemy began with a description of the sophisticated instruments that he used and may have perfected himself and the methods of observation. All the distances between the celestial bodies are determined by angular measurements in degrees, minutes and seconds and expressed trigonometrically by the ratio of the intercepted chord to the radius, which is assigned the value of one and is also subdivided according to the hexagesimal system. To facilitate his computations Ptolemy prepared a table of chords at half-degree intervals from one to 180 degrees. These measurements were used to locate the position of stars in reference to meridians and their elevation in reference to the plane of the equator and the ecliptic, respectively. Ptolemy also discussed the precession of equinoxes and corrected earlier astronomic measurements according to the precession. He assumed the precession to be one degree per century but Hipparchus, positing the precession at 1.3 degrees, had been closer to the correct value of 1.4 degrees. Based on these methods and his observations Ptolemy included tables showing the positions of over a thousand fixed stars and their degrees of brightness. With these and the description of the geocentric system Ptolemaic astronomy retained its validity well into the 17th century until the findings of Copernicus, Brahe and Kepler.

The authority of Ptolemy's work was such that it completely overshadowed and probably thus caused the loss of most previous treatises on the subject, including the heliocentric theory of Aristarchus of Samos, which Hipparchus had rejected and which Ptolemy never mentioned. We know something about Aristarchus' genius from one of his books which survives. In his *On the Sizes and Distances of the Sun and the Moon*, Aristarchus presented ingenious and flawless geometric procedures to arrive at exact values, but unfortunately the observations and the angle measurements available were so far off the mark as to make the results worthless despite the correctness of his methods. An even bolder pioneering effort was his heliocentric planetary system, in which he anticipated Copernicus by a thousand years.

We know Aristarchus' theory only from second-hand comments. The most important is a short paragraph in Archimedes' *Sand-Reckoner* (1.4-7) in which he cites Aristarchus' opinion to the effect that:

the fixed stars and the sun remain motionless while the earth revolves in the circumference of a circle about the sun which lies in the middle of its orbit, and that the sphere of the fixed stars, situated about the same center as the sun, is so great that the circle in which he supposes it to revolve has such a proportion to the distance of the fixed stars as the center of the sphere bears to its surface.

The last, somewhat fuzzy, statement implies that the whole sphere defined by the earth's orbit is like a point in comparison to the distance of the fixed stars from the earth. Aristarchus' radical vision of an almost infinite universe must have followed the observation that there was no change in the angle at which fixed stars were observed at various times and thus from various positions of the earth. It had been accepted that distances on the surface of the earth were small enough in comparison to the distance to the fixed star heaven that the lines of sight from different locations appeared parallel. But the displacement of an observer along the earth's orbit around the sun would be so much larger that the absence of parallactic change indicated a vastly greater universe than had been generally assumed. This bold idea was too enormous for Aristarchus' contemporaries to accept, just as it was the reason why 1700 years later Tycho Brahe could not accept the Copernican theory. Besides, in both cases there were all the religious and philosophical prejudices that militated against the removal of the earth from its motionless position at the center of the universe. Thus the Aristarchan system was rejected and all but forgotten while the Ptolemaic retained its uncontested dominance for the next 14 centuries.

The *megiste syntaxis* became the *Almagest* when it was first translated into Arabic in the 8th century. Several other Arab translations followed between the 9th and 13th centuries. It was first translated from Arabic into Latin in the 12th century by John of Seville and shortly thereafter a Latin translation from the Greek appeared in Sicily. Two epitomized versions of Ptolemaic astronomy were published in print in 1492 and 1496 respectively, both in Italy. The first printed editions of the full text of the *Almagest* were the following: a Latin translation from the Arabic, prepared by

Gerard of Cremona in 1175 and edited by Peter Liechtenstein in
Venice in 1515; a Latin version from the Greek by George of Tre-
bizond, printed in Venice in 1528. The first printed Greek text,
edited by Simon Grynaeus, was published in Basel in 1538.

Ptolemy's Geography

An achievement of nearly the importance of Ptolemy's astronomy
was his work on geography. The *geographike hyphegesis* was another textbook that summarized the accumulated knowledge in its
field and remained authoritative in cartography for several centuries. But, while Ptolemy's astronomy retained the validity of both
the methodology and the data obtained by the practical application
of his methods, the lasting importance of Ptolemy's geography lay
in establishing the principles of mathematical geography; the actual
results, due to the lack of reliable measurements and the absence
of celestial fixes, were so inaccurate that they were of little value.

Ptolemy drew on the work of his predecessors: Eratosthenes,
Hipparchus, Posidonius, and especially Marinus of Tyre. And, just
as in the *Almagest*, he contributed much of his own conceptual,
mathematical, and organizing genius. In the first introductory book
Ptolemy gives his estimate of the size of the earth. Eratosthenes,
head of the Alexandrian Library from 234-192 BC, had calculated
the circumference of the earth by measuring the distance between
two locations on the same meridian and correlating this distance
with the difference between the two angles of incidence of the sun-
rays at the solstice at both points. Extrapolating from the relationship between the distance and the angular difference he calculated
the circumference corresponding to 360 degrees. He arrived at a
figure equivalent to 37,500 kilometers. This was an excellent approximation to the correct measurement of 40,120 kilometers. Unfortunately, however, Ptolemy preferred the figure of 26,785 kilometers given by the Stoic philosopher Posidonius. We do not know
how Posidonius arrived at this measurement nor why Ptolemy accepted it. This was another source of errors in Ptolemy's tables and,
presumably, maps.

With a network of meridians of longitude and parallels of latitude Ptolemy provided the system which allows one to locate any point on the globe, and he proposed various methods of projection. Ptolemy, following Eratosthenes, established his parallels according to the length of the longest day of the year in different latitudes. For Ptolemy, as for most inhabitants of the classical lands, the Mediterranean was the focus of the known world. Therefore, he made the parallel which he thought to be running through Rhodes and Gibraltar and roughly bisecting the Mediterranean (our 30 degrees N) the axis of his system. From this zero-latitude he placed his parallels in one hour intervals north and south according to the length of the longest day. To the south his knowledge reached as far as Meroe in Nubia, today's Aswan, where the day at solstice is 13 hours long (roughly latitude 17 N.); to the north somewhere along the Dnieper between latitudes 60 and 65 N., where he believed the longest day to be 16 hours. He counted his longitudes eastward from the meridian of the Canary Islands, the westernmost land he knew, to the east end of Asia, which he thought to be a distance of 180 degrees. Actually the Eurasian continent spans only 130 degrees. As George Sarton suggests, this error and his underestimation of the length of the earth's circumference may have helped twelve centuries later to deceive Columbus about the distance to India.[2]

The book includes a list of approximately 8,000 localities with their longitudes and latitudes according to his grid. But, since most of his information was based on primitive surveys, dead reckoning, hearsay, and guess, the data are generally quite incorrect; yet the theoretical system would eventually lead to modern cartography, but this had to wait for the voyages of discovery and the invention of printing and copper engraving.

Ptolemy's geography or cosmology, as it was called more often, was commented on by Arab geographers in the 10th century, and the Greek text was translated into Latin by Giacomo d'Angelo in 1409. The first printed edition in Latin was prepared by Herrmann Liechtenstein in Vincenza in 1457. The first Greek text, edited by Erasmus of Rotterdam, was printed by Froben in Basel in 1533.

Galen's Medical Science

Claudius Galenus was a prolific writer. The fairly complete early
modern edition by Gottlieb Kuhn (*Galeni opera omnia*, [Leipzig
1821-33]) consists of 22 thick volumes and contains the 122 treatises known at that time. A few more have been recovered from
Arabic translations since then. Galen was born around AD 130 in
Pergamum, which, with its library and Asclepeion, rivaled Alexandria as a center of learning. Its sanctuary of the healer-god Ascle-
pius was one of the three most renowned medical establishments of
the Greek world, offering divine as well as medical succor to the
sick. The others were Cos, the residence of Galen's predecessor
Hippocrates, and Epidaurus. After receiving a thorough philosophic education from representatives of the four main schools,
Platonic, Aristotelian, Stoic and Epicurean, Galen devoted himself
to eleven years of studies in anatomy and medicine in Pergamum,
Smyrna, Corinth, and Alexandria. At the age of 28 he was appointed surgeon to the troop of gladiators in the arena of Pergamum, a position which he held for four years until a war with the
neighboring Galatians put an end to the gladiatorial games. One
can hardly imagine a better opportunity for a budding surgeon to
gain experience than a prolonged internship in the bloody arena.
After that he served as army surgeon and finally as court physician
to the emperor Marcus Aurelius and his son Commodus from 169-
192. After Commodus was murdered he retired to Pergamum,
where he died around AD 200 at the age of 70. Although Galen
drew on the knowledge of his predecessors, especially the Hippocratic writings, and the work of the physicians at the Museum of
Alexandria, much of his knowledge was based on his own research
and experience.

Hippocrates had been active on the Aegean island of Cos in the
late 5th century BC. He undoubtedly was the author of many of the
treatises ascribed to him, but it also seems quite clear that much
that went under his name in the Hippocratic corpus was the work
of later writers. Through their continuous involvement in warfare
and hand-to-hand fighting the Greeks had gained considerable ex-

perience in anatomy and the functioning of the human body. Already in Homer one finds amazingly realistic descriptions of the effects of wounds on various parts and organs of the body, and we hear that skilled physicians were in great demand. In opposition to that empirical tradition some abstract medical theories had been promoted on philosophical grounds. For instance, the theory of the four humors was probably derived from the Pythagorean doctrine of the harmony of opposites through correct mathematical proportions. Thus, health was viewed as the proper balance of the body-fluids: blood, yellow bile, phlegm, and black bile. Disease was ascribed to a disturbance of the proper ratio between them, and it was the physician's task to restore the balance. Their mixture was also thought to determine the temperament of a person and we still use the terms sanguine, phlegmatic, choleric, and melancholy to describe different moods. Hippocrates and his followers, on the whole, stressed empiricism. The Hippocratic writers were at their best in their exact descriptions of symptoms and the pathological sequences of events in the course of illnesses. They were conscious of the importance of diet and held a strong belief in the influence of climate and environment. Hippocrates recognized the brain as the seat of consciousness and emotions, an insight that was later discredited by Aristotle.

Knowledge of the human body was considerably increased by two physicians at the Museum of Alexandria. Herophilus and his younger successor Erasistratus, active in the 3d century BC, performed dissections of cadavers and advanced the knowledge of anatomy. They are also reported to have performed vivisection on condemned criminals, a report that may be or may not be based on truth. Herophilus described the digestive system, and discovered much about the nervous system, and reinstituted the brain as the center of mental activity. Erasistratus developed a theory on the circulatory system, according to which the veins carried the blood-flow while the arteries were filled with air. Blood was thought to be continuously produced from food and air and to be used up by the body as nourishment. Very little seems to have been added to medical science between Erasistratus and Galen.

Galen's approach was thoroughly scientific. He wrote books on anatomy, biology, surgery, therapy, and pharmacology. He had firsthand knowledge of the human bone and muscular structures, but his knowledge of the interior organs was derived from the dissection of animals, mainly monkeys. In his textbook on anatomical procedures, *de anatomicis administrationibus* (following mediaeval and renaissance usage it is still customary to refer to Galen's works by their Latin names), he implies the difficulties in obtaining human subjects for dissection or autopsy:[3]

> It is still possible to see something of human bones I, at least have done so often by breaking open a grave or tomb... If you have no luck in seeing anything like that, dissect an ape ...if you have no ape, other animals must serve...

Of course there was the difficulty of discerning small structures with the naked eye:[4]

> ... we hold it best to study the details which are hard to see, in bodies of large sized animals. I mean oxen, horses, asses, mules, and others like these.

Without human specimens, without microscope, without chemistry, Galen still opened the way to much new understanding.

Galen came about 500 years after Erasistratus. During all that time it had been an unsolved problem how blood could enter from the venous system into the arterial system, as there was no apparent communication between the two; the veins connected with the right ventricle of the heart, and the arteries originated from the left ventricle. The two chambers were separated by the solid wall of the *septum* between them. Thus, since no blood could enter the arteries from the veins, the arteries were thought to be filled by air. But Galen's experience as surgeon and his experiments with animals had convinced him that the arteries were always filled with blood. Therefore he surmised correctly that venous blood flowed from the right ventricle into the lungs, where it absorbed air and entered the left chamber of the heart. But he still thought that the arterial blood was used up by the body as nourishment like the venous blood. It was not until the 17th century that the true nature of blood circulation as a closed loop was discovered by William Harvey and confirmed by the microscopic discovery of the pulmonary capillaries by Marcello Malpighi. Although Galen never realized the full impact of his findings Harvey repeatedly acknowledged his debt to him.

Galen described how to diagnose fever by counting the pulse. His discoveries about the nervous system were an outstanding achievement. He recognized that the brain, through the spinal cord and the nerves, regulated all voluntary movements of the body. One of his most influential works was a treatise in 17 books on the anatomy and functions of the parts of the human body (*de usu partium corporis humani*). Inspired by Aristotle's teleology Galen saw in the perfect adaptation of each organ to its function the design of a providence of infinite wisdom. This view contributed to the later popularity of his works among Christians and Moslems. Galen's most important work was *The Art of Healing* (*de methodo medendi*), in the Middle Ages commonly called "The Great Art" (*megatechne* or *ars magna*) in 14 books. He also addressed to a friend a shorter version in two books, entitled *ad Glauconem de medendi methodo*, known as the *therapeutica*. This was further condensed under the title *ars medica*. Referred to as "The Small Art" (*microtechne* or *ars parva*), it became the most popular of his works and existed in many manuscripts in Greek, Latin, Syriac, Arabic and Hebrew. Galen still subscribed to the concept of the four humors and wrote on the subject under the title *de temperamentis et de inequali intemperie*.

He discussed many of his predecessors and contemporaries, often in a polemic fashion. It should be noted that his writings included an autobiography and his bibliography. Both are firsts in scientific literature, and because of them we know more about Galen's life than that of other ancient writers. His bibliography is of great value in helping to distinguish his authentic works from later attributions.[5]

The Galenic tradition of medicine was never interrupted in the Byzantine empire and the Near East. His works were lost to western Europe after the collapse of the West Roman empire until they

were translated into Latin from Arabic in the 11th and 12th centuries and then made their full impact with the advent of print.
Philippus Pincius printed a Latin edition of Galen's works in
Venice in 1490, while the first printed text in Greek was the *thera-
peutika*, printed by Zacharias Callierges in Venice in 1500. In 1521
the treatise on the humors, edited by Thomas Linacre was published by Siberch in Cambridge. This was the first book printed in
Greek type in England. The first complete edition of Galen's
known works in Greek was published by Aldus Manutius in Venice
in 1525. In Paris, Basel, Lyon and Venice alone 481 editions of
works by Galen were published during the Renaissance period--
not including summaries (Siegel 69). Galen's works had become
the universal medical curriculum and provided the Renaissance
with the starting point and the experimental methods for the development of modern anatomy and medicine. The medical scientists took their inspiration from him, rather than "freeing themselves" from him; just as they built on Aristotle, rather than
"shaking off his shackles" as some modern historians of science like
to assert.

Dionysius Thrax' Greek Grammar[6]

Dionysius' *Art of Grammar* (*techne grammatike*) shaped the way
that grammar was to be taught and studied in the Western world
until our own time. Dionysius (170-90 BC) was a pupil of
Aristarchus of Samothrace (216 -144 BC), perhaps the greatest of
the librarians and *philologoi* at the Alexandrian library. Because of
the political upheavals in Egypt in 145/144 BC Dionysius left
Alexandria and went to Rhodes. The close relationship between
Rhodes and Rome enabled him to help spread the influence of the
Alexandrian scholars to the West. Like his teacher, Aristarchus, he
was mainly interested in interpreting Homer and he wrote commentaries on the Homeric poems. His only surviving work, however, is his grammar, which is also the earliest surviving classical
schoolbook on grammar. In the 4th century BC a much more sophisticated system of linguistics had been developed by Panini in

India, but it did not became known in the West until recently and thus had no influence on European developments.

The *Art* is a small, very concise textbook, barely 50 pages in modern print. Because of its terseness many explanatory notes were subsequently added by the Byzantine scholars. It begins with a few definitions, then classifies the letters as vowels, long or short, diphthongs, and consonants; then syllables, long, short or indeterminate; finally eight parts of speech: nouns with three genders and five case inflections; verbs with their moods, voices, tenses, persons, numbers, and conjugation; participles sharing the functions of nouns and verbs, then the article, pronoun, prepositions, adverbs, and conjunctions. It contained no attempt at syntax or composition. Although the grammar was developed from Greek and for Greek and remained the basis of textbooks in the Greek East through Byzantine times, it was used in the same form to teach Latin, and all later Latin grammars are its offspring. Its influence on the West in the Middle Ages and the Renaissance came not through direct use of the book, but from the fact that its system had become traditional and was used by all writers of Latin grammars and later grammars for any European language.

When interest in Greek revived in Florence and the Greek scholar Chrysolaras was invited by Salutati in 1396 to teach that language he wrote his own question-and-answer textbook (*erotemata*) based on Dionysius' grammar. The *Art of Grammar* did not appear in print until 1715; its system, however, was the customary and only approach to teaching language in the Western world. Since the Indo-European languages are all more or less closely related and have similar structures the method remained quite adequate. It was only in modern times, when ethnologists and anthropologists found a need to analyse and describe languages with structures and phonetics that are totally different from the Indo-European, that a new approach had to be found. Modern linguistics developed in response to this need and reached back to Panini's techniques. Dionysius Thrax' *techne*, however, is still alive and well in many Western schools.

Justinian's Law Code

A compilation that cannot properly be called a textbook and was entirely of Roman origin, rather than Hellenistic, was the Justinian *corpus iuris civilis*. The Romans had nurtured from earliest times a strong sentiment for tradition and orderly procedures based on custom (*mos maiorum*). This respect for the past expressed itself in a high regard for precedent in the application of laws. Court procedings and decisions were preserved in archives for future reference. Nationalistic pride in the Roman institutions and the rights of citizens had generated a strong feeling for due process and equality before the law. Expertise in questions of law and court procedure became a great asset for those seeking political power in the late republic and subsequently for bureaucrats and administrators in the empire. The legal expert (*iuris prudens*) and advocate (*respondens*) were respected professionals representative of the oratorical tradition. Legal manuals for reference and training and dissertations by learned jurists, especially during the 2nd century after Christ, added to a growing body of legal literature. In the later empire law schools were established in Rome, Beirut and Constantinople.

The emperor Justinian (518-565) created a commission of jurists to codify all valid laws in a form designed to eliminate current controversies. The result was the *corpus iuris civilis*, the final comprehensive compilation of Roman law, which consists of three parts. The first part, issued in 529 and revised in 534, was the *Code of Justinian*, containing all laws and imperial edicts with validity throughout the empire. The second part, the *Digest*, issued in 533, consisted of abstracts from the writings of the most prominent jurists, arranged for easy reference. The third part, the *institutiones*, was a textbook for the instruction of students. The whole *corpus* was to be the only source of law to be used in the courts and to be taught in the law schools.

In the 13th century, with the growth of independent cities and secular government, there arose a need for civil laws and constitutions, and the only available models were those of antiquity. The study of Roman law became part of the university curriculum and was based mainly on the Justinian corpus. The study of Roman law was instrumental in reawakening an interest in Roman institutions and history. In Italy the study of Roman historians and writers such as Cicero brought the realization of the changes that the Latin language had undergone. The study of Roman law played a considerable part in the growing enthusiasm for classical Latin and thus the rediscovery of the ancient literature that led to the beginning of Renaissance humanism. Eventually Roman law became the basis of all Western law, including English common law, to a greater degree than is generally realized. The very ideas of individual rights and due process are a legacy of Rome.

Justinian's *corpus* of Roman law was the last chapter in the codification of the Greek-Roman cultural heritage. All the other works discussed in the foregoing were written before the year AD 200.

Notes

1. The following relies heavily on George Sarton, *A History of Science* (Cambridge, Mass. 1959)

2. *A History of Science*

3. Charles Singer, *The Discovery of the Circulation of the Blood* (London 1956), 3-7. R. E. Siegel, *Galen's System of Physiology and Medicine* (Basel 1968), 28

4. Siegel, 101

5. Siegel, 69

6. Rudolf Pfeiffer, *History of Classical Scholarship* (Oxford 1968), 266-272

Bibliography

John Adams   *Adams Family Correspondence*, edited by L. H. Butterfield, 4 vols. (Cambridge, Mass. 1963-73)

--   *Diary and Autobiography of John Adams*, edited by L. H. Butterfield, 4 vols. (Cambridge, Mass. 1962)

--   *The Works of John Adams*, 10 vols. (Boston 1850-56)

--   *The Adams-Jefferson Letters*, edited by L. J. Cappon, (Chapel Hill 1959)

F. E. Adcock   *The Greek and Macedonian Art of War* (1957)

H. B. Adelmann   *Marcello Malpighi and the Evolution of Embryology*, 5 vols. (Ithaca 1967)

Thomas Africa   "Copernicus' Relation to Aristarchus and Pythagoras", *Isis* 52 (1961), 403-9

M. L. Albert & L. K. Obler   *The Bilingual Brain: Neurolinguistic Aspects of Bilingualism* (New York & London 1978)

W. F. Albright   *Archaeology and the Religion of Israel* (4th ed. Garden City, N. Y. 1968)

--   *From the Stone Age to Christianity* (4th ed. Garden City, N. Y. 1957)

— —   *The Vocalization of the Egyptian Syllabic Orthography* (New Haven 1934)

— —   *The Archaeology of Palestine* (New York 1963)

— —   *Yahweh and the Gods of Canaan* (New York 1968)

Jaques Amyot   See: Plutarch

Shimon Applebaum   *Jews and Greeks in Ancient Cyrene* (Leiden 1979)

Aristarchus   *Aristarchus of Samos, the Ancient Copernicus*, text and trans. by Thomas Heath (Oxford 1913)

Aristotle   *The Basic Works of Aristotle* edited by R. McKeon, based on the Oxford translation of 1931, (Chicago 1941)

M. C. Astour   *Hellenosemitica* (Leiden 1965)

M. M. Austin   *The Hellenistic World from Alexander to the Roman Conquest* (Cambridge 1981)

Ernst Badian   "Alexander the Great and the Unity of Mankind" *Historia* 7 (1958), 425-444

— —   *Studies in Greek and Roman History* (New York 1964)

Hans Baron   "Fifteenth Century Civilization and Renaissance", in *New Cambridge Modern History*, vol. 1 (1957)

— —   *The Crisis of the Early Italian Renaissance* (Princeton 1966)

Carola Baumgardt   *Johannes Kepler: Life and Letters* (New York 1951)

F. A. G. Beck   *Greek Education*, 450-350 B.C. (New York 1964)

--   *Album of Greek Education* (Sydney 1975)

E. L. Bennett Jr.   *Mycenaean Studies* (Madison 1964)

H. S. Bennett   *English Books and Readers, 1475-1557*, (Cambridge 1969)

--   *English Books and Readers, 1558-1603* (Cambridge 1965)

--   *English Books and Readers, 1603-1640* (Cambridge 1970)

D. F. Benson   In J. T. Guthrie, *Aspects of Reading Acquisition* (Baltimore and London 1976), 7-8

C. & L. Bergren   *The Literacy Process: A Practice in Domestication or Liberation* (London 1975)

Bruno Bettelheim & Karen Zelan   *On Learning to Read: The Child's Fascination with Reading* (New York 1982)

P. G. Bietenholz   *Basle and France in the Sixteenth Century: The Basle Humanists and Printers in their Contacts with Francophone Culture*, (Toronto 1971)

Theodor Birt   *Die Buchrolle in der Kunst* (Leipzig 1907)

C. W. Blegen   "Inscriptions on Geometric Pottery from Hymettos", *American Journal of Archaeology* 38 (1934), 10-28

340   *Bibliography*

Allan Bloom   *The Closing of the American Mind* (New
                     York 1987)

J. M. Blythe   "The Mixed Constitution in Thomas
                     Aquinas", *Journal of the History of Ideas*
                     47 (1986), 547-565

R.R. Bolgar   *The Classical Heritage and its Beneficia-
                     ries: From the Carolingian Age to the End
                     of the Renaissance* (New York 1964)

J. D. Bolter   *Turing's Man, Western Culture in the Com-
                     puter Age* (Chapel Hill, 1984)

S. F. Bonner   *The Education of A Roman* (Liverpool
                     1950)
T. A. Boring   "Literacy in Ancient Sparta", *Mnemosyne*,
                     suppl. 54 (1979)

C. M. Bowra   *Homer* (London 1972)

J. H. Breasted   *The Conquest of Civilization* (New York
                     1938)

Walter Burkert   *Weisheit und Wissenshaft* (Nuremberg
                     1962)

John Burnet   *Early Greek Philosophy* (London 1892)

Alfred Burns   "The Fragments of Philolaos and Aristo-
                     tle's Account in Metaphysics A", *Classica
                     et Mediaevalia* 25 (1966), 93-128

-- --   The Tunnel of Eupalinus and the Tunnel
                     Problem of Hero of Alexandria", *Isis* 62
                     (1970), 170-185

-- --   Athenian Literacy in the Fifth Century
                     B.C , *Journal of the History of Ideas* 42
                     (1981), 371-387

--   "Hippodamus and the Planned City", *Historia* 25, 414-428

J. B. Bury   *A History of Greece to the Death of Alexander the Great* (3d. edition London 1959)

Joseph Campbell   *The Masks of God: Primitive Mythology* (New York 1959, 1969)

--   *The Masks of God: Occidental Mythology* (New York 1964, 3d printing 1971)

David Caplan.   *Biological Perspectives on Language* A. R. Lecours &   (Cambridge, Mass. & London 1984) Allan Smith

Rhys Carpenter   "The Antiquity of the Greek Alphabet", *American Journal of Archaeology* 37 (1933), 8-29; "The Greek Alphabet Again" *AJA* 42 (1938), 58-69

J. B. Carroll &   *Towards a Literate Society: The Report of* J. S. Chall (edd.)   *the Committee on Reading of the National Academy of Education* (New York 1975)

Max Cary   *History of the Greek World from 323 to 146 BC* (2nd ed., reprinted London 1963)

Ernst Cassirer   *The Philosophy of the Enlightenment* (Boston 1951)

George Cawkwell   *Philip of Macedon* (London & Boston 1978)

Carlo Cipolla   *Literacy and Development in the West* (London 1969)

John Chadwick   *The Mycenaean World* (Cambridge 1976)

H. F. Cherniss	*Aristotle's Criticism of Presocratic Philosophy* (Baltimore 1935)
Noam Chomsky	*Language and Mind* (New York 1968)
--	*Reflections on Language* (New York 1975)
Marshall Clagett	*Archimedes in the Middle Ages I: The Arabo-Latin Tradition* (Madison 1964)
Colin Clair	*A History of European Printing* (London & New York 1976)
--	*Christopher Plantin* (London 1960)
M. C. R. Cohen	*La Grande Invention de I a Écriture et son Évolution* (Paris 1958)
H. S. Commager	*Jefferson, Nationalism and the Enlightenment* (New York 1975)
F. M. Cornford	*From Religion to Philosophy: A Study in the Origins of Western Speculation* (New York 1957)
R. M. Cook & A. G. Woodhead	"The Diffusion of the Greek Alphabet", *American Journal of Archaeology* 63 (1959), 175
David Cressy	*Literacy and the Social Order* (Cambridge 1980)
R. G. Damerell	*Education's Smoking Gun* (New York 1985)
R. B. Davis	*A Colonial Southern Bookshelf: Reading in the 18th Century* (Athens, Georgia 1979)

J. A. Davison   "Literature and Literacy in Ancient Greece", *Phoenix* 16 (1962), 213-232

Allen Debus, ed.   *Science, Medicine and Society in the Renaissance*, in honor of Walter Pagel, (New York 1974)

– –   *Man and Nature in the Renaissance* (Cambridge 1978)

V.R.d.A. Desborough   *The Greek Dark Ages* (London 1972)

J. A. Deutsch, ed.   *The Physiological Basis of Memory* (New York 1973)

Hermann Diels   *Die Fragmente der Vorsokratiker* (Berlin 1954)

W. B. Dinsmoor   *The Architecture of Ancient Greece* (London 1950)

David Diringer   *The Alphabet* (3rd ed. London 1968)

– –   *Writing* (New York 1962)

Sterling Dow   "Minoan and Mycenaean Literacy" in *The Cambridge Ancient History* vol. 2, pt. 1, 3d. ed. 1973)

Stillman Drake   "Early Science and the Printed Book: The Spread of Science beyond the University", *Renaissance and Reformation* 6 (1970), 38-52

G. R. Driver   *Semitic Writing from Pictograph to Alphabet* (London 1948)

T. J. Dunbabin   *The Greeks and their Near Eastern Neighbors* (London 1957)

Samuel Edgerton	*The Renaissance Rediscovery of Linear Perspective* (New York 1975)
Elisabeth Eisenstein	*The Printing Press as an Agent of Change* (Cambridge 1979)
H. C. Elliot	*The Shape of Intelligence, the Evolution of the Human Brain* (New York 1969)
W. B. Essman & Shiushu Nakajima, edd.	*Current Biochemical Approaches to Learning* (New York 1973)
Arthur Evans	*The Palace of Minos*, 4 vols. (London 1921- 1935)
Margit Falkner	*Zur Frühgeschichte des Griechischen Alphabetes* (Vienna 1958)
Ellis Farneworth (ed. and tr.)	*The Works of Nicholas Machiavel* (London 1772)
M. I. Finley	*The World of Odysseus* (New York 1954)
Erich Frank	*Plato und die sogenannten Pythagoreer* (Halle 1923)
Henri Frankfort	"The Last Predynastic Period in Babylonia", *Cambridge Ancient History*, vol., 1 chpt. 12
Paulo Freire	*The Politics of Liberation: Culture, Power and Liberation* (South Hadley, Mass. 1985)
J. D. French, ed.	*Frontiers of Brain Research* (New York 1962)

Kurt von Fritz — *Grundprobleme der Geschichte der Antiken Wissenschaft* (Berlin and New York 1971)

— — — *Philosophie und Sprachlicher Ausdruck* (Darmstadt 1963)

— — — *Die Griechische Geschichtschreibung* (Berlin 1967)

C. H. Gadd — "The Cities of Babylonia" in *CAH* v.1 chpt. 13; "Babylonia, 2120-1800 BC", *CAH* v.1 chpt. 22; "Hammurabi and the End of his Dynasty" *CAH* v.2 chpt. 5

J. A. Gade — *The Life and Times of Tycho Brahe* (Princeton 1947)

Galileo Galilei — *Sidereus Nuncius* (Venice 1610)

— — — *Dialogue Concerning the Two Chief World Systems*, translated by Stillman Drake, Foreword by Albert Einstein (California U.P., Berkeley, 1967)

— — — *Discoveries and Opinions of Galileo*, ed. and tr. by Stillman Drake, (New York 1957)

L. V. Garulaitis — *Printing and Publishing in Fifteenth Century Venice* (Chicago & London 1976)

I. J. Gelb — *A Study of Writing* (Chicago 1963)

Edward Gibbon — *The History of the Decline and Fall of the Roman Empire*, 8 vols. (Philadelphia 1804-5)

Owen Gingerich, ed.   *The Nature of Scientific Discovery*,
                        Copernican Symposium 1975,
                        (Washington, D.C. 1975), 403-409

— —   "Copernicus and the Impact of Printing",
                        in A. Beer and K. A. Strand, eds. *Vistas in
                        Astronomy* (Oxford 1975)

Jack Goody   "Literacy, Criticism and the Growth of
                        Knowledge", in J. Ben-Davis & T. Nichols
                        Clark, edd., *Culture and its Creators: Es-
                        says in Honor of Edward Shilds* (Chicago
                        1977)

Jack Goody, ed.   *Literacy in Traditional Societies*
                        (Cambridge 1968)

C. H. Gordon   *The Common Background of Greek and
                        Hebrew Civilizations* (New York 1965)

J. W. Gough   *John Locke's Political Philosophy* (Oxford,
                        2nd edition 1973)

H. J. Graff   *The Literacy Myth* (London 1979)

— —   *The Legacies of Literacy* (Bloomington
                        1987)

H. J. Graff (ed.)   *Literacy and Social Development in the
                        West: A Reader* (Cambridge 1981)

Michael Grant   *From Alexander to Cleopatra, the Hel-
                        lenistic World* (New York 1982)

— —   *The History of Ancient Israel* (New York
                        1984)

— —   *The Climax of Rome*

W. S. Gray · *The Teaching of Reading and Writing* (UNESCO, Paris 1956)

P. F. Grendler · *The Roman Inquisition and the Venetian Press 1540-1605* (Princeton 1977)

G. T. Griffith, ed. · *Alexander the Great: The Main Problems* (Cambridge 1966)

E. S. Gruen · *The Last Generation of the Roman Republic* (Berkeley 1974)

-- · *The Hellenistic World and the Coming of Rome*, 2 vols. (Berkley 1984)

Margherita Guarducci · "La culla dell' alphabeto greco", in *Geras Antoniou Keramopolou* (Athens 1953)

R. M. Gummere · *The American Colonial Mind and the Classical Tradition* (Cambridge, Mass. 1963)

-- · *Seven Wise Men of Colonial America* (Cambridge, Mass. 1967)

J. T. Guthrie, ed. · *Comprehension and Teaching* (International Reading Association 1981)

-- · *Aspects of Reading Acquisition* (Baltimore and London 1976)

W. K. C. Guthrie · *A History of Greek Philosophy* (Cambridge 1962)

Moses Hadas · *Hellenistic Culture, Fusion and Diffusion* (1959)

-- · *A History of Latin Literature* (New York 1952)

Alexander Hamilton   *Works of Alexander Hamilton*, edited by Henry Cabot Lodge, 12 vols. (New York 1904)

— —   *Papers of Alexander Hamilton*, edited by H. C. Syrett, (New York 1961 -)

Stuart Hampshire   *The Age of Reason: The 17th Century Philosophers* (New York 1956)

G. M. A. Hanfmann   "Ionia, Leader or Follower", *Harvard Studies in Classical Philology* 61 (1953), 1-37

F. D. Harvey   "Literacy in the Athenian Democracy", *Revue des Études Grecques* 79 (1966), 585-635

William Harvey   *Exercitatio anatomica de circulatione sanguinis in animalibus* (Frankfurt 1628)

— —   *An Anatomical Disputation Concerning the Movement of Heart and Blood in Living Creatures,* translated by Gweneth Whitteridge (Oxford 1976)

M.B.Hatzopoulos & L. D. Loukopoulos   *Philip of Macedon* (Athens 1980)

E. A. Havelock   *Preface to Plato* (Harvard 1963)

— —   *Prologue to Greek Literacy* (Cincinnati 1971)

— —   *The Literate Revolution in Greece and its Cultural Consequences* (Princeton 1982)

— —   *The Muse Learns to Write: Reflections on Orality and Literacy from Antiquity to the Present* (New Haven and London 1986)

Gilbert Highet	*The Classical Tradition* (8th printing Oxford 1978)
G. D. M. Hinton & J. A. Anderson	*Parallel Models of Associative Memory* (Hillsdale, N.J. 1981)
E. D. Hirsch Jr.	*Cultural Literacy* (Boston 1987)
Rudolf Hirsch	*Printing, Selling and Reading, 1450-1550* (Wiesbaden 1967)
Thomas Hobbes	*Leviathan - Parts One and Two*, By H. W. Schneider, ed. (New York 1958)
Robert Hope Simpson & J. F. Lazenby	*The Catalogue of Ships in Homer's Iliad* (Oxford 1970)
S. H. Horn	*Biblical Archaeology - a Generation of Discovery*, (Washington 1985)
F. W. Householder	"More on Mycenaean," *Classical Journal* 54 (1959), 379-383
J. S. Hutchinson	"Mycenaean Kingdoms and Medieval Estates", *Historia* 26 (1977), 1-23
H. R. Immerwahr	"Book Rolls on Attic Vases", *Classical, Medieval and Renaissance Studies in Honor of Berthold Louis Ullman*, (Rome 1964), 17-48
H. A. Innis	*Empire an Communications*, 2nd ed., revised by M. Q. Innis (Toronto 1972)
--	*The Bias of Communication* (Toronto 1951)

L.A.Jacobovits, ed.	*Readings in the Psychology of Language*
Werner Jaeger	*Paideia*, transl. by Gilbert Highet (Oxford 1939)
Thomas Jefferson	*The Writings of Thomas Jefferson*, Memorial Edition, 20 vols. (Washington, D.C. 1905)
– –	*Papers of Thomas Jefferson*, edited by J. P. Boyd, (Princeton 1950)
L. H. Jeffery	*The Local Scripts of Archaic Greece* (Oxford 1961)
J. L. Jepsen, G. G. Simpson & Ernst Mayr, edd.	*Genetics, Paleontology and Evolution,* (Princeton 1949)
C. H. Kahn	*Anaximander and the Origins of Greek Cosmology* (New York 1960)
F. G. Kenyon	*Books and Readers in Ancient Greece and Rome* (Oxford 1951)
G. S. Kirk	*The Songs of Homer* (Cambridge 1962)
– –	*Myth - Its Meanings and Functions in Ancient and Other Cultures* (Cambridge 1961)
– –	*Homer and the Oral Tradition* (Cambridge 1976)
G. S. Kirk & J. E. Raven	*The Presocratic Philosophers* (Cambridge 1962)
Teuvo Kohonen	*Associative Memory* (Berlin 1977)

Jonathan Kozol	*Illiterate America* (Garden City, N.Y. 1985)
C.H. Kraeling & R. M. Adams, edd.	*City Invincible* (Chicago 1960)
S. N. Kramer	*The Sumerians, Their History, Culture and Character* (Chicago 1963)
– –	*Sumerian Mythology* (New York 1961)
– –	*History Begins in Sumer* (London 1958)
P. O. Kristeller	*Renaissance Thought: The Classic, Scholastic, and Humanistic Strains* (New York 1961)
– –	*Renaissance Thought II* (New York 1965)
T. S. Kuhn	*The Copernican Revolution* (Cambridge, Mass. 1957)
– –	*The Structure of Scientific Revolutions* (Chicago 1970)
R. A. Lanham	*Literacy and the Survival of Humanism* (New Haven, 1983)
Wilhelm Larfeld	*Handbuch der Griechischen Epigraphik* (Munich 1914)
Richmond Lattimore, tr.	*The Iliad of Homer* (Chicago 1951)
E. H. Lenneberg	*Biological Foundations of Language* (New York 1967)
Kenneth Levine	*The Social Context of Literacy* (London 1986)

– –	*Becoming Literate*, research report (University of Nottingham 1980)
John Locke	*Two Tracts on Government*, by Philip Abrams, ed. and tr. (Cambridge 1967)
– –	*Two Treatises of Goverment*, by Peter Laslett, ed. and tr. (Cambridge 1967)
– –	*Essay on Human Understanding*, ed. R. I. Aaron (Oxford 1937)
K. A. Lockridge	*Literacy in Colonial New England* (New York 1974)
R. K. Logan	*The Alphabet Effect* (New York 1986)
A. O. Lovejoy	*The Great Chain of Being* (Cambridge, Mass. 1948)
A. B. Lord	*The Singer of Tales* (Cambridge, Mass. 1960)
J. V. Luce	*Homer and the Heroic Age* (New York 1975)
– –	*The End of Atlantis* (London 1969)
Martin Luther	*Luther's Works*, edited by C. Bergendorff and H. T. Lehmann, (Philadelphia 1958)
J. B. McDiarmid	"Theophrastus on the Presocratic Causes", *Harvard Studies in Classical Philology* 61 (1953)
Richard McKeon	*Introduction to Aristotle* (2nd ed. Chicago 1973)

Marshall McLuhan — *The Gutenberg Galaxy: The Making of Typographical Man* (Toronto 1962)

— — *Understanding Media: The Extensions of Man* (New York 1965)

Elio Maggio — *Psychophysiology of Learning and Memory* (Springfield 1971)

M. E. L. Mallowan — *Early Mesopotamia and Iran* (London 1965)

Frank Manuel — *A Portrait of Isaac Newton* (Cambridge, Mass. 1968)

H. I. Marrou — *Histoire de l'éducation dans l'antiquité* (Paris 1948)

Mariusz Maruscewski — *Language Communication and the Brain* (The Hague 1975)

Olivier Masson — *Les inscriptions Chypriotes syllabiques* (Paris 1961)

Ernst Mayr — *Animal Species and Evolution* (Cambridge, Mass. 1963)

R. E, Meiggs & David Lewis — *Selection of Greek Historical Inscriptions to the End of the Fifth Century BC* (Oxford 1969)

James Mellaart — *Earliest Civilizations of the Near East* (London 1965)

B. D. Meritt — *Epigraphica Attica* (Harvard 1940)

Valerie Miller — *Between Struggle and Hope: The Nicaraguan Literacy Crusade* (Boulder and London 1985)

C.L.S. Montesquieu	*Oeuvres Complètes*, R. Caillois ed. (Paris 1951)
Lewis Mumford	*Technics and Civilization* (New York 1963)
Gilbert Murray	*Five Stages of Greek Religion* (3d. ed. New York 1955)
G. E. Mylonas	*Mycenae and the Mycenaean Age* (Princeton 1966)
Joseph Naveh	"Some Semitic Epigraphical Considerations on the Antiquity of the Greek Alphabet", *American Journal of Archaeology* 77 (1973)
– –	*Early History of the Alphabet* (Jerusalem 1982)
Joseph Needham	*Science and Civilization in China*, vol. 5, part 1: "Paper and Printing" by Tsien Tsuen-Hsuin, (Cambridge 1985)
Wilhelm Nestle	*Vom Mythos zum Logos* (Stuttgart 1942)
Otto Neugebauer	*The Exact Sciences in Antiquity* (Princeton 1952)
Isaac Newton	*Mathematical Principles of Natural Philosophy*, edited by Florian Cajori, (Berkeley 1946)
M. P. Nilsson	"Die Übernahme und Entwicklung des Alphabets durch die Griechen", *Opuscula* 2 (Lund 1952), pp. 1029-1056
– –	*The Minoan-Mycenaean Religion and its Survival in Greek Religion* (Lund 1950)

– –   *The Mycenaean Origin of Greek Mythology*
                             (Berkeley 1932)

Thomas North   See: Plutarch

J. A. Notopoulos   Mnemosyne in Oral Literature", *TAPA* 69
                             (1938), 465ff.

G. A. Ojemann &   The Bilingual Brain", *Archives of Neurol-*
H. A. Whitaker   *ogy* 35 (1978), 409-412

G. A. Ojemann &   Localization of Memory, Syntax and
Catherine Mateer   Sequential Motor-Phoneme Identification
                             Systems", *Science* 205 (1979), 1401-1403

G. A. Ojemann   "Brain Organization for Language from
                             the Perspective of electrical stimulation
                             Mapping", *The Behavioral & Brain Sci-*
                             ences 6 (1983), 189-206

D. R. Olsen,   *Literacy, Language, and Learning*
Nancy Torrance &   (Cambridge 1985)
Angela Hildyard, edd.

J. P. Olivier   *Les Scribes de Cnossos* (Rome 1967)

W. J. Ong   *Orality and Literacy: The Technologizing*
                             of the Word (London 1982)

A. L. Oppenheim   *Ancient Mesopotamia* (Chicago 1964)

C. E. Osgood &   *Psycholinguistics* (Bloomington 1965)
T. A. Seboek, edd.

John Oxenham   *Literacy, Writing, Reading, and Social*
                             Organisation (London 1980)

D. L. Page   *History and the Homeric Iliad* (Berkeley
                             1959)

--   *The Homeric Odyssey* (London 1966)

Walter Pagel &   "Vesalius and Paracelsus", *Medical History*
P. M. Rattansi   8 (1964), 309-334

L. R. Palmer   *The Interpretation of Mycenaean Greek Texts* (Oxford 1963)

Antonie Pannekock   *A History of Astronomy* (London 1961)

Erwin Panofsky   *The Life and Art of Albrecht Dürer* (Princeton 1955)

M. B. Parkes   "The Literacy of the Laity", in David Daiches and Anthony Thorlby (edd.) *The Medieval World* (London 1973)

Milman Parry   *The Making of Homeric Verse* ed. A. Parry (Oxford 1971)

--   *Les Formules et la metrique d'Homère* (Paris 1926)

--   *L'Epithete traditionelle chez Homère* (Paris 1928)

--   "Studies in the Epic Technique of Oral Verse Making", *Harvard Studies in Classical Philology* 41 (1930), 43 (1932)

Robert Pattison   *On Literacy - The Politics of the Word from Homer to the Age of Rock* (Oxford 1982)

Wilder Penfield   *The Mystery of the Mind* (Princeton 1975)

Wilder Penfield &   *Speech and Brain Mechanisms* (Princeton
Lamar Roberts   1959)

F. E. Peters	*The Harvest of Hellenism: A History of the Near East From Alexander, the Great to the Triumph of Christianity* (New York 1970)
Rudolf Pfeiffer	*History of Classical Scholarship from the Beginnings to the End of the Hellenistic Age* (Oxford 1968)
– –	*History of Classical Scholarship 1300 to 1850* (Oxford, Clarendon 1976)
Gerhard Pfohl, ed.	*Das Alphabet, Entstehung und Entwicklung der griechischen Schrift* (Darmstadt 1968)
J. A. Philip	*Pythagoras and Early Pythagoreanism* (Toronto 1966)
Jean Piaget	*The Child and Reality,* (New York 1973)
– –	*Language and Thought of the Child* (London 1932)
– –	*The Principles of Genetic Epistemology* (New York 1972)
Jean Piaget & Barbel Inhelder	*Memory and Intelligence* (New York 1973)
Plato	*The Republic of Plato,* tr. by F. M. Cornford, (Oxford 1941, reprinted 1945)
Pliny	*The Letters of the Younger Pliny,* tr. by Betty Radice, (New York 1963)

Plutarch	*Lives of the Noble Grecians and Romans Englished by Sir Thomas North Anno 1579* 6 vols. (London 1895-6), (after the French translation by Jaques Amyot (Paris 1559)
H. L. Pinner	*The World of Books in Classical Antiquity* (Leiden 1948)
K. R. Popper & J. C. Eccles	*The Self and its Brain* (Heidelberg 1977)
Derek de S. Price	*Science since Babylon*, (New Haven 1975)
J.B. Pritchard, ed.	*The Ancient Near East* (Princeton 1958)
Leopold Prowe	*Nicolaus Copernicus*, vol .2 *Urkunden*, (Berlin 1884)
Anthony Raubitschek	"Plato and Minos", *Quaderni di storia* 3 (1976), 233-238
Meyer Reinhold	*Classica Americana: The Greek and Roman Heritage in the United States* (Detroit 1984)
– –	*The Classick Pages: Classical Reading of Eighteenth Century Americans* (University Park, Pa. 1975)
Colin Renfrew	*The Emergence of Civilization, the Cyclades and the Aegean in the Third Millennium B.C.* (London 1972)
V.M. Rentel	*Psychological Aspects of Reading and Learning* S.A. Corson & B.R.Dunn (ed's) (Amsterdam 1985)
H. J. Rose	*A Handbook of Greek Mythology* (New York 1959)

Steve Rose — *The Conscious Brain* (New York 1973)

Edward Rosen — *Three Copernican Treatises*, (3rd ed. New York 1971)

— — "Was Copernicus a Neoplatonist?", *Journal of the History of Ideas*, vol. 44 (1983), 667

— — "Kepler's Early Writings", *Journal of the History of Ideas*, vol. 46 (1985), 449

— — "The Dissolution of the Solid Celestial Spheres", *JHI*. 46, 13-31

David Ross — *Aristotle* (2nd ed. London 1949)

M. I. Rostovtzeff — *The Social and Economic History of the Hellenistic World*, 3 vols. (Oxford 1941)

George Roux — *Ancient Iraq* (London 1964)

Geoffrey Sampson — *Writing Systems* (Stanford 1985)

Giorgio de Santillana — *The Origins of Scientific Thought, from Anaximander to Proclus, 600 BC to 300 AD* (Chicago 1961)

G. de Santillana & Hertha v. Dechend — *Hamlet's Mill: An Essay on Myth and the Frame of Time* (Boston 1969)

George Sarton — *Six Wings, Men of Science in the Renaisance* (Bloomington, Indiana 1957)

— — *A History of Science* (Cambridge, Ma. 1959)

Denise Schmandt-Besserat — "From Tokens to Tablets, a Reevaluation of the So-Called Numerical Tablets" *Visible Language* 15 (1981), 321-344.

--	"The Emergence of Recording", *American Anthropologist* 84 (1982), 872-6
--	"An Ancient Token System: The Precursors to Numerals and Writing", *Archaeology* 39 (1986), 32-39.
C. B. Schmitt	*Studies in Renaissance Philosophy and Science: Aristotle and the Renaissance* (Cambridge, Mass. 1983)
Michael Shallis	*The Silicon Idol* (Oxford 1984)
G. M. Shepherd	*The Synaptic Organization of the Brain* (Oxford 1974)
G. G. Simpson	*Biology of Man* (New York 1964)
--	*This View of Life* (New York 1964)
R. E. Siegel	*Galen's System of Physiology and Medicine: An Analysis of his Doctrines and Observations on Bloodflow, Respiration, Tumors and Internal Diseases* (Basel 1968)
Charles Singer	*A Short History of Scientific Ideas to 1900* (Oxford, Clarendon 1959)
--	*A History of Technology*, 7 vols. (Oxford 1954-78)
--	*The Discovery of the Circulation of the Blood* (reprinted London 1956)
Frank Smith	*Reading Without Nonsense* (2nd ed. New York 1985)
Bruno Snell	*The Discovery of the Mind* (Harvard 1953)

A. M. Snodgrass   *The Dark Age of Greece* (Edinburgh 1971)

R. W. Southern   *The Making of the Middle Age* (New Haven 1967)

P. M. Spurlin   *Rousseau in America, 1760-1809* (University of Alabama 1969)

--   *Montesquieu in America 1760-1801* (New York 1969)

--   *The French Enlightenment in America* (Athens, Georgia 1984)

S. H. Steinberg   *Five Hundred Years of Printing* (Bristol 1961)

George Steiner   *After Babel: Aspects of Language and Translation* (Oxford 1975)

Tina Stiefel   "The Heresy of Science: A Twelfth Century Conceptual Revolution", *Isis* 68 (1977), 347-362

Bryan Stock   *The Implications of Literacy* (Princeton 1983)

B. V. Street   *Literacy in Theory and Practice* (Cambridge 1984)

Michael Stubbs   *Language, Schools and Classrooms* (London 1976)

--   *Language and Literacy* (London 1980)

Ronald Syme   *The Roman Revolution* (Oxford 1939)

W. W. Tarn   *Alexander the Great* (Oxford 1941)

L. R. Taylor   *Party Politics in the Age of Caesar*
(Berkeley 1949)

– –   *The Divinity of the Roman Emperor*
(American Philological Association 1931)

Victor Tcherikover   *Hellenistic Civilization and the Jews* (New
York 1970)

J. W. Thompson   *The Literacy of the Laity in the Middle
Ages* (New York 1963)

M. N. Tod   *A Selection of Greek Historical Inscriptions*
(Oxford 1946)

E. G. Turner   *Athenian Books in the Fifth and Fourth
Centuries BC,* Inaugural Lecture, Univer-
sity College (London 1951)

B. L. Ullman   "How Old is the Greek Alphabet?" *American Journal of Archaeology* 38 (1934)

Walter Ullman: *Mediaeval Foundations of Renaissance
Humanism* (London 1977)

UNDP   *The Experimental World Literacy Pro-
gramme* (The Unesco Press, Paris 1976)

Eugene Vanderpool   *Ostracism at Athens* (Cincinnati 1970)

Michael Ventris &   *Documents in Mycenaean Greek*
Joseph Chadwick   (Cambridge 1956)

Emily Vermeule   *Greece in the Bronze Age* (Chicago 1964)

Leon Voet   *The Golden Compasses: A History and
Evaluation of the Printing and Publishing
Activities of the Officina Plantiniana at
Antwerp,* 5 vols. (Amsterdam 1969)

A. J. B. Wace   *Mycenae - An Archaeological History and Guide* (New York 1964)

A. J. B. Wace &   *A Companion to Homer* (London 1962)
F. H. Stubbings

H. T. Wade-Gery   *The Poet of the Iliad* (Cambridge 1952)

B. L. v.d. Waerden   *Science Awakening* (Oxford 1961)

F. W. Walbank   *The Hellenistic World* (Brighton and Atlantic Highlands 1981)

Ian Watt   *The Rise of the Novel* (Berkeley 1967)

Charles Webster   *The Great Instauration: Science, Medicine and Reform 1626-1660* (London 1975)

T. B. L. Webster   *From Mycenae to Homer* (London 1964)

R. S. Westman, ed.   *The Copernican Achievement* (Los Angeles 1975)

C. H. Whitman   *Homer and the Heroic Tradition* (Harvard 1958)

R. F. Willets   *The Civilization of Ancient Crete* (Berkeley 1977)

– –   *Cretan Cults and Festivals* (London 1962)

Leonard Woodbury   "Aristophanes' *Frogs* and Athenian Literacy", *Transactions of the American Philological Association* 106 (1976), 349-357

A. G. Woodhead   *The Study of Greek Inscriptions* (Cambridge 1949)

E. & C. Zeller ed's., Nicolai Copernici Thorunensis *de revolutionibus orbium celestium libri sex* (Munich, Oldenbourg 1949)

Eduardo Zeller *La Filosofia dei Greci*, edited and enlarged by Rudolfo Mondolfo, (3d ed. Florence 1951)

S. P. Zervos "On the Development of Mathematical Intuition; on the Genesis of Geometry", *Tensor* 26 (1972), 397-461

Ladislav Zgusta "Graeco Latin Bilingualism in the Roman Empire", *Studies in Language Learning* 1 (1976)

Index

The series STUDIA CLASSICA is designed to examine various aspects of the Graeco-Roman world syntopically. That is, it treats the traditional areas of scholarship dealing with ancient Greece and Rome — literature, history, philosophy, archaeology, art history — from more than one point of view. Examples of pertinent studies would be: a sociological approach to Greek later comedy; the psychology of Ovid's love (or exile) poetry; the demography of Athenian oratory.

The series editors are:

Anthony J. Podlecki
Department of Classics
The University of British Columbia
Vancouver, B.C. CANADA
V6T IN5

John C. Overbeck
State University of New York
    at Albany
Albany, New York 12222